Living as the Community of God

Moses Speaks to the Church in Deuteronomy

Phillip G. Camp

CROSSLINK PUBLISHING

Living as the Community of God: Moses Speaks to the Church in Deuteronomy

D CrossLink Publishing
C www.crosslinkpublishing.com

Copyright, © 2014 Phillip G. Camp

ISBN 978-1-936746-98-9

Library of Congress Control Number: 2014931037

Contents

Abbreviations for English Translations

ESV	English Standard Version
KJV	King James Version
NAB	New American Bible
NASB	New American Standard Bible
NIV	New International Version
NKJV	New King James Version
NLT	New Living Translation
NRSV	New Revised Standard Version
RSV	Revised Standard Version

I dedicate this book to my sons,
Jim, Davis, and Timothy.
I pray that my wife Amy and I can faithfully inscribe the
Word of God in their hearts that they may enjoy the life
God intends for them, fulfill God's purposes
for them in his divine mission,
and keep the faith alive for the generation they will one day raise.

Acknowledgements

The journey toward Deuteronomy becoming one of my favorite books of the Bible and this book as an attempt to help others see the value of Deuteronomy began with a class on Deuteronomy at Princeton Theological Seminary under Dr. Patrick Miller. Dr. Miller was a wonderful teacher, and his class showed me the value of Deuteronomy as a living word of God to the church today, revealing so much about the nature of God and its rich guidance for Christian living. My love for the book grew through my doctoral research at Union Theological Seminary in Richmond, Virginia, as Deuteronomy played a major role in my dissertation. Finally, I have been given the privilege over the last several years to teach Deuteronomy on the graduate and undergraduate levels at Lipscomb University and to teach and preach from Deuteronomy in various churches.

This book is a product of my researching, reading, writing, and teaching on Deuteronomy for many years, and of numerous conversations in classes and churches. I am grateful to my students and the church members who helped me test and shape my thoughts on Deuteronomy. Special thanks go to my friend and former student Craig "Dusty" Katzenmiller, who read the manuscript, offering corrections and constructive insights.

I am continually grateful for the support of my family. My wife Amy is a constant source of support (in every way imaginable). My sons Jim, Davis, and Timothy are a blessing and remind me of the importance of passing on the faith to the next generation. My parents Jim and Edith Camp, have also been a constant support to me and are primarily responsible for passing the faith on to me.

Introduction: Why Bother with Deuteronomy?

Deuteronomy[1] is an engaging and vital book! Perhaps you have never heard such a claim before. Let us be honest here. If you asked someone to list their top ten favorite books of the Bible, Deuteronomy probably would not make most lists (or the top twenty or sixty for that matter!). This book of laws and curses, or so the popular perception goes, often seems boring and irrelevant. But wait! Perhaps there is more here than meets the eye. A closer look at Deuteronomy reveals a book that is important to today's Christian. In fact, with apologies to David Letterman, here are ten reasons Deuteronomy matters for the Christian:

(1) It shows what it means to be in a *faithful relationship with God* and invites us into such a relationship.
(2) It highlights the *grace of God* for his people and for all people.
(3) It teaches a great deal about the *nature of God*: his love, mercy, justice, righteousness, faithfulness, etc.
(4) It shows the *nature of community life* for God's people.
(5) It reveals the *missiological purpose* of the people of God, their role in his plan.
(6) It illustrates how the people of God are *to respond to a religiously pluralistic and materialistic world*.
(7) It teaches us a great deal about the *nature and performance of worship*.
(8) It teaches us how to *rightly order our lives*—where the priorities are.
(9) It is *one of the most influential books on the rest of the Bible*. The basic theologies of (at the least) Joshua, Judges, 1 and 2 Samuel, 1 and 2 Kings, and Jeremiah are rooted in Deuteronomy, and it is one of the most cited Old Testament books in the New Testament. Note, for

example, that all of Jesus' responses to Satan in the temptation narratives are drawn from Deuteronomy (Matt. 4:1–11; Luke 4:1–13; cf. Deut. 8:3; 6:13, 16)!

(10) *It is Christian Scripture.* According to Paul, "All Scripture is God-breathed and is useful for teaching, rebuking, correcting and training in righteousness so that the man of God may be thoroughly equipped for every good work" (2 Tim. 3:16–17, NIV).

But What Does the Old Testament Law Have to Do with Christians?

The question of the Christian's relationship to the Law is too broad to cover in detail here, and that discussion is ongoing among Christians. So, in the interest of full disclosure, I assume the following with respect to the Old Testament law and the Christian.[2] First, the Law contains the stipulations of the covenant between God and Israel. Therefore, it is ancient Israel's covenant with God, not ours. Second, the Law has found its fulfillment or goal in Jesus Christ, who was anticipated by the Law in that all of the Old Testament points to Jesus in some way (cf. Luke 24:25–27, 44). Jesus also modeled perfectly the trustful obedience Israel had been called to in the Law and thus embodied ideal Israel.[3] Third, Christians are under the new covenant (see Luke 22:20; Heb. 8:6–13; 12:22–24; cf. Jer. 31:31–34) and therefore the specific stipulations of the Law are not binding upon Christians. Fourth, though the Old Testament law is not our covenant, it is still God's word to us (see again 2 Tim. 3:16–17). Therefore, we must somehow hear God's word to us through Deuteronomy and the Old Testament law as a whole.[4]

How to hear God's word to us in Deuteronomy also becomes problematic, and again the "how" is an ongoing discussion among Christians. After all, Deuteronomy was written for a specific group of people (the ancient Israelites) who lived thousands of years ago in a distant land and distinct culture (Palestine and, more broadly, the ancient Near East), a largely agrarian people who looked at the world differently than we do. Two solutions often presented are unsatisfactory. First, it will not do to say that the ethical or moral laws are relevant while the civil and ritual laws are not. This position would say laws like, "You shall not kill" and "Do not oppress the widow and the orphan" speak to us, but laws about kings, freeing slaves, unclean foods, and sacrifices do not. The Old Testament law itself, however, makes no rigid distinctions between moral, civil, and ritual laws, largely because Israel saw life under the Law holistically. A second position is that only the Old Testament laws that are "renewed" in the New Testament apply to Christians. While this is perhaps true as far as it goes, it is too limiting. Again, all of the Old Testament is God's word for Christians, so we must "listen" to all of it. Furthermore, the New Testament writers clearly find relevance in Deuteronomy for Christians beyond "renewing" certain laws (cf. 1 Cor. 9:9–10; 1 Tim. 5:17–18; cf. Deut. 25:4).

How then do we hear the ancient words in Deuteronomy (and in the Law in general) as a word to Christians today? The following considerations guide my discussion of the laws in Deuteronomy. First, one might simply ask how keeping a given law in Israel would have demonstrated love of God and/or love of neighbor, which Jesus says is the crux of the entire Law (Matt. 22:36–40; cf. Rom. 13:9; Gal. 5:14). A second question to ask then is: what ideal or goal for God's people is commanded or illustrated? That is, how would keeping a particular law make Israel into the kind of community God wanted them to be? What would a society that kept these laws look like, and why would that matter?[5] Third, in light of the other questions, we must ask the theological question: what does this text say or reveal about God? What does a given discourse or stipulation reveal about who God is and what is important to him, about his purposes, and about his mission for his people?

The answers to these broader questions will then guide our hearing of the Law as the living word of God to us today. More questions will then move us in that direction. How is the same kind of love for God or love for neighbor manifest in our own day and time? How would those goals and ideals for Israel look in our own setting, recognizing that the particulars of their time are often not the same as ours? And, of course, it may be that we will not find any sort of "go and do likewise" application. Instead, the relevance may be, and certainly ultimately in some sense always is, to draw our attention and reflection on God. That is, the relevance of the text may not be "go and do" something but rather "come and see" what an awesome, mighty God we serve. Through asking the theological questions, we come to understand more and more about our God, often in ways that challenge long-held beliefs. The result may even make us uncomfortable, because in coming to know more of this God, we realize how little we know him and how he refuses to be contained by our simplistic thinking and systems. And, thus, we are moved to confession and praise.

Orientation to Deuteronomy

To understand God's word to his people through Deuteronomy, it is helpful to have some sense of the setting and form of the book. There is a great deal of discussion among biblical scholars about the authorship, composition, and date of Deuteronomy. Commentary introductions and Old Testament introductions can give the reader an abundance of details on these debates. For my purposes, I will examine the book's own presentation of its setting, and our concern will be the canonical (final, authoritative) form of the book.

Deuteronomy presents itself as the words of Moses to a new generation of Israelites on the border of the Promised Land about forty years after the exodus from Egypt, as they prepare to enter the land: "These are the words that Moses spoke to all Israel beyond the Jordan..." (1:1). However, the text quickly makes it clear that Moses speaks at God's command (1:3).[6] Moses' words are a restatement and exposition of the Horeb/Sinai Law (*Torah*) of God for the children of the exodus generation, a generation not permitted to enter the land because of rebellion against God (see Num. 13–14). The new generation now camps in the plain of Moab, on the east side of the Jordan River, just across from the Promised Land. They are the people who will go in and conquer the land God has given them. This *Torah* will tell the people how to live as the people of God in the land once they gain possession of it, so that they may enjoy life and blessing and they may fulfill God's larger purposes for them by mediating his blessings to other nations (cf. Gen. 12:3).

Within the larger biblical story, Deuteronomy forms something of a bridge or transition point, looking both back and forward. Looking back, Deuteronomy recalls God's mighty acts leading up to the time just before they take the land. Israel is now reminded of their origins, going back to the calling of and promises to Abraham, Isaac, and Jacob. Faithful to his promises, God made the descendants of these men into a great nation, and God was fulfilling his promises to bless this nation in the land he had promised to their ancestors. Moses reiterates that Israel's salvation is from God, who liberated them from bondage in Egypt by defeating Pharaoh and the forces of Egypt with mighty signs and wonders. God brought them through the sea and into the wilderness, where he met their every need as he led them toward the land of promise. Moses reminds Israel of their continual rebellion against God, culminating in their refusal to enter the Promised Land and thus forfeiting their right to enter it. But he also reminds Israel of their God-given victories in the wilderness over those who would stand in the way of their reception of God's promises.

Looking forward, Deuteronomy anticipates life in the land as the people of God. Deuteronomy promises the blessings that will result from obedience to God and warns against turning away from God to other gods. Indeed, it fully anticipates Israel's forsaking their covenant with God and presents the consequences of such a choice—the curses, which culminate in Israel's banishment from the land. But even then, a word offering hope of restoration appears. The books that follow Deuteronomy (Joshua, Judges, 1 and 2 Samuel, 1 and 2 Kings)[7] play out the ups and downs of Israel's relationship with God—the good, the bad, and the ugly.

What Is Deuteronomy?

A number of suggestions have been made regarding the form or genre (type of literature) of Deuteronomy, which is an important question since form relates to the function or purpose of the work. In fact, one may justifiably note elements of more than one genre in Deuteronomy. Among those suggested by scholars, three are particularly helpful as we consider Deuteronomy's word for us today: covenant, constitution, and catechism.

(1) Covenant. Scholars have long recognized that Deuteronomy roughly follows the outline of an ancient Near Eastern suzerainty-vassal treaty,[8] and Deuteronomy claims this form for itself (see especially Deut. 29). Like these ancient treaties, Deuteronomy has a preamble (1:1–5), a historical prologue rehearsing the relationship between the parties involved (1:6–4:49), general stipulations or obligations (chaps. 5–11), specific stipulations or obligations (chaps. 12–26), and blessings and curses (chaps. 27–28), and it ends with reference to witnesses and provisions for public reading (chaps. 29–34).

Such treaties or covenants were made between the king of a powerful nation (the suzerain) and the king of a weaker nation subject to the more powerful nation (the vassal). Within these treaties were the expectations and obligations for both parties. The vassals were usually obligated to render absolute loyalty to the suzerain, pay an annual tribute of precious metals and produce, and report any hints of rebellion against the suzerain's authority. The suzerain, in turn, promised to protect loyal vassals, but rebellious vassals were subject to punishment.

Deuteronomy takes this form—without importing all aspects of the nature of the relationship between a suzerain and a vassal—to characterize the relationship between God and Israel. God, as the suzerain, promises to bless Israel with protection, agricultural abundance, fertility of wombs, and the like. Israel, in turn, must render uncompromised loyalty to Yahweh (God's name in the Old Testament, rendered LORD in English Bibles).[9] If they are not loyal, Yahweh will then send the curses against Israel. However, as we will see later, the curses in Deuteronomy are ultimately redemptive in purpose.

Thus, the form as well as the content of Deuteronomy reminds Israel that they are in a covenant relationship with God that entails real responsibilities and that has real consequences. God is Israel's King, their Lord, who has placed certain obligations upon them, obligations that serve God's larger redemptive purposes not only for Israel but for all of creation. Because of this relationship, even the laws that seemingly have to do with human-to-human issues are ultimately divine-human issues.

(2) Constitution. Admittedly, to describe Deuteronomy as a constitution, or polity, for the people of Israel is anachronistic, but the content of Deuteronomy at least indicates that this is another way of characterizing the book. This view suggests that Deuteronomy represents a "comprehensive social charter" showing how Israel is to live in relationship to God and to one another in the land.[10] In a manner similar to the Constitution of the United States of America, Deuteronomy lays out rights, restrictions, and responsibilities of the people of Israel, and it enshrines special protections against potentially abusive exercises of power.

Deuteronomy is often characterized as a law book, which in some sense it is, but such a view leads the mischaracterization of Deuteronomy as merely a listing of regulations. To be sure, regulations or stipulations are there, but the term "law" misses the personal relational aspect between God and Israel and among Israelites that Deuteronomy so clearly demonstrates. Indeed, the Hebrew word translated "law," *Torah*, is much broader than simply the idea of rules and regulations. It carries the connotations of guidance, teaching, and instruction. That does not mean, however, that Deuteronomy contains just good advice that Israel should follow. Israel was expected to obey or keep *Torah* to enjoy the blessings of the land and fulfill their larger purposes among the nations.

Looking at Deuteronomy as a constitution points more to its content and function in Israel. On the one hand, it called Israel into a trusting relationship with God and showed them how to live out that relationship on a daily basis. Thus, they were called to exclusive loyalty to God, and, by living out that relationship with God, to live justly and righteously with one another. How they treated one another had a direct bearing on their relationship with God, and their relationship with God had a direct bearing on how they treated one another. Deuteronomy as constitution sets the parameters of those relationships, showing how Israel, as the people of God, was to live in relationship with their God and with one another. If, in some sense, living under the Constitution defines what it means to be an American, so Israel's living under the *Torah* in Deuteronomy defined what it meant to be an Israelite.

(3) Catechism. Churches are interested in teaching their children the content and practice of the faith, and some churches do this formally in classes for children who have reached a certain age and level of understanding. This process is known as catechesis, and the content of the teaching is called the catechism. Although the terminology is again anachronistic when applied to Deuteronomy, "catechism" helpfully describes the emphasis in Deuteronomy on passing on and explaining Israel's faith to the children of the Israelites (cf. Deut. 4:9–10; 6:1–9, 20–25; 31:10–13).[11] That is, one of the explicit expectations in Deuteronomy is that each generation will teach subsequent generations to live in loving and obedient relationship with God. They are taught not only the commands of the *Torah* but, more significantly, about the God who gave the *Torah* to Israel. Otherwise, the children may abandon the life-giving relationship with God and larger purposes that God has for Israel.

Perhaps looking at Deuteronomy from these three perspectives—covenant, constitution, and catechism—will help us see already some of the relevance Deuteronomy has for the Christian community. We are children of God brought into a loving, covenantal relationship with him through faith in Jesus Christ. Jesus' death and resurrection initiated the new covenant that has made that relationship with God possible, and it is a relationship that brings both blessings and creates demands on those who participate. That is, we confess that Jesus is not only our savior and friend, but also that Jesus is Lord. Living under the lordship of Jesus Christ then sets the direction for how we live as the people of God today in relationship with God and with others. Finally, we recognize that for our children to enjoy the benefits of the covenant relationship with God and to fulfill God's purposes for their lives, we must pass on the content of our faith to our children. We teach our children not merely a set of doctrines but, more importantly, about God, who revealed himself in the *Torah* to Israel and most fully in the Word incarnate, his Son, Jesus Christ.

Some Notes on Using this Book

The book will move for the most part section by section through Deuteronomy, though in some places it will follow a more topical approach. To fully understand the discussion, I recommend that you first read the portions of Deuteronomy given at the start of each chapter. After all, the point of this book is to get you into the book of Deuteronomy.

This book presents a general overview of Deuteronomy rather than an examination of every detail. That is, this book looks more at the forest than the trees. Since the goal is to give the big picture, particularly the theological emphases of the text and its relevance to the community of God today, not every verse or every law will be covered in detail, though every section will be touched upon. Consult the "Index to Texts in Deuteronomy" for references to particular portions of Deuteronomy.

Each chapter divides the discussion of a given passage or passages from Deuteronomy into three parts. First, there is a brief discussion of the passage itself. The second section, "The God of the Community," discusses the theological emphases of the text within Deuteronomy and the Bible in general. The third section, "Guidance for Today's Community," suggests ways these texts continue to speak to the church today. The use of "Guidance" is intentional in keeping with the understanding of *Torah* as guidance or instruction rather than simply a list of rules or commands. The *Torah* of Deuteronomy continues to offer guidance for the church on what it means and what it looks like to be the community of God.

I have included several endnotes. Some simply cite sources for the information or ideas presented. Others, however, are designed to give the reader additional information to illuminate the biblical text, raise issues related to the text and its use, and point the reader to resources that may be helpful.

Chapter 1

Are We There Yet?

Read: *Deuteronomy 1:1–2:1*

euteronomy begins on what might be considered a low note: a rehearsal of the failings of the previous generation of Israelites. The new generation of Israelites hears from Moses something that few people would care to hear: an attack cataloging the spiritual and moral failings of their parents and grandparents. However, as this new generation prepares to cross the Jordan into the Promised Land, Moses reminds them of what prevented their parents from entering forty years earlier.

A Long Trip (1:1–8)

The first eight verses of Deuteronomy present what seems like a fairly uninteresting listing of place names, which give Israel's current location (v. 1), and it then moves to what seems like an irrelevant statement: "It takes eleven days to go from Horeb to Kadesh Barnea by the Mount Seir road" (v. 2, NIV). Why give what appears to be such a minor detail? Kadesh Barnea is where the previous generation rebelled against God by refusing to go in and take the Promised Land (see v. 19; cf. Num. 13–14), a story that Moses will rehearse in the verses that follow. That generation was eleven days away from where they would begin their march into Canaan, but, as verse 3 reminds, the eleven-day trip ultimately took forty years! They certainly knew it should take only eleven days having gone that way once before, but, because of their rebellion, the trip to the land would take a lifetime. So now, even as God orders the children of that generation to break camp and move out (vv. 6–8), this new generation of Israelites must hear the dangers of rebellion against their God.

However, possession of the land has really taken much more than forty years. As the reference to Abraham, Isaac, and Jacob (v. 8) reminds the reader, it has taken hundreds of years. In those years, God has remained faithful to his promises to the ancestors, beginning with Abraham, Isaac, and Jacob. In keeping with his promises to the patriarchs, God increased their descendants' numbers, so that by the time they left Egypt, they were "as numerous as the stars of heaven" (v. 10; cf. Gen 15:5, 22:17, 26:4). His faithfulness in this area should have led Israel to trust him with respect to his promises concerning the land. But God's faithfulness was met by their faithlessness. This reminder in the opening verses of Deuteronomy serves, on one level, as a point of contrast between God's fidelity and Israel's lack of it.

Moses and Israel's Leaders (1:9–18)

The reference to ancestors and the fulfillment of one of the promises to them also segues into the discussion of Moses' appointment of leaders over the tribes (vv. 9–18). The people's numbers grew, and, for this, Moses praised God and prayed that their numbers continue to increase. However, overseeing them became a burden to Moses. So Moses, with the agreement of the people, organized Israel into units and subunits within the tribes.[12] While judicial decisions were obviously part of his intention, it also seemed that Moses was organizing the people for the march to and invasion of Canaan. The qualifications for the leaders were that they be wise, understanding, and knowledgeable or known (i.e., men of standing within the community). The judges were then charged to decide cases fairly without regard to the parties' ethnicity or standing. They were to carry out their responsibility fearlessly, because their authority came from God. Moses then would only hear those cases too hard for the judges to decide.[13]

Spying and Rebelling (1:19–2:1)

Though the earlier generation was organized and prepared to go to and into Canaan, they set out for a place few of them would ever reach. Arriving in Kadesh Barnea, Moses encouraged the people to go in and take the land God has given them, again, invoking the promise to the ancestors (v. 20). He told the people, "Do not fear or be dismayed" (v. 21). God was giving them the land. With all that they have witnessed in Egypt and the wilderness, surely, they could trust God in this matter and go ahead boldly.

But the people had another idea. They wanted to send in spies to scout out the best routes and possible obstacles. Was this a lack of faith on their part? It may suggest they lacked full faith in God at this point, or that they were simply thinking in "practical" terms, *which can be the same thing as lack of faith*. But Moses agreed, perhaps seeing this as an opportunity to embolden them by allowing them to see that the land was everything God had promised.[14]

If encouragement was Moses' intent, the plan failed miserably. The spies indeed saw the goodness of the land, but they also saw something else: huge people, Anakites,[15] in sky-high fortresses! This was a hyperbolic description, no doubt, but one that terrified the people. Rebellion against God followed. The people managed to take the clearest demonstration of God's care and love for them and twist it into the claim that the Lord hated them and was luring them to their destruction. The exodus from Egypt—the very deed that demonstrated that no people could stand against God—in their fear-filled, melting hearts became evidence not of God's deliverance from death but of his delivering them to death. Rather than a father who lovingly carried his children through the wilderness (v. 31), they now saw God as one who was going to let foreigners carry away their own children (v. 39).

Moses' attempts to embolden them, recounting God's mighty acts on their behalf, fell on deaf ears. He reminded them that God would fight for them, as they themselves had seen in Egypt. But that was then, not now. They could not hear his words because they had heard the reports of whom and what stood against them. Memory failed, and then faith failed.

Their decision not to go in would not matter much in the grand scheme of things, perhaps, had their decision simply affected them. But it did not. It affected God and God's purposes. He had made promises to the ancestors, promises intended not merely for them but for the blessing of all his creation (Gen. 12:1–3; see the discussion on

Deut. 4:5–8), and no generation of his people would thwart those promises. So God responded, as he often does, by letting those who rebel against him have what they want. If they did not want to move into the land, then they could have what they desired; they would not go in. He sent them back toward the Red Sea, ironically, the place where God struck the final and decisive blow against the Egyptians.

Of that generation of adults, only Joshua and Caleb would see the land. They become the forerunners of God's faithful remnant throughout Israel's history and signal the hope that God's purposes will continue even in the midst of judgment. They stand with the seven thousand who did not bow to Baal in Elijah's day (1 Kings 19:14–18); with Naomi, Ruth, and Boaz in the apostasy-filled period of the judges; and with Jeremiah, Obed-Melech, and the sons of Shaphan in the days before the fall of Judah (Jer. 26:24; 38:1–13; 39:16–18). They are those who refused to be swayed by popular sentiment and faithless surrender when the call of God pointed them toward what seemed to be overwhelming odds. They stood their ground because they trusted the God who was faithful to the patriarchs and who delivered his people from Egypt.

Perhaps the instruction to go toward the Red Sea reminded the people of what God did for them there, or perhaps they were just tired of the wilderness, but something evokes confession of sin and of a willingness to obey. They determined to go in and fight, despite God's warning through Moses against it. Submission to God means submission to his word, and his word is now to go the other direction. They presumptuously assumed that if they decided to obey God when it suited them and so fight when they were ready, God would come along. However, they soon learned that God was not at their beck and call, that he could not be launched against their enemies when they chose. So they were routed.

The chapter closes on a scary note: Moses told them that despite their weeping, "the Lord did not listen to your voice or give ear to you." God stopped listening? Perhaps weeping before the Lord is not the same thing as turning to the Lord. Their weeping seemed to have less to do with sorrow for disregarding the Lord's warning than for not getting what they now decided they wanted after all.

The God of the Community

The number of ways the opening chapter of Deuteronomy describes God is in itself amazing. God is: one who speaks to his people (v. 6, 19); who gives the land (vv. 8, 21, 25, 39); who blesses his people (vv. 10–11); who is the authority behind justice (v. 17); who fights for and delivers his people (vv. 29–30); who is like a father to his people (v. 31); who guides his people (v. 33); who can be angered (v. 34, 37) and yet is merciful, not only in fighting for and guiding his people but even in warning them against resisting his command (v. 42); and who refuses to hear the pleas of his rebellious people (v. 45). Other descriptions could be added, but this list gets at what all of Deuteronomy demonstrates: God will be with, bless, and fight for his people when they obey his commands, but he will become angry and withhold his blessing and protection when they rebel against his command. Yet, despite the rebellion of his people and his anger, he exercises justice and mercy.

Mount Horeb (aka Sinai) marked the starting point of a new relationship between God and Israel. Already, their relationship was established through God's promises to Abraham, Isaac, and Jacob, and God showed himself faithful to that relationship, both in increasing Israel's numbers (vv. 9–11) and in delivering them from Egypt (vv. 29–31). But at Horeb, the relationship took an added dimension as all Israel entered into a covenant with God in which he would be their God and they would be his people. The covenant relationship involved blessings, to be sure, but it also entailed responsibilities or obligations. Israel entered its special role in God's divine plan, a role that Israel must fulfill. As had already been seen, any particular generation that failed to honor the covenant by disobeying God would also fail to attain the promised blessings.

However, God's anger will not cause him to break covenant faithfulness for his part even when Israel is unfaithful. Thus, he preserves a new generation, and, as will be seen in the rest of Deuteronomy, lays before them the same opportunity to choose or refuse blessing. Furthermore, God's consistent faithfulness to the promises to Abraham, Isaac, and Jacob stand to provide a background for God's consistent faithfulness toward the Israelites despite their rebellions. God has said he will grant the land to the descendants of Abraham, and he will make good on that promise.[16] In these ways, God's faithfulness is also evidence of his mercy.

The recitation of Israel's history in Deuteronomy 1 becomes something of a preview for the struggles that will follow in generations to come, as seen in the biblical account of Israel from Joshua to Malachi. Israel will constantly rebel against God, and God will send judgment. Yet God will also ultimately restore. Also, the Old Testament demonstrates and claims repeatedly that God has remained faithful to his side of the covenant, placing the blame for breaking the covenant squarely upon Israel (see, e.g., 2 Kings 17:7–23; Neh. 8–9; Isa. 5:1–7; Jer. 2). Rebellion against God is such a tragedy, because his people then forfeit all the blessings that he intends and desires to lavish upon them. Moreover, they rejected their role in God's great plan for history. Instead, they languished in a barren waste with little more to do than anticipate their own deaths.

Thus, a truly frightening claim closes out this chapter: God refused to fight for his people and paid no attention to the weeping of his people. If they did not want to seize the promises of God, and if they did not trust God when he was present among them, he would shut himself off from them (cf. Jer. 7:16; 11:14; 14:11–12).

Guidance for Today's Community

What are we who have entered the new covenant through Christ to hear in all of this? Surely, this does not mean that we have to walk on eggshells, wondering every minute if God is for us or against us, wondering whether we are damned or saved. The promise of the Scripture is that in Christ, God is absolutely for us, and so no power can stand against us (Rom. 8:31–39). There is no condemnation for those who are in Christ Jesus (Rom. 8:1). Neither did Israel have to worry day in and out whether they were under God's blessing. The issue was not whether a sin or sins removed them from God's favor because sacrifice was instituted to deal with sin (see Lev. 4–6). The issue was presumption and rebellion against God, as if they said, "We simply do not care what you command, God. We will not obey." The issue was rejecting the good of God by claiming that God, in fact, had an evil intent. This issue was rejecting the call of God upon their lives. To do so meant forfeiting the blessing and gift of God. To do so meant that God would no longer fight for his people and will in fact send judgment upon them.

Committing sins is not the same thing as rebellion, but we must ask ourselves whether we are denying the will of God for our lives as a community and as members of the community. Do we say, at least by what we do, "We know you have called your church to this, but that way is hard and scary, so we will not walk it"—the way of trusting God despite obstacles, of going where and when he says, "go"? Of course, Jesus called us to the narrow way (Matt. 7:13–14), a way marked by self-denial and cross-bearing (Matt. 16:24–25; Mark 8:34–35; Luke 9:23–24). But it is our walk, or the direction of our walk, that determines whether we remain under the blessing of God (1 John 1:5–7). As was the case for Israel, so is the case for the church. Life is found in going the way God commands, not in choosing our own way.

We refuse to live lives of purity and integrity because it sets us too much apart from the culture at large. We refuse to engage those who are poor or in need because they live in dangerous neighborhoods, and we might get hurt. We refuse to trust God for provision and protection, thinking we must put our trust in governments, businesses, or our own devices to supply these. We know the call to come out and be distinct (2 Cor. 6:17) but prefer the supposed security of a comfortable and conforming Christianity. Deuteronomy 1 stands as a warning to those Christians who reject the calling, guidance, and security of God or who seek it on their own terms. How often has such a rejection delayed or caused us to miss out on the gift of God and fail in God's purposes for us? Deuteronomy 1 also offers hope that God is consistently faithful to his promises and purposes.

Chapter 2

Give and Take

Read: *Deuteronomy 2:2–3:29*

D euteronomy presents an interesting tension with respect to the land that Israel is promised: the land is presented as both a gift from God and as something that Israel must take for themselves. To be sure, as noted in the last chapter, Israel cannot take the land *by themselves*, but they must participate in seizing the land that God has granted to them. God will fight with them and for them, but they must also fight, following their God into the land. Only on this basis, of trusting God enough to go in and take what he says is theirs, may they actually obtain what he has given them. They must seize the gift of God. Several times in Deuteronomy 1 this concept was stated (emphasis mine):

> See, *I have set* the land before you. *Go in and take possession* of the land that the Lord swore to your fathers, to Abraham, to Isaac, and to Jacob, to give to them and to their offspring after them. (1:8)

> See, *the Lord your God has set* the land before you. *Go up, take possession*, as the Lord, the God of your fathers, has told you. Do not fear or be dismayed. (1:21)

> And as for your little ones, who you said would become a prey, and your children, who today have no knowledge of good or evil, they shall go in there. And to them *I will give it*, and *they shall possess it*. (1:39)

This understanding of the relationship between gift and taking possession continues into chapters 2–3, and, in fact, throughout the book. Still, as a comparison between 1:8, 1:21, and 1:39 suggests, there is an "already/not yet" understanding of the gift. Already, God has granted the land; it was theirs for the taking. But they have not yet taken it, though they may if they will go in and do so, as God has instructed.

The Neighbor's Territory (2:2–23)

Before, the new generation of Israelites can take their own territory, however, they must first pass through territories they are not allowed to possess. Chapter 2 begins with a listing of three nations whose land Israel is not permitted to take: Edom, Moab, and Ammon.[17] Why does God forbid Israel to take their land? Because God has given these nations the land they occupy. Israel's territory is specifically delimited by God.[18]

> Turn and take your journey, and go to the hill country of the Amorites and to all their neighbors in the Arabah, in the hill country and in the lowland and in the Negeb and by the seacoast, the land of the Canaanites, and Lebanon, as far as the great river, the river Euphrates. (1:7)

> Every place on which the sole of your foot treads shall be yours. Your territory shall be from the wilderness to the Lebanon and from the River, the river Euphrates, to the western sea. (11:24)

God adds to this the Transjordan (on the east side of the Jordan River) territory occupied by the Reubenites, Gadites, and half the tribe of Manasseh (3:12–17), but their lands do not infringe on the territory of Edom, Moab, and Ammon.[19] In other places, the scope of the land is presented in terms of the nations to be conquered rather than geographical markers (Deut. 7:1; 20:17).[20] Thus, Israel has its land assigned and may not encroach upon what God has given to others, what falls outside God's gift to Israel.

Thus, Israel learns that not only can God deliver territories to nations, but that God has, in fact, done so already. Not only did he grant these other nations their territories, but they each also overcame enemies as imposing as the Anakites (2:11, 21), presumably because God fought for the Edomites, Moabites, and Ammonites (see 2:21). By telling this to the Israelites, Moses aims to evoke among the people the trust that God will do the same for them. Furthermore, in the midst of this discussion, Moses reiterates the costs of failing to trust God in this respect by referring to destruction of the previous generation through the thirty-eight years of wandering in the wilderness (2:14–15).

The Defeat of Two Kings (2:24–3:20)

In contrast to the lands of the Edomites, Ammonites, and Moabites, Israel was permitted to take over the territory of two kings: Sihon (2:24–37) and Og (3:1–11).[21] Both are identified as Amorite kings who ruled east of the Jordan (3:8). If Israel has doubts about God's willingness or ability to defeat the Amorites west of the Jordan (cf. 1:27), he has demonstrated that he is both willing and able to do so, using these kings as examples. Note in 2:24 that God said to Israel, "*I have given into your hand* Sihon the Amorite, king of Heshbon, and his land." Then Israel is commanded, "Begin *to take possession of it*" (also v. 31).[22] Again, the gift is, in one sense, already granted, but they must seize it.

The defeat and takeover of the territory of these kings foreshadows what God will do to the Amorites and other nations on the other side of the river. God indicated as much to Israel when he told them that the coming defeat of Sihon's kingdom would be the start of the "dread and fear" of Israel to fall on all nations (2:25; cf. 11:25). The testimonies of Rahab (Josh 2:10) and the Gibeonites (Josh 9:10) indicate that this is, in fact, what happened. Furthermore, in language recalling how God set up Pharaoh for defeat in Egypt, Moses said that God "hardened his [Sihon's] spirit and made his heart obstinate" (2:30). The word translated "hardened" by the ESV is the same word used in Exodus 7:3 for what God did to Pharaoh's heart.[23]

As Israel prepared to meet Og, king of Bashan, God told Moses, "Do not fear him" (3:2). The exhortation seems needed for two reasons. First, Og had sixty-six cities "with high walls, gates, and bars" (vv. 4–5; cf. 1:28). Second, Og himself was "left of the remnant of the Rephaim" (3:11), a people who are linked with those dreaded, huge Anakites (Deut. 2:11). His bed, thirteen feet long and six feet wide, suggests that Og was huge as well. While such a large bed could simply be a sign of kingly excess, in this context, especially given the linkage of Og to the Rephaites, the inclusion of the dimensions of the bed surely is intended to suggest that King Og was a huge obstacle like the Anakites.

Thus, from the perspective of the generation Moses presently addresses, the reminder about the victories over Sihon and Og functions to show that God, who gives the land and calls his people to take it, will also enable his people to do so, as he has shown them already. Israel fought, but they succeeded because God delivered the enemy into their hands (2:33). They learned that neither the dreaded fortified cities of the Amorites nor the huge, intimidating people of the land can withstand them when God fights with them. God has given them the land, and nothing can prevent them from taking it, except their own faithlessness.

Another aspect of the gift of the land comes into play in the discussion of the division of the land among the Transjordan tribes. In verse 20, these two and a half tribes are told that they must help the remaining tribes take their land west of the Jordan River. Only when all of the people have obtained "rest" in the land can any enjoy "rest." That is, only when all of the people have their allotments and are enjoying security and prosperity in the land—God's blessing in the land—do any of the individual tribes have the right to enjoy it. The gift of the land is a gift to the whole community of God, and taking the land is the obligation of the whole community.[24]

Moses Excluded from the Land (3:21–29)

The fact that Moses will not cross over into the land negates neither the gift of the land nor Israel's responsibility to take it. Joshua will lead in Moses' place. Moses will get a glimpse of the land, much as the spies did, but his own exclusion from the land will serve as a final reminder of how the refusal to obey God means forfeiting the gift of God.[25]

The God of the Community

Gift and Obligation

God is presented as both the one who gives the land, and, though he commands that Israel seize the gift, God is also the one who enables Israel to do so.[26] Already, we have seen that unless God goes with them, they cannot defeat the inhabitants of Canaan. Yet God has demonstrated through the defeat of Sihon and Og that all of those things that caused Israel to doubt whether they could take the land were no obstacle when God was with them. Even Moses' impending death is not seen as an obstacle to the fulfillment of the promise.

Thus, Israel must respond to God's gift of the land not only by trusting him when he tells them to take it, but also by remaining obedient to him once they enter the land, a fact that will become clear as Deuteronomy progresses. One may ask why God would have Israel fight instead of simply wiping out the inhabitants with a plague or some similarly devastating means that did not require Israel to be directly involved. It seems that God has invited Israel into real participation in his divine purposes. There is actual divine-human cooperation going on here. God has chosen to work through people, and they become the partners in and instruments of his purposes. Faith is built not merely in experiencing the blessing of God but also, even chiefly, in walking with God and trusting that his people will prevail through him, despite glaring obstacles in their path.

The obligation to seize the promises, however, is not simply an obligation to God. It is also an obligation toward the other members of the community. Israel's covenant with God is a community covenant and thus entails responsibilities toward others in the community. One could not be content with simply getting his or her due. There was nothing due the individual or single tribe that was also not granted to the community as a whole. That is, no one was permitted to simply think in terms of "me, myself, and I." Israel was to think in terms of "us, ourselves, and we." Thus, the Transjordan tribes must fight alongside their fellow Israelites until all can enjoy the rest God provides in the land.

God's Sovereignty over the Nations

God is able to give Israel their land because he is the God over all lands and peoples, whether they acknowledge him or not. Thus, Edom, Moab, and Ammon dwell where they do because God has given them the land after driving out the previous inhabitants. That God moves out the previous inhabitants, however, suggests that no nation can presume a right to the land in perpetuity, apart from the will of God. Even Israel will be reminded that, just as the Canaanites will be removed to make room for the Israelites, so the Israelites can be removed if they refuse to obey God.

Do Not Fear

God tells Moses, "Do not fear" Og (3:2), one of six times in Deuteronomy this *command* appears (see also 1:21; 20:1, 3; 31:6, 8). Israel need not fear because: God has given them the land (1:21); God has handed the enemy over to them (3:2); and God will be with them in their battles and fights for them (20:1, 3). Furthermore, Joshua need not fear because God is with him and will never leave or forsake him (31:6, 8). Thus, Deuteronomy couches the command not to fear in the promise, presence, purposes, and protection of God. As Israel has seen, they need not fear what lay ahead because they can look back and see what God has done.

"Do not fear" (or some form of it) is the most frequent command in the Bible. In most cases, the command is either from God to an individual or to Israel or it is from someone (humans or angels) who imparts the command to encourage others, couching it in what God will do. As with Deuteronomy, the promise, presence, purposes, and protection of God—and Christ and the Spirit in the New Testament—give the motivation to carry out the command.[27]

Though it seems unusual to command someone not to be afraid, those who trust in God have good reason to obey this command. God is stronger than all challengers and all potential threats to his people or purposes. The key to obeying the command is to see that God's victories in the past give confidence for the present and future. This is particularly true in light of his victory through Christ over sin and death by the cross and resurrection of Christ. So, as the well-known words of Romans 8:31–39 remind us, absolutely nothing and no one in heaven above or on earth below "will be able to separate us from the love of God in Christ Jesus our Lord."

Rest

Deuteronomy 3:20 introduces the theological concept of "rest," which is a way of describing God's provision and protection for Israel in the land (see also 12:10 and 25:19). Once Israel seizes the land, ideally, they need not worry about enemies from the outside or need on the inside. God will grant them all they need in the land. God has redeemed them from the fear, oppression, and deprivation of slavery in Egypt, a fact which they commemorate weekly by enjoying rest and granting rest to others on the Sabbath (5:13–15). And, in the land, they will remain secure from threats, as long as they remain committed to God as demonstrated through covenant obedience.

Full enjoyment of the rest was slow in coming to Israel and fleeting when it did come, largely because of their rebellion. Following Joshua's conquest, Israel had its rest initially (Josh 21:44; 22:4; 23:1), but Israel's failure to keep the covenant, as described in the book of Judges, meant that Israel was once again subject to foreign oppressors. With David, the man after God's own heart, rest was once again achieved, as he—through God's help—subdued all of Israel's enemies (2 Sam 7:1, 11). This then set the stage for another development in the understanding of rest, one anticipated in Deuteronomy 12:10. God would choose a place for his sanctuary and there will dwell among his people in a special way. Note then that 1 Kings brackets the account of the building of the temple with Solomon's declarations that God has given rest "on every side" from enemies and disasters (1 Kings 5:4; 8:56). At the dedication of the temple, Solomon indicates that the building of the temple marks the completion of the rest promised by God through Moses.[28] However, that rest is soon forfeited as Solomon and most of his successors in both the northern and southern Israelite kingdoms rebel against God, culminating in the eventual destruction and exile of both nations. In addition, when Jerusalem falls and a foreign oppressor exiles its population, the invaders also destroyed the temple, which is a sure sign that God's people no longer enjoy God's rest. Still, even in exile, God through his prophets gives hope of renewed rest (e.g., Jer. 31:2).

From a New Testament perspective, that rest is not linked to a place but a person: Jesus Christ. In Matthew, Jesus says, "Come to me, all who labor and are heavy laden, and I will give you rest. Take my yoke upon you, and learn from me, for I am gentle and lowly in heart, and you will find rest for your souls" (Matt. 11:28–29). It is interesting to note as well, in association with this promise of rest, that Matthew also brackets his gospel with the presence of God in Jesus. At the beginning, Matthew refers to the prophecy concerning Immanuel, which means "God with us" (1:23; cf. Isa 7:14), and, at the end, Jesus promises, "I am with you always" (28:20). In John, Jesus offers those who trust in him both provision, living water (4:10–14) and the bread of life (6:35–59), and protection as the good shepherd (10:11–18), all elements of the OT concept of rest now found in Jesus himself. Those who maintain their trust in Jesus find the rest in him that was never completely achieved in the conquest and its aftermath because of Israel's faithlessness (Heb. 4:1–11).

Guidance for Today's Community

God has granted us ultimate protection and provision, or rest, in Jesus Christ. Like Israel, God has invited us into his divine purposes, calling us through the Son. Theological traditions argue concerning the extent to which humans can make freewill responses to the call of God, and Deuteronomy itself will suggest that divine aid is needed to respond appropriately or fully (cf. Deut. 10:16; 30:6). However, the repeated examples of the Scripture show that believers did respond in some way to accept what God had given them. The disciples leave behind boats and tax booths to follow Jesus (Matt. 8:18–22; 9:9, et al.). The people on Pentecost and the Philippian jailer ask what they must do and do it (Acts 2:37–41; 16:29–34). Responding to the gift in these ways makes it no less a gift than taking the paper off a present on Christmas morning does. Through Christ, God has given to us his protection and provision, blessing and hope. In Christ, God has given us a role in his greater purposes.

However, like Israel, we can allow fear or doubt to cause us to turn our backs on the call and gift of God. We fear not being able to provide food and shelter for ourselves and our families, so we refuse the gift of God's provision as we seek our own self-sufficiency. We fear the confrontations that our Christian walk may create with family, employers, or the government. We fear the cost or imposition following Christ will make on our lives. So we rebel against God's purposes, never experiencing the joy of rest in Jesus. But the call to us, as to Israel, is: "Do not be afraid! Trust God, accept his gifts, and enjoy his blessings."

Admittedly, this is more easily said than done. We recognize that following Christ can lead to deprivation and physical harm, as Jesus and Apostle Paul both taught and illustrated in their own lives. However, as Jesus showed and Paul lived out, the resurrection means that neither of these are the last words. The last words are life and blessing. As we live between the times, we are like Israel on the border of the Promised Land. To an extent, we experience the blessings of God, to be sure, but not the full realization of the promised blessings. Trusting God to obtain those blessings will mean giving up the comfort of what we know for something hinted at and revealed in glimpses but not fully known. Will we trust the God who has shown himself repeatedly faithful, especially in the resurrection of Jesus, and who controls the destinies of nations? Or will we wander about, never fully trusting, and so let fear and doubt control us?

Perhaps, as we encourage one another not to fear, we would do well to offer our witness to one another about our experiences and the experiences of others of the provision and protection of God, or what makes us trust Him when these things are not so obvious. We see in the Scripture that God indeed fought for Israel and provided for them inside and outside the land, but we sometimes forget that God did not stop working through and for his people when the last page of the Bible was written. Sharing the stories of God's presence and work among us today reminds us that God, who told Israel to take the land and who raised Jesus from the dead, continues to fight for and provide for his people. So we need not fear. We need to move forward in trust and seize the gift of God.

We will also do well to remember that none of us can enjoy the rest until all of us do. That is, it will not do to say, "I have mine. Good luck getting yours." Like the Transjordan tribes, we must fight on behalf of our brothers and sisters who do not enjoy the provision and security that we have. Just as the Jordan River was not a true boundary to the relationship and obligation between the tribes, so national, economic, racial, and gender boundaries do not stand between us and those who are also seeking to obtain the blessings of God. Paul said that in Christ the significance of such boundaries for God's children disappears (Gal. 3:26–29; Eph. 2:11–22). So we are called to put our full enjoyment of these blessings on hold, until we help our fellow Christians everywhere, across various boundaries, to enjoy the gifts of God.

What does mutuality look like? At the very least, it would mean sacrificing our means to better the lot of our poor and suffering brothers and sisters in Christ, although that alone can simply be a means of salving our consciences without ever recognizing the covenantal relationship we share. Thus, it also calls for personal engagement across the boundaries, walking beside those who are cut off from food, clothing, homes, and the like, and helping them find their promised rest.

Chapter 3

What Is Going on Here?

Read: *Deuteronomy 4:1–43*

D euteronomy 4 gets at the heart of what it means for Israel to be Israel as God intended them to be. God delivered Israel from Egypt and was bringing them into the Promised Land for a reason. And that reason is not simply for their enjoyment. In fact, Deuteronomy 4 shows that it has never been simply about Israel itself. God certainly intends to bless Israel, but God's purposes for Israel move well beyond this particular people. Israel is God's instrument in his larger saving purposes. The land of Canaan is not an end for Israel but a means for God to use Israel in service to the nations. Thus, this chapter stands between the recitation of Israel's past faithlessness and God's faithfulness in chapters 1–3, and the giving of the *Torah*, God's divine instruction beginning in 4:44. Faithfulness not only matters for their relationship to God but also for God's purposes for them. Israel has a mission![29]

Call for Obedience (4:1–4)

The first four verses call for obedience to the "statutes and the rules" (ESV; "statutes and ordinances" NRSV),[30] that is, to the individual regulations in the *Torah*, as a condition for taking and living in the land. And Israel cannot be selective in obedience, taking out commands that do not suit them, nor can they replace the stipulations with ones they prefer to keep. Keeping the decrees is the way to life, and this is illustrated vividly by focusing on a past violation of the command against the worship of other gods. At Baal Peor, those who chose to worship Baal were destroyed while those who remained faithful to God remain alive (cf. Num. 25:1–15). Obedience is a matter of life and death for Israel.

Israel as a Witness to the Nations (4:5–8)

Beyond Israel's own survival, these verses reveal why obedience matters: Others will be watching! Living as the community of God not only affects the people of God and their relationship with God and with each other, but it also bears witness to the larger world about the God whom Israel serves. Thus, by living according to the commandments of God, Israel begins to fulfill one of the promises of God to Abraham that "all of the peoples of the earth will be blessed through you" (Gen. 12:3, NIV).

That is, God will put Israel on display for the world. Thus, it seems no mere accident of history that the land God has given Israel is, in some ways, geographically the center of the ancient world. Take a look at a map of the ancient Near East. To the south of Israel is Egypt, which for centuries was a major player on the world stage. To the east is Mesopotamia, home of several significant empires, particularly Assyria and Babylon. To the north were the Hittite Empire and other peoples of the Asia Minor. Two major north-south highways passed through Israelite territory: the King's Highway on the east of the Jordan River and the Via Maris (Way of the Sea) along the Mediterranean coast. Thus, Canaan was the thoroughfare, or crossroads, as the major nations to the north and west (that have to circle the Arabian Desert and come through Canaan from the north) interacted with Egypt and the Arabian nations in trade, diplomacy, or warfare. Add to that the port city of Tyre in neighboring Phoenicia, from which goods and merchants from across the Mediterranean entered the Palestine/Canaan,[31] and Israel had a prime location for God to show them off.

To what exactly does Israel bear witness? According to verses 5–8, Israel demonstrates their "wisdom" and "understanding" to the nations that presumably learn about the statues of God, because they hear the reports of those who have seen Israel keeping those statutes. That is, as people from the nations pass through the land to trade or fight, they would, ideally, look around and notice something different. Unlike where they come from, in Israel there is a people who worships only one God, Yahweh. Because they worship this one God, they treat one another and even the aliens (non-Israelite residents) well. They give rest and eventually freedom to their servants. They do not charge one another interest, and so they do not profit from another's misfortune. Indeed, there are no poor in the land. Their officials and judges grant true justice, regardless of the claimants' wealth or status. They do not invest all power in a single king or individual, but power is spread out. Women are not treated as sexual objects merely to be cast off when they no longer please their husbands. Their religious celebrations include all levels of society.[32] And, in keeping the commands of their God, Israel enjoys the provision and protection of this God. As the nations pass through, what they should see and report at home is a place where everything is different, and it is different because these people keep the commands of this single God they profess. This is not wisdom like the wisdom the foreigners know at home, but something else. This wisdom creates a new kind of community that in many ways sets it apart from the world around it and bears witness to the God who gave these commands. It is, in fact, God's wisdom.

Not only are the people of Israel seen as distinct, but ultimately it is their God, Yahweh, who is seen as distinct. He is a God who is near and hears their prayers. He is not like the distant, mysterious, capricious gods of the nations, but a nearby God who responds to the prayers of the Israelites. He is not a God whom they can anger for unknown reasons and then must seek to appease. He is a God who, because he has given his commandments, makes clear when and why he is either pleased or displeased with his people.

Of course, Israel can successfully carry out this witnessing function only if they keep the commands and decrees. So the issue for Israel throughout their history will be: What do the nations see? Do they see something distinct among the Israelites as they pass through, and so begin to raise questions about this God whom Israel serves? Or will they pass through and see exactly what they see at home—a place where the rich and powerful trample the poor and weak, where justice is had at a price, where human life is often cheap, and where the nation's god is viewed as a partisan of the powerful?

God Alone (4:9–40)

These verses root Israel's witnessing function in Yahweh, the one God they are to serve to the exclusion of all others. Israel's exclusive relationship with God is the foundation upon which all of the commands and statutes, indeed the entire covenant, was built. If they reject this God, their God, then there is no reason to accept the stipulations of their covenant relationship with him. Who they are and will be as a people flows from their singular devotion to the God who brought them out of Egypt and is bringing them into the land he has given them. As Moses will point out later, the very nature of their community life is bound up in the character of their God, Yahweh (see Deut. 10:12–22). To abandon this God or to compromise their understanding of him through the worship of idols and false gods, gods who do not share his character, is to compromise the character and nature of their covenant and thus of their witness.

So Moses calls them to protect their special understanding of God, and thus their relationship with him, by keeping alive their communal and historical memory of him. Memory and keeping that memory alive by passing it on to the subsequent generations becomes one of the primary ways Israel will maintain their exclusive devotion to God. Moses calls them to remember their experience of God at Horeb, which was in fact mostly the previous generation's experience. But Moses here models what he calls the people to do. He imaginatively brings the new generation before the mountain, making them participants in the historical memory. There he reminds them that when they encountered God, they saw a terrible mixture of dark and light, clouds and fire, but they did not see God. Instead, they heard God. Thus, God can never be reduced to an idol of any kind, because they have not seen God and nothing in creation approximates God. Further, idols cannot speak, but their God does speak. They have heard him. So any idol of God reduces God, making him less than the God who brought them out of Egypt and who entered covenant relationship with them at Horeb. It makes him into some other god.

Israel is further reminded that their God is a jealous God (v. 24) who will not sit by and accept reduction to a no-god, an idol. Nor will he allow them to divide their loyalty between him and other gods who are imaged. He is a jealous God. That is, he is zealous for his relationship with Israel. So strong is that zeal or passion that God will not sit idly by and let them violate their relationship. He will step in and do something about it. Indeed, if Israel chooses against God, and thus against his purposes for them, he will punish them, with exile from the land if need be.

However, the fact that God also will allow those who then seek him to return and that he will show them mercy suggests the nature of his judgment upon them. First, God's judgment takes the form of letting them have what they seek. If they desire to serve other gods, then Yahweh God will let them do so in the gods' own land and out of the Promised Land. But ultimately, the point is redemption. The aim is to force them to see the folly of serving other gods and to have them turn wholeheartedly to their God. Then they will experience his restoration and his mercy. For even if they violate the covenant, God is faithful to the covenant and promises to the ancestors, both for the sakes of their descendants and the redemptive purposes he has for their descendants.

Moses highlights God's uniqueness relative to other gods in a variety of ways. Israel's God cannot be physically likened to anything in creation (vv. 15–20). Israel alone has heard their God speak (v. 33).[33] No other god has delivered a nation in the way Israel's God delivered Israel from Egypt and into the Promised Land (vv. 34–38).

But Moses moves beyond claiming that Israel's God is unique among gods to twice claiming that there is no other god (vv. 35, 39). Moses' point is not that God is the best or strongest God among gods, but that he is the only God. This indeed would sound strange to the ears of Israel's neighbors. These neighbors would understand a nation's fidelity to its main god, but not to the exclusion of all other gods. But whatever any other nation would call a god, it is not so for Israel.[34] Yahweh alone is Israel's God, who does for Israel what the nations believe their multiplicity of gods do for them. Israel's God does even more. Israel bears witness to this God in their exclusive loyalty to him and thus in their obedience to his commands.

Cities of Refuge (4:41–43)

The inclusion of the Transjordan cities of refuge here is somewhat puzzling. They would seem to fit better with the general discussion of these cities in 19:1–13. While the existence of such cities certainly reflects God's mercy and concern to protect innocent life, the point here may simply be to round out matters east of the Jordan before turning the focus more specifically to life in the land.

The God of the Community

Obedience to Commands

Though obedience to the commands of the *Torah* could degenerate into the kind of justification or salvation by law-keeping that Paul argues against in Romans and Galatians, Israel did not believe that keeping the commands saved them. God saved them, as Deuteronomy repeatedly highlights in recalling God's deliverance of Israel from Egypt. The decrees and commands are rather the stipulations of the Horeb covenant between God and Israel. To be sure, keeping the covenant is not an option, and obtaining the land and remaining in it is contingent on obedience to these commands. Such obedience is the trusting response to the God who delivered Israel and who has called them to bear witness to his nature to the nations. Such obedience demonstrates what it means to be the people of God—what it looks like.

Though the commands can be corrupted into a burden, as Jesus himself noted (Matt 23:4), they were never intended to be such. As Deuteronomy repeatedly notes, in keeping the commands, Israel would have life (4:1; 5:33; 8:1; 30:6, 15–20). Elsewhere, Israel celebrates the commands and covenant of God as something good, beautiful, and life-giving, most notably the longest chapter in the Bible, Psalm 119.

A Jealous and Judging Yet Merciful God

The result of obedience is blessing in the land that God has given Israel, but disobedience results in curse or judgment. One cannot read Deuteronomy and escape the conclusion that the God of Israel has judged and will judge his people for rebellion against him. But God's judgment is not the judgment of a capricious God. First, he does not judge without cause, and, in Israel's case, the cause is violation of the covenant. However, by knowing the covenant, Israel should understand what will keep them in the situation of blessing rather than judgment. They have the *Torah* and so know what God has called them to be and do. Second, the fact that God holds out the possibility of return for Israel, that he promises to restore them, indicates that his judgment is purposeful. The purpose is not to destroy Israel, though he will punish their wickedness, at times at the cost of many their lives if their rebellion goes unabated. Rather, the purpose of judgment is remedial and ultimately redemptive. In judgment, Israel is to see that other gods are impotent and that their God, Yahweh, alone speaks and acts on behalf of his people.

Therefore, one should not understand God's jealousy as the crazed mistrust of a suspicious lover. Instead, it should be understood as God's passion for the relationship with Israel, a passion rooted in his promise to and love for Israel's ancestors. It is his zeal to protect the exclusive relationship with this nation, not only for their own good but also for the sake of his larger purposes. Israel cannot bear witness to the uniqueness of their God if they continually serve other gods, reduce their God to an idol, or treat him as though he were simply one of many gods.

But even through judgment, God makes his mercy evident in the refusal to give up on them or destroy them and in his willingness to restore them. This is a mercy that is witnessed again and again in the Scripture. When Israel rebelled at Sinai with the calf image, God forgave and restored them (Exod. 32–34). When Israel rebelled in the wilderness (Num. 13–14), refusing to go into the land, God preserved the children so that his promises could continue. During the period of the judges, God repeatedly raised up deliverers—"judges"—for his rebellious people. During the monarchies of Israel and Judah, God sent prophet after prophet to warn them (2 Kings 17:13, 23). Even in exile, God offered hope through his prophets and eventually brought restoration. And God's mercy on the rebellious and sinners is most clearly seen in that "while we were still sinners, Christ died for us" (Rom. 5:8), and when we as God's people sin, if we confess, "he is faithful and just to forgive us our sins and to cleanse us from all unrighteousness" (1 John 1:9).

God Is Unique

Israel's living out the covenant is supposed to suggest something about Israel's God. As we will note later, God calls Israel to live out *his* character in keeping the covenant. Furthermore, Israel shows that their God cannot simply be equated with or put alongside whatever the nations might call a god. Israel is to worship and serve God exclusively. There is a distinction between their God and the multiplicity of the gods the nations serve, not the least of which is that this God is able (and willing!) to provide all of their needs. Thus, Israel need not look elsewhere. Also, unlike the gods of the nations, Yahweh God is not identified with the elements of creation and cannot be imaged by them. He is not a mute and impotent god, as are the gods of the nations. Rather, he is the God who has spoken to Israel and acted on their behalf. Deuteronomy's claim is that their God is *the* God, and Israel need not and cannot look elsewhere.

The Mission of God's People

God has chosen to involve human beings in his plan to redeem creation, and, in particular, he chose the offspring of Abraham, Isaac, and Jacob—that is, the Israelites (Gen. 12:3). Israel was to bear witness to the world about the wisdom and uniqueness of Yahweh, the God of Israel, over against whatever anyone else called a god. Israel bore witness to this by obedience to the commands of God, which reflected the character of the God they confessed. This obedience would set them apart and get the attention of those passing through, and, from there, their attention would be directed to God. Israel's mission was so important, both for their own sake and for the sake of the nations, that God would not allow Israel to thwart it permanently by their rebellion. His zeal for Israel, his passion for that relationship, expands to a zeal for his whole creation, a world "God so loved" (John 3:16).

Guidance for the Today's Community

Trust and Obey

While keeping commands no more saves Christians than it did Israel, still we are—like Israel—to obey the commands of the Lord. In doing so, we submit to the one we call "Lord" and we live out our salvation. In keeping his commands, we demonstrate our love for Jesus (John 14:15, 24). Furthermore, obeying Jesus allows us to remain in the love of God, following the example of Jesus (John 15:10). Indeed, in obedience, we imitate our Lord (John 13:13–14; Phil 2:5–8).

God's Judgment and Mercy

Despite claims by some to the contrary, the God of the Old Testament *is* the God of the New Testament, the one Jesus calls "Father." Nor, as some seem to imply, did God undergo a radical personality change after having a child. Despite the caricature of the God of the OT as wrathful and judging, bear in mind that the most frequent qualities ascribed to God in the Old Testament are graciousness, mercy, and compassion (e.g., Exod. 34:6; Pss. 86:15, 103:8, 111:4, 112:4, 145:8; Joel 2:13; Jonah 4:2). On the other hand, the subject of hell comes up only in the New Testament, and usually on the lips of Jesus (e.g., Matt. 5:29–30; 25:41, 46). That is, it will not do to separate the God in the Old Testament and New Testament on the basis of judgment and mercy. Furthermore, we must bear in mind that God's judgment and jealously are for the sake of the relationship with his people and his redemptive purpose in the world. That is, God's jealously and judgment are subsumed under his love, mercy, and grace. God's zeal for and protection of his relationship with us, even at times through judgment, is intended to keep us close to him, the source of life, and to draw us back into our divinely given mission.

Our Mission

Like Israel, Christians are likewise called to a witnessing function, a mission. However, our mission has shifted from a people on display in a distinct land to a sent people from many nations to many nations (Matt. 28:19–20). We, too, bear witness to this unique, wise, jealous, yet merciful God who intends to redeem all creation. While we often think of mission as sending missionaries into foreign lands, and it does involve this, we also need to consider mission as being out and about in the our own corners of the world as salt and light (Matt. 5:13–16). In part, this mission involves living lives that reflect our devotion to our God, the God of Israel, revealed most fully in Jesus Christ. That is, we cannot show the world that our God is all-sufficient for us then put our trust in and seek blessing from things other than God (e.g., wealth, status, national pride, and military superiority). Nor can we simply agree that anything anyone else calls "God" is in fact the God of the Bible and the church. From time to time, surveys come out reporting that a large majority of Americans believe in God, and that sounds great. But then if you ask those surveyed to define or clarify what they mean by "God," you will find that the answers vary greatly and often depart drastically from the God revealed in the Scripture.

In carrying out our mission, we live in conformity to God's will to point others to God the Father, the Son, and the Holy Spirit. We do so by allowing others to see us living lives faithfully submitted to Jesus' commands, and, to the degree we can, modeling the life of Jesus. We become salt and light so that others may see our good deeds and glorify God (Matt. 5:16). Therefore, doing good cannot be seen as a manipulative or marketing tool to get people to church before we pull a bait-and-switch. Rather, as we do good things in the name of Jesus for the benefit of others, what we want is for them to see something different than what they see in the world at large. Rather than seeing those who are self-seeking, unloving, violent, or those who do good only when it has a benefit for them, they should see in us those who seek the good of others, who love all, who are peacemakers, and who serve without seeking benefits (including feeling good about serving!). This in turn may lead them to ask, "Why are you doing this?" And this question then provides an opportunity to talk about the amazing God we serve. Conversion is God's responsibility. Our mission is bringing God before people by living Christlike lives.

Chapter 4

Ordering Life, Part 1: Love of God

Read: *Deuteronomy 4:44–5:11*

What matters most in life? How should the community of God's people order its life? This next section of Deuteronomy begins to answer that question, laying out the general precepts that will guide Israel's life as a witnessing community. As the people prepare to move across the Jordan River and take the land God has given to them, Moses speaks the *Torah*, God's instruction on living in the land. All Israel is called upon to hear and learn the stipulations of the covenant that God made with them at Horeb (Sinai).[35]

Notice in Deuteronomy 5:3–5 that Moses addresses this new generation as though they were the ones who heard God speak at Mount Horeb. In reality, it was not them (except perhaps for older ones who were children then) but their parents who had heard God at Horeb. This is a common rhetorical device in Deuteronomy. Moses often addresses the current generation as though they are the original participants of the exodus from Egypt and those who entered the covenant at Horeb. From now on, every subsequent generation will be transported back in their imaginations to their ancestors' day to experience the Horeb event for themselves and to commit themselves to the covenant. By imagination and memory, they are linked to the past and participate in it, and they then provide the link for the next generation to participate in the story of God's creation of the nation Israel. Thus, the covenant is not a dead word to a past generation, but a living word to each generation in Israel.

As this generation prepares to reaffirm the covenant, they are reminded of the living God who spoke to them and who has acted on their behalf already in the exodus and the victories on the east side of the Jordan River (4:44–5:6). Indeed, it is imperative to understand that the laws and decrees that follow are rooted precisely in Israel's relationship with their God who brought them out of Egypt (5:6). Thus, these commandments are not timeless "principles" dropped from heaven for everyone everywhere. These are God's words to his people Israel, telling them how to live as the people of God among the nations, thus, enabling them to live out God's purposes for them.[36]

The Ten Commandments (or Ten Words or Decalogue)[37] provide a starting point for the rest of the stipulations of the covenant. The Ten Commandments are fairly general, giving the bigger picture of what the community of God is to be, but they set trajectories for the other stipulations, which give more details regarding the community's life.[38] These commandments get at the heart of what it means to be God's people, and they invite reflection on how Israel should practice each commandment in day-to-day living, even beyond the situations envisioned in the individual laws that follow. This is important to bear in mind because, as with any law, the stipulations of the Law do not (and could not!) cover every possible situation in the life of Israel. Thus, the Ten Commandments call Israel to apply the commandments in situations that may yet arise and that are not specifically covered in the *Torah* stipulations.[39]

It has often been noted that the Ten Commandments divide along the lines of the more vertically directed commands, those that have to do with Israel's relationship to God (commands 1–3), and the more horizontally directed commands, those having to do with relationships among Israelites (commands 5–10). The fourth commandment, on Sabbath, then serves as a transitional commandment with both horizontal and vertical aspects. While this division is generally appropriate, it must be stated that neither group is exclusively horizontal or vertical in orientation. Israel's obedience to the "vertical" commands, their exclusive loyalty and submission to God, deeply affects how they relate to their fellow Israelites and others. Likewise, how they treat their fellow Israelites is reflective of their relationship with God and affects their mission in bearing witness to him through how they treat others. The Sabbath command, as the "transition," illustrates this beautifully by showing that what Israel does for others on the Sabbath is a reflection of what God has done for them.

In addition, Christopher Wright has shown how the ordering of the commandments reflects a scale of values or priorities that are to be reflected in the lives of the people. That scale, beginning with the most important is: God (the first three commandments), the welfare of society as a whole (the Sabbath commandment), family (fifth commandment), individual human life (sixth commandment), sex (seventh commandment), and property (last three commandments). He also notes astutely that our modern society has "almost precisely inverted this order of priorities."[40] But again, these priorities cannot be separated. They are mutually interrelated and rooted in *the* priority for Israel, Yahweh their God.

The First Commandment: No Other Gods (5:7)

Deuteronomy has already illustrated what is commanded here: there is no god for Israel except Yahweh, the God who brought them out of Egypt. In terms of translation, as the footnotes in many Bibles make clear, the command can be rendered "you shall have no other gods *before* me" or "no other gods *besides* me." The former could suggest that other gods are permitted, though Yahweh would have priority. The latter is more interpretive but gets at the meaning better. The phrase translated "before" or "besides" has the idea of being present or in the presence of, so a good translation would be, "Do not let another god come into our [Yahweh's and Israel's] presence together."[41] The emphasis here is not on an abstract notion of monotheism, that Yahweh is the only God, but on Israel's relationship to Yahweh. Despite whatever anyone else considers gods, for Israel, Yahweh is the *only* God. "*You, Israel,* shall have no other god." Yahweh is the God who made and fulfills the promises to their ancestors, who brought them out of slavery in Egypt, who spoke to them "face-to-face" on the mountain, and who entered the covenant with them at Horeb. He alone is God for them.

The Second Commandment: No Images (5:8–10)

Since the previous commandment prohibits Israel from having other gods, which presumably would include idols of those gods, this command probably intends mainly to prohibit attempts to image

Yahweh. However, idols of any sort are ruled out for Israel, and the reference to God's jealousy in verse 9 broadens the prohibition to cover any idol, whether an image of Yahweh or another god.

Already, in 4:15–19, we saw that Israel could not approximate God with an image of anything in creation, because they had not seen God. They heard him, but they did not see him. Images would allow Israel to confuse the Creator with the created, both by what is imaged and by the stone, wood, or metal used in the image. Also, by focusing on a single object, the image could identify God with only one sphere of activity, again, denying his all-sufficiency for Israel. Finally, since in the world around Israel idols were the medium for humans to meet the needs of the gods (for example, feeding them), images of Yahweh would suggest that he was somehow dependent upon and could even be manipulated by them. The portable nature of many idols could suggest the latter as well.

This commandment is accompanied by both warning and encouragement. God will punish those who "hate" him—that is, show covenantal disloyalty—by worshipping idols. That punishment will extend to their children, grandchildren, and great-grandchildren. However, his love will last a thousand generations for those who love him. In the former case, one may question how or why God would punish children for the sins of their parents (cf. 24:16).[42] Of course, it could simply imply that subsequent generations will suffer the consequences of their parents' actions. That is, the children will suffer the effects of God's judgment as well, whether it comes via famine, disease, invasion, or exile. So parents are advised to consider the effects of their actions upon their children. Another or additional possibility is that "the third and fourth generation" refers to the multigenerational households in Israel. Perhaps the suggestion is that any punishment for idolatry on the parents (i.e., the head of the household) has an immediate effect on those living under their roof. Or it could imply that all the members of the multigenerational household are following the lead of the parents and also worshipping idols (cf. 13:6–11). If so, their punishment is for their own disobedience.[43] Again, this would caution the parents to think about how what they do affects their families.

In sharp, hugely unbalanced contrast to the punishment on those who hate God, those who love God are rewarded to the thousandth generation! Showing love to God is here equated with obedience, and the concept of "love" itself has covenantal connotations in the larger culture around Israel. Thus, God and Israel demonstrate love, in the covenant context, by what they do. God loves by fulfilling the covenantal blessings, and Israel loves by obeying God. However, this covenantal understanding of love does not rule out genuine affection between God and Israel. While punishment on the children for the sins of the parents tends to capture our attention, the real focus should be the disparity between the consequences for the disobedient and the obedient. If taken literally, God shows love to the thousandth generation—250 times greater than his punishment to those who hate him. However, rather than taking the statement literally, it probably ought to be understood as "an unimaginably long time."

The Third Commandment: Do Not Misuse God's Name (5:11)

The third commandment is traditionally rendered something like, "Do not take the Lord's name in vain." The word translated "in vain" indicates deceitfully, emptily, or with futility. In Exodus 23:1, this word is connected with witnesses giving false reports. In Psalm 12:2, it is in parallel to flattering lips and a deceitful heart, and, in Psalm 26:4, it is in parallel to hypocrites, that is, those who pretend to be what they are not. In Psalms 60:11 and 108:12, it has to do with the uselessness of human aid compared to God's help. Thus, the sense of the word is to take the name of Yahweh on one's lips for false, deceitful, and even useless or empty purposes. Oaths in a judicial setting may have been the primary intent, where one would invoke Yahweh's name to ensure the truth of his or her testimony. But it expands beyond that to any situation where human claims, pledges, or covenants are supported by an appeal to God's name. Thus, for example, the prophet who claimed to speak for Yahweh, when Yahweh had not, in fact, spoken to him, would violate this commandment (cf. Deut. 18:15–22). Failing to fulfill vows made in Yahweh's name would flow out of the commandment (23:21–23). This commandment could also prevent magical uses of God's name.

Israel's God cannot be manipulated, and they should not try to do so through magic, a means others in the ancient world believed one could use to manipulate their gods. Finally, it also warns against irreverent or unthinking uses of God's name.

The God of the Community

The first three commandments establish Israel's priority. It is not so much God first, then whatever else second, third, fourth, and so on. God is *the* priority for Israel, and whatever else Israel does and whatever else Israel is flows out of the recognition that Yahweh is God alone for Israel, distinct and apart from all of creation—unlike anything else others call "god," and not subject to human reduction or manipulation.

The First Commandment

To pursue other gods means rejecting Israel's God, Yahweh, as an exclusive covenant partner. By extension, then, to worship other gods is to deny that Yahweh is all-sufficient to provide for and protect his people. Israel has no need of other gods because Yahweh does all for them that the nations believe their manifold gods do for them, and he does more.[44] He has invited them into a true relationship and given them a role in his redemptive purposes. The community's life and purpose are found in this God and him alone. To pursue other gods denies his uniqueness and undermines their role as Yahweh's witnesses to the nations.

God sees devotion to other gods as personal betrayal. God takes it so seriously that he commands Israel to execute prophets who encourage people to follow other gods, family members to join in executing their own flesh and blood who serve other gods, and Israel to completely destroy Israelite towns that follow other gods (Deut. 13). On the other hand, in keeping the commandment by recognizing only Yahweh as their God, Israel remains in that covenant relationship in which God promises to richly bless them. It sets up a relationship that touches every aspect of their lives. They will enjoy life in fellowship with God and with one another. Furthermore, their lives in that relationship become an invitation for the nations around them to inquire why in the world one God is sufficient for these people.

The Second Commandment

Idolatry, in the popular imagination reduces and limits God, confuses him with created things, and lumps him in among what other people consider gods. But God absolutely refuses such degradation or confusion. Making images of God fails to recognize who he is and what he does, compared to the effectively impotent gods that other nations serve. Idolatry fails to hold up God as unique and thus will fail to draw the nations to him. Therefore, God prohibits any images of himself along with the prohibition on worship of other gods (and their idols).

On the other hand, stated positively, this commandment, along with the first commandment, invites Israel to constantly be aware of the uniqueness of their God. He is qualitatively and quantitatively distinct from whatever else others call a god. He is a God worthy of their love and obedience because he is unlike anything else in all of creation, indeed, because all of creation is his creation. Furthermore, he is a God worthy of their love and obedience, because he has demonstrated his love and faithfulness in ways that no other gods could or have done for them through the exodus and through the covenant relationship.

The Third Commandment

God's people must take his divine name seriously. When Israel invokes his name in an oath or contractual situation, they are essentially invoking his reputation and power. To do so and then disregard the oath or agreement, or to use it as a means to twist or manipulate the truth for one's own benefit, reflects poorly on the name of the God they confess. God's name, and God himself, becomes a means to an end. Thus, God is no longer recognized as their Creator and Sovereign. Such usage lessens and cheapens God in Israel, and, by extension, among those who hear of this God, perhaps in the false oaths and deceitful promises of his people. Thus, their witness about this God is corrupted. Beyond that, misusing the Lord's name in this way could have real-life disastrous consequences in Israel. If an oath was evoked in Yahweh's name in a court case, the testimony could affect the life or livelihood of the one on trial.

Just as idolatry can reduce God in the eyes of his people and others, so can invoking his name for false or futile purposes. God will not allow himself to be so reduced in the eyes and actions of his people. They are called to recognize him as the God who delivers and sustains them, and thus they must not rely on their own devices, whether it is idols they have made with their hands or false oaths or magical incantations to get what they want. Furthermore, his faithfulness to the covenant means that he aims to protect those who could be injured by the false oaths and promises made in his name, typically those people who are among the weak of society and have little recourse if the justice system is corrupted in this way. Also, God's faithfulness to the promises of Abraham, especially his intent to bless all people through Abraham's descendants, is placed in jeopardy if those descendants do not take their own God seriously.

Stated positively, the third command calls Israel to hold God's name, and thus God himself (since his name involves his reputation and character), in high regard. By refusing to use God's name to their own ends, they recognize that he is God, who is to be revered rather than used. They tell the world around them that this God is unique and not subject to the same trivialization and manipulation that other gods are.

Guidance for Today's Community

As with Israel, God is not simply the number one priority for Christians; God is *the priority*. The way we may think of our relationship to God, in terms of priorities, is God first, family second, then whatever else (work, golf, gardening, karaoke) third, fourth, etc. But this is a mistake. This view compartmentalizes our lives, giving God perhaps the biggest percentage (at least we claim to do so) but treating the various aspects of our lives in isolation. Instead, God is *the* priority of our lives. Everything else we are and everything else we do flows from that exclusive relationship. He has saved us through his Son, Jesus Christ, and has sealed us with his Holy Spirit, and, in doing so, he has laid exclusive claim to our lives. The first three commandments demonstrate what is to shape and guide Israel's life and ours: exclusive loyalty to God that neither reduces nor compromises him.

The first commandment reminds us that we, too, are called to exclusive loyalty to the Lord God, and that we can put our full trust in him as the one who is all-sufficient. It prevents us from farming out responsibility for our lives to people (including ourselves) or things that we believe will secure us or provide for us; that is, our other gods. We do not put our faith in financial planning, medical institutions, government, and military to grant us the things we need, because we trust that God is all-sufficient to provide for us. As with Israel, this does not mean that we do not work to earn a living or take safety precautions, but we do so with the understanding that we cannot in any final way secure our lives by these means. We know that they are all weak, temporary, and ultimately cannot be relied upon. We know this from experience. People lose jobs or become injured so that they cannot work. Despite our fences, inoculations, seat belts, and safety helmets, children still get hurt and many still die. Markets crash, terrorists slip through our defenses, and human strength fails. Thus, we seek first his kingdom of God and his righteousness in our jobs, family life, political involvement, and so on, and we trust that he will provide the things we need as well (Matt. 6:33). Such a radical trust then bears witness to the larger world that our security and hope rest solely in the God we confess. There is no other before or besides him for us.

The second commandment then complements the first by warning us against reducing the all-sufficient God, making him less than God. We are reminded that a reduced god, one who can be confused with creation or manipulated, really is not all-sufficient after all. Indeed, it is not God at all. What we call God becomes simply one more tool in our efforts to manage our own lives. If something eventually comes up that we cannot handle—disaster, depression, death, etc.—we then trot him out as the last hope, but only one hope among others and one that many people will gladly blame if things do not work out as desired.

But the second commandment also reminds us of the uniqueness of the God we serve. He cannot simply be set on a shelf next to other so-called gods or be identified with them. He cannot be confused with what he has created, including nature (sun, trees, humans), biological impulses (sex, satisfaction of needs), or human devices (ingenuity, technology, wealth). He is the God who lives and speaks and acts. He is *the* God who so loved the world that he gave his one and only Son.

At this point, it is worth noting that there is a difference between what the ancient world called gods and what we often call gods today, at least when asked in a Sunday school class to identify our modern gods. In Sunday school, the list usually starts with money, then moves to things like ourselves, our military, status, or political power. The difference is that, unlike the so-called gods of the ancient world, some of these modern gods have power, at least for a time. For example, people with money can live more securely and get things done that they could not do without that money. That is, unlike a statue of Baal or Zeus, money works. I can pray, "O Baal give me food" and nothing will happen, but I can take my money to the grocery store and stock up. So what is the connection between serving impotent gods in the ancient world and a "god" like money today? Both reveal what is ultimately an attempt by humans to direct their own fates or manage their own lives. Idolatry has less to do with reverence than with attempts to sway or appease the gods so that the worshipper could get on with his life. Money and our other modern idols are used for the same purpose. So both lead to the self-delusion that we can, somehow, control our lives, and this lie turns us from trust in the One who truly has our lives in his hands.

The third commandment speaks to us along these lines as well, when we think about idolatry as an attempt to manipulate God. Consider the ways we can invoke God's name in attempts to bend his will to ours, instead of our wills to his, and thus try to retain control. Christians are often taught that if they will but say a certain prayer or perform certain ritual, God somehow becomes like a vending machine producing a predictable and expected result.[45] However, this view likewise reduces God because, in our minds, he is no longer free to be God but is subject to our desires and to our manipulations. But God will not be coerced or manipulated. We trust that he will care for us, not because we have somehow forced his hand, but because he has promised to do so and has shown himself faithful to that promise among his people.

The third commandment also reminds us of our witness as those who confess faith in God the Father, Son, and Spirit. When we invoke God's name, whether in contracts, oaths, or covenants (e.g., marriage), how seriously we take those pledges reflects not only on our personal integrity but our respect and devotion for the God we confess. If we can simply throw around his name lightly to accomplish our ends, then we testify to the world that neither we nor they should take God seriously. Thus, we should constantly be aware and suspicious of those who invoke God-language to their own selfish ends, whether it is companies that know "religion sells" or politicians who wrap their political agendas in God-language (beware of the politicians who appear in churches around election time!).

In this regard, it is also worth reflecting on the covenant we make in baptism, which is done *in the name of* the Father, Son, and Holy Spirit. Baptism is a sign of the covenant we have entered with God, much as circumcision was for Israel (Col. 2:11–12), and in it we have clothed ourselves in Christ (Gal. 3:27). In baptism, we commit ourselves wholeheartedly to God who saves us by the resurrection of Jesus Christ (1 Pet. 3:21), and we die to sin that we might live for Christ (Rom. 6:3–4). Thus, to reject the discipleship to which Jesus has called us, to live as though we are lords of our own lives and Jesus is merely a useful prop at times to make us feel good or to get our way, is to take the Lord's name in vain.

Finally, lest we simply hear these commands individualistically, we must remember that they are delivered to the community of God's people. While they certainly have relevance to our lives individually, we also need to reflect on how they speak to us as the people of God. If individuals can turn wealth, status, power, and self-reliance into gods or idols, so can churches. A church that believes it can only survive if it has a certain amount of money in the bank is veering away from dependence on God. A church that glories in its size or finds its identity primarily in its nationality instead of its God has dropped a knee to other gods. A church who sees its hope of survival tied up in a strong national defense to protect religious freedom and its road to influence through strong political connections no longer sees God as all-sufficient. Furthermore, when a church does not live up to its commitments and calling or simply thinks it is sufficient to wear the name of Christ apart from its calling to reflect Christ in the world, that church has taken its Lord's name in vain.

Chapter 5

Ordering Life, Part 2: Love of Neighbor

Read: *Deuteronomy 5:12–5:33*

The remaining seven commandments are more focused on human relationships. Already, we have seen that all of Israel's life grows out of its exclusive relationship with God. The fourth through tenth commandments point to how the members of a God-centered community relate to one another, but with implications for how they relate to God.[46]

The Fourth Commandment: Observe the Sabbath (5:12–15)

The Sabbath[47] was not a day of worship, *per se*, akin to Sunday for Christians. The details of what the ancient Israelites did on the Sabbath are obscure, because the focus is on what they are not to do: work. The one thing they are told to do is to remember what God has done for them.

The Sabbath commandment forms a transition between the first three commandments and the final six by holding Israel's gaze simultaneously on what God has done for them and on what they are to do for one another. God provided Israel with rest by freeing them from Egypt, and they remember their deliverance from forced labor by ceasing their labor on the seventh day.[48] Thus, Sabbath focuses their attention on the God who gave them rest. At the same time, the command calls upon Israel to *provide* rest, not only for family members, but everyone else in the community—from slaves to foreigners to the animals. Note that the command specifies that the rest is to be given "that your male servant and your female servant may rest as well as you." The command is for all Israel but has special application and benefit for those who would not otherwise experience such a rest. As is frequently the case in Deuteronomy, special care is taken to watch out for those who were among the lower levels of the socioeconomic system. So the entire community comes to a halt in a regular observance and enjoyment of the rest God provided for them, and, in providing rest, they become imitators of their God.[49]

The God of the Community

The Sabbath observance illustrates a principle of Israel's community life, namely, that Israelites live their lives in imitation of the God they serve. This principle will be spelled out further in 10:14–19, but here it is shown most fundamentally. Just as Israel was granted rest by God, so Israel grants rest.

The implications of Sabbath extend further. First, by ceasing to work and running the risk of loss that could occur by not working, Israel is reminded that God will provide for them in the land of promise. Keep in mind the anticipation of life in the land as "rest" (Deut. 3:20; 12:10; 25:19). This result of Sabbath observance corresponds nicely with the version of the command in Exodus 20:8–11, which focuses on God as creator, and thus the one whom they can trust to supply their needs. Though the Israelites work the land and care for their livestock, they must remember that all they have comes from God. Sabbath serves, in the midst of their prosperity, as a safeguard against forgetting who God is and what he has done for them, a danger that Moses repeatedly warns Israel against (e.g., Deut. 6:10–12; 8:10–20). Furthermore, in this light, the renewal of focus each week on God as provider prevents the idolatry of work and of self-reliance.

Second, Sabbath sets Israel apart as unique within the world around them. When Israel stops working every seventh day, a practice found nowhere else in the ancient Near East, they mark themselves as distinct. But it is not distinction simply for the sake of distinction. Their rest serves as a witness to those who see them, and, as a result, raises questions about this God they serve. How can they stop working when the crops must be planted or harvested, when the borders must be defended, and when commerce must go on to survive? They can because they trust their God, Yahweh, to care for them.

Third, Sabbath becomes the great equalizer in the Israelite community. It is the reminder that all Israel was once enslaved, that they shared a common deliverance, and now that all in Israel share a common rest serves to put everyone on the same level: all are objects of God's mercy and salvation. Though different social and economic levels will develop in Israel, Sabbath observance relativizes them all. In this regard as well, the Deuteronomy and Exodus versions of the commandment mesh well. Both remind of commonalities rather than differences. Deuteronomy's version points to a common salvation, and the Exodus version, being rooted in Creation, to the fact that all humans are created in God's image (cf. Gen. 1:26–28).

Guidance for Today's Community

The first question on many people's minds after a discussion of the Sabbath is, "Do Christians have to take a day off, too?" I am already nervous about the question, because it can reveal a tendency toward legalism and miss the focus on God that comes in our observing a rest. This is precisely the problem Jesus encountered with Pharisees in the New Testament: rules about Sabbath-keeping overwhelmed the purpose of Sabbath-keeping. There is no direct command for Christians to take any day off, though clearly Sunday eventually became such a day for many. We do gather for worship as a community on the first day of the week, but that does not necessarily demand that the whole day be taken off. Indeed, for some, such has never been a possibility. In the early church, many of the Christians were slaves of non-Christian masters and could not take a day off. Likewise, today, many have jobs that require them to work on Sunday, and I certainly would not want to use this commandment to induce guilt. Some have no choice because of who employs them or the demands of their jobs (e.g., firemen or emergency room doctors and nurses). Others have to work to make ends meet, which is more of an indictment on the affluent employers and consumers—and the Christian community when those people are in our midst—than the worker. But the principle of Sabbath, the idea of taking and providing rest, remains important for the Christian community for a number of reasons. The "how" may differ. Some may not work on a given day. Some may block off time within each day to cease. The "why" is more important than the "how."

First, while the Sabbath was not originally a day for formal corporate worship in Israel as Sunday is for Christians, it did have a worshipful aspect in its recognition of who God was for Israel: their creator, sustainer, and deliverer. Thus, Sabbath can inform how we worship as Christians. In our community's worship, we renew our focus and reorient our lives by remembering that God has created us, provides for us, and has redeemed us through Jesus Christ. Sabbath reminds us to rest, to cease from our work, because we have a Creator, Provider, and Redeemer. We did not create or redeem ourselves, and ultimately we do not secure our lives. Sabbath observance says to each of us, "There is a God, and you are not him."

Second, we are reminded of our calling to be Christlike, particularly to those within the community but also to those alien to our community. We not only enjoy rest, but we also *give* rest—to our family members, to those who work for us, to the poor and needy—by finding ways to alleviate their distresses. One question that often comes up when I teach on the Sabbath is whether Christians should patronize restaurants on Sunday. The thinking is that by eating at these places, we are forcing people to work. However, whether we go or not probably would not have much effect on whether the restaurant was open on Sunday, and we should not expect everyone else to conform to our religious traditions. Indeed, many may really need that Sunday job to put food on their tables. So, perhaps, in this case, the way we can provide rest is twofold. First, we can avoid being overdemanding and obnoxious to the servers. Sadly, I have heard over and over again from those who have been servers that the after-church crowd often accounts for the most disagreeable and rude customers. Second, we can tip really well to help relieve some of the servers' burdens.[50]

Third, Sabbath becomes the great equalizer in our Christian communities. As we grant rest in imitation of the Lord who gives us rest (Matt. 11:28–29), social and economic class distinctions should disappear. No longer should the rich be favored over the poor (James 2:1–13). Distinctions of gender, ethnicity, and social station are lost in the grace freely bestowed on all (Gal. 3:27–28). Indeed, Sabbath reminds us that Christians are all alike in that "for all have sinned and fall short of the glory of God, and are justified by his grace as a gift, through the redemption that is in Christ Jesus" (Rom. 3:23–24).

Fourth, some kind of Sabbath observance, enjoying and granting rest, still serves as a witness today. It sets us apart as unique. When others see that we take a break from our hectic, success-driven, status-driven, profit-driven society and simply stop, questions arise. When they see by our rest that we do not think our own survival, much less the survival of our company or our world is in our hands, questions arise. When they see that we grant rest to employees while paying them as well as anyone else so they need not worry about making ends meet, questions arise. When we free our children from their extracurricular activity-filled, stressed, success-driven lives and require them to rest, questions arise.

Our participation in the Lord's Supper mirrors the principle of Sabbath in many of these ways.[51] The bread and wine remind us of and make us participants in the body and blood of Jesus through which God has saved us (Matt. 26:26–29; Mark 14:22–25; Luke 22:14–20; 1 Cor. 10:16–17). In saving us, God created us as a community that enjoys the rest of Jesus' easy yoke (Matt. 11:28–29) and anticipates that final rest when Jesus returns (Heb. 4:1–11). Also, the Lord's Supper reminds us of our common salvation in Jesus Christ and thus calls on us within the body of Christ to reject the world's social and economic distinctions (1 Cor. 11:17–34).[52]

The Fifth Commandment: Honor Your Parents (5:16)

The commandment to honor parents is addressed to all Israel and therefore applies to any child, but perhaps it applies especially in adults' relationships with their parents. The word translated "honor" in this commandment has the basic meaning of "to be heavy." Thus, to paraphrase, Israelites are to give due weight or significance to their parents, both their mother and their father. The opposite of honoring parents is, thus, to treat them lightly as suggested by Deuteronomy 27:16, where a curse is pronounced on those who dishonor their parents. The word translated "dishonors" can also mean "to treat lightly."[53]

That is, the fifth commandment calls on Israelites to respect, obey, and care for their parents. The respect in this case is not respect that is earned but respect that is due simply because they are the parents. While

45

respect would certainly include speaking well of one's parents, it is most clearly manifested in obedience to them. The significance of this expectation of respect and obedience becomes clear in Deuteronomy 21:18–21, where a "stubborn and rebellious son" who refuses to heed his parents' correction is executed. This law also suggests that honoring parents means living an honorable life that reflects well on one's parents. Finally, honoring parents means caring for them in their old age. Just as they provided for and cared for the child as he or she grew, so it becomes the child's obligation to meet the needs of their parents.

The motivation for honoring parents is that those who do so may live long and well in the land God has given them. The well-being of the community is somehow tied to the observance of this commandment. Since, in the context of a command on honoring parents, Israel is reminded that God has given them the land, perhaps the implication is that how they honor their parents becomes reflective of how they honor God. People given to dishonor on the fundamental societal level of the parent-child relationship are also likely to show dishonor to authority on all levels of society, culminating with dishonor, and hence disobedience, to God. And Israel is warned that rebellion against God's authority will ultimately lead to expulsion from the land. On the other hand, those who grow up honoring their parents are formed to honor authority within the community and ultimately to honor God. In this case, as the commandment suggests, Israelites will enjoy life and prosperity in the land. Hence, honoring parents has implications for the community at large—in intracommunity relationships and the community's relationship with God.

The God of the Community

Submission to one's parents demonstrated a respect for their God-given authority and therefore by extension a respect for God's authority. Refusal to submit to authority on the fundamental level of the parent-child relationship could be evidence of a rebellious streak that will manifest itself in a refusal to accept God's authority. Put another way, children who refuse to respect their parents are likely to show disrespect to God as well. If this is the case, then the community becomes useless as a witness for God. Why would anyone else honor God if Israel refuses to do so?

Honoring parents, submitting to their instruction, becomes important in Israel also because parents are a primary means for passing down the *Torah* from generation to generation. Other means are used, but Israelite parents are to teach the commands of God to their children always and everywhere (Deut. 6:6–9). Children who submit to their parents will submit to their parents' *Torah* instructions, hence, creating a community submissive to God, allowing them to remain in the land and enjoy the blessings of God. Those who refuse to respect and obey their parents will disregard the *Torah* for themselves and fail to pass it on to their own children, creating a situation ripe for forgetting and then forsaking their God. This situation will then lead to expulsion from the land.

On another level, the care for parents implied in this command is consistent with Deuteronomy's overall call to care for those who do not have the means or ability to care for themselves. When the elderly can no longer provide for themselves, they are at the mercy of others, much like the widow, orphan, and alien. Thus, the children step up to insure that their parents are properly cared for. This call is consistent with Jesus' rebuke of the Pharisees for allowing people to disregard this commandment and not care for their parents in the name of a presumed higher religious act (cf. Mark 7:9–13). It is also consistent with Paul's call for Christians to care for elderly widows in their family and his insistence that one who does not "has denied the faith and is worse than an unbeliever" (1 Tim. 5:3–8).

Guidance for Today's Community

God's people today are likewise called to respect, obey, and care for their parents. Interestingly, nowhere in the Old or New Testaments is the call to honor *good* parents but simply parents. Drawing on the fifth commandment, Paul tells Christian children—again, not simply little ones but adult children as well—to obey their parents "for this is right" (Eph. 6:1). He does not argue the point; he simply asserts that it is the right thing to do. Thus, we esteem our parents, care for them, and, yes, obey them.

As in ancient Israel, refusal to submit to the basic level of authority—parents—has ripple effects both with the community of

God and larger societal authorities. Christians who do not honor their parents are far less likely to honor their church's elders (cf. 1 Tim. 5:17), the governmental authorities, and ultimately God himself. If we resist the notion that refusing to honor parents leads to refusing to honor God, keep in mind that in not honoring our parents, we are disobeying God. Over the past several generations, the notion of submitting to any authority, much less the idea of God-ordained authority (cf. Rom. 13:1–7), has become repugnant to many.[54] Thus, honoring parents and other authorities becomes countercultural, drawing the attention of others to the uniqueness of the Christian community. Of course, if a parent or any other authority told us to do something against the will of God, then we could not submit and would answer with Peter and John: "We must obey God rather than men" (Acts 5:29; cf. 4:19). But usually our balking at authority falls far short of this standard.

In the church, as in Israel, parents are the first and most important source for passing on faith from one generation to the next (cf. 2 Tim. 1:5). Parents are called upon to raise their children "in the discipline and instruction of the Lord" (Eph. 6:4). In a church where children of all ages honor their parents, the atmosphere is cultivated to keep the faith alive across generations. In a church where children do not honor their parents and their parents' teaching on faith, a true faith in God can disappear within a generation or two even if the church continues the rituals. In this case, honoring parents means honoring the traditions and teachings of the parents. Even when changes are made within the church to relate to the current culture, it cannot be done with the disrespectful attitude that says, "These old people don't know what they are talking about!" or "Who needs them anymore?" The result will be a childish church acting in childish ways that will find the same struggles occurring when its children grow up, if they are still even a part of the church.

Honoring our parents also means that we care for them in their old age. Paul argues that caring for parents and grandparents is a way for children to repay them (1 Tim. 5:4). As we care for them, we continue to show them deference and respect, which means we treat elderly parents as adults and not children. If our parents become too weak to feed, clothe, and groom themselves, we may find ourselves doing for them as they once did for us: spoon feeding, bathing, even changing them. However, we do not let those similarities with caring for a child cause us to regard them as children.

Admittedly, such care can become a strain on the children physically, financially, and emotionally, but probably no more so than the children were to the parents. But even if the burden is heavier, we remind ourselves that life is not about pleasing ourselves but about bearing witness to the God we serve. What a marvelous witness it becomes when the world at large sees us caring for our elderly parents even when it creates a strain, because we love them and because we love the Lord. The community also bears witness when it helps those children who are so honoring their parents with the burden and when it honors its many "moms" and "dads" in the faith, whether they have their own children or not, by caring for them in their old age (cf. 1 Tim. 5:3).

Should we then put our parents in nursing homes? This question often gets asked in light of this commandment. Certainly, there are times when a nursing home is an appropriate option for a parent who needs specialized care. But it would be incumbent upon the children to investigate the quality of care given in the home and to be with their parents often. If Christians simply use a nursing home, no matter how nice it is, as a place to warehouse elderly parents and keep them out of sight and mind until they die, then it does violate this commandment. But there can be a witness for the church as well when it makes sure that their own parents are not forgotten in these institutions and when they even look after others people's parents there.

The Sixth Commandment: Do Not Kill (5:17)

Many versions of the Bible translate the sixth commandment as "Do not *murder*," but the word used here can indicate murder (e.g., Num. 35:16, 21, 31; Deut. 22:26) or unintentional killing (Num. 35:6, 11, 25, 28; Deut. 4:42; 19:3, 4, 6; Josh. 20:3, 5), though it is used much more in the case of the former than the latter.[55] Given later stipulations in Deuteronomy, the commandment does not exclude killing in war (20:1–18) or capital punishment (e.g., Deut. 13:10; 17:5–6; 21:21-23; 22:21–24). Thus, the translation "Do not murder" does seem to be what the command is getting at. However, since the word has a broader meaning, perhaps it is better to translate the command "Do not kill." This translation gives it the broadest possible application and requires those who would take human life to justify why such killing should be considered permissible.[56] In Israel, human life is to be respected and protected.

The God of the Community

The commandment against killing is rooted in the fact that God gives life to humans who are created in his image, rather than an abstract notion of the sanctity of life (Gen. 9:5–6). To simply say that life can never be taken, human or otherwise, runs into obstacles with the rest of the Law.[57] Furthermore, since God alone grants life, it is God's prerogative alone to decide under what circumstances human life can be taken away, whether it be judicially, by direct divine judgment, or simply letting life runs its course. The protection of human life is so important that when the innocent are killed, the community faces curse until there is justice for the victim (cf. Gen. 9:5; 1 Kings 2:31–33; 2 Kings 24:1–4; Jer. 22:17–19).

Deuteronomy repeatedly illustrates the importance of avoiding innocent bloodshed and unnecessary bloodshed. First, judicial execution requires two or more witnesses to insure that an innocent person is not put to death (Deut. 17:6–7). Second, the stipulations for cities of refuge prevent someone who accidentally kills from being murdered in revenge while allowing for the execution of the one who intentionally kills (Deut. 19:1–13). Third, even an unsolved death requires atonement and a declaration of innocence by the community, lest the people be held responsible (Deut. 21:1–9). Fourth, parents are not to be executed for the crimes of their children nor children for the crimes of their parents (Deut. 24:16).[58] Fifth, even in cases of war against enemies outside the land, Israel is to first offer terms of surrender, and if those terms are refused, only the men (i.e., those who would be combatants) are killed (Deut. 20:10–15).[59]

Given God's special care for the vulnerable, the prohibition on killing can also be extended to include the indirect taking of life through conspiracy, injustice, or deprivation. That is, if Israelites lie to have an enemy executed (see below on giving false testimony) or if they deprive a person of the means of livelihood through confiscation of their land (cf. Deut. 19:14) or by failing to pay their wages, they could be taking a life (cf. Deut. 24:14–15; James 5:1–6).

Viewed positively, the commandment calls for respecting and protecting human life. The command invites God's people to recognize their common identity as those created in the image of God as well as their common mortality. Thus, it leads to proactive steps to protect and preserve life. In Deuteronomy, this would include providing for the poor through gifts (15:7–11), tithes (26:12), or gleaning (24:19–22), as well as safety precautions in home construction to avoid shedding innocent blood (22:8).

It does not take a great leap of the imagination to see where a community that no longer recognizes the image of God in the other and that no longer protects life will go. Members of such a community regard human life as merely a commodity to be exploited for personal gain or an obstacle to be overcome for the same reason. Life becomes graded, with survival of the fittest as the rule. Those who can, through power or means, protect themselves will do so at the expense of those who cannot, which, of course, is the complete opposite of what God calls his people to do. God's people take special notice and care of those who do not have within themselves the means of protection.

Guidance for Today's Community

The sixth commandment calls us to consider all human life as valuable, because every human is created in the image of God. While certainly we refrain from taking life, the commandment also invites us to explore ways in which we can promote life. Thus, for example, not only do we take a stand against abortion, but we find proactive means to prevent situations that lead to abortion. That is, we as a community provide support and care for the mother and the child. Not only do we refrain from raising a hand against the poor and the immigrant, but we seek ways to aid their survival and human dignity.

Jesus, of course, traces a trajectory from this commandment against killing to that which can kill community life as quickly as anything: acting out of anger. Too many stories are told of churches splitting because someone did not get his or her way, then the name-calling began, and the community eventually became divided or simply dried up. So deadly is the situation to the people of God that Jesus says that reconciliation must occur before one can make an offering to God (Matt. 5:21–26)—in our context, praise, worship, and pleas for forgiveness. To prevent the death of relationships or the community, Jesus calls for reconciliation. Of course, it is not easy to reconcile, but imagine the witness of a community that struggles through its heated differences and repairs the damage versus the witness of the church that splits or constantly fights.

Finally, this valuing of human life has to inform our discussions and debates about issues like war and capital punishment. As suggested, this commandment in the context of the Law does not forbid either. However, in light of Jesus' command to love one's enemies and the fact that he submitted to unjust treatment and death rather than taking up the sword, many Christians see the use of violence by Christians as antithetical to the gospel. Others, however, believe that valuing human life means that violence and even killing are at times justified to combat injustice and to preserve life and well-being on a larger scale. It would be a mistake to label the latter position pro-killing or pro-violence because the ultimate aim is peace and justice. Therefore, this understanding is not the same as baptizing with religious language a society's violence against the weak or against other societies for its own selfish ends. And simply accepting in principle that killing may at times be justified does not permit a Christian to assume or accept that every war is justified under the patriotic assumption that our national cause is always the right and just cause. Nor is every state execution justified simply because a legal authority sanctions it. Justice is much more complex, nuanced, and context-specific to allow generalities to overwhelm particularities. One must take into account whether capital punishment is carried out justly in our day and whether it serves the same ends it did for ancient Israel.[60]

The Seventh Commandment: Do Not Commit Adultery (5:18)

The seventh commandment protects the covenant of marriage. In ancient Israel, the prohibition means that a man could not have sex with another man's wife or fiancée. A woman in Israel committed adultery by sleeping with a married man or, if she is engaged or married, with any other man. The command does not exclude an Israelite man from having multiple wives or concubines, nor does it specifically forbid premarital sex. However, note that a man who has sex with an unmarried, unengaged woman acquires a new wife (cf. Exod. 22:16–17; Deut. 22:28–29)!

On one level, such a law would safeguard property and inheritance issues by making clear whose children were whose. On a more significant level, the law serves to protect the community from the instability created by adultery. Jealousy, mistrust, and rage erupt. Family and communal ties are strained and broken by adultery. Thus, elsewhere in the *Torah*, the death penalty is proscribed for the adulterer and the adulteress (see Deut. 22:13–24).

The God of the Community

God's concern for the community is evident in this commandment that protects the basic family relationship and protects the stability and well-being of the family. This stability then, in turn, promotes stability within the clan, the tribe, and the community at large. Since life and relationships were so interconnected in Israel, a violation of the basic relationship rippled throughout the community as a whole.

From another point of view, the marriage covenant becomes a proving ground for Israel's ability to keep the covenant in general, and in particular, their covenant with God. Fidelity to the marriage covenant, through the joys and the trials, teaches Israelites what it means to enter and remain in covenant over a lifetime. It is little wonder then that the covenant relationship between God and Israel is often symbolized in terms of a marriage, and with matters such as idolatry, adultery (e.g., Hos. 1–3; Jer. 3:1–15; Ezek. 16, 23).[61] The same marriage image is picked up in the New Testament to describe the relationship between Jesus and the church (Matt. 22:2–14; 2 Cor. 11:2; Rev. 19:7–9; cf. Eph. 5:25–33).

Indeed, honoring the marriage covenant becomes one of the primary places where love of God and neighbor are demonstrated. Love of God is not only shown in obedience to the command of God against adultery but also in the refusal to make self-seeking pleasure a god in its own right. Love of neighbor—and here neighbor means both one's spouse, one's family, and the larger community—is demonstrated in the refusal to inflict the emotional and relational damage spawned by adultery.

Guidance for Today's Community

The seventh commandment reminds the Christian community of our need to protect the marriage covenant. Many of us have witnessed the devastation that an extramarital affair creates in a family. The innocent spouse and the children are devastated. Very often, the damage extends in two directions, as both partners in the adulterous union sacrifice the stability and happiness of their households. If the marriage survives, trust becomes difficult to rebuild and maintain between husband and wife, as well as within the extended family. If the marriage does not survive, then divorce severs the family, inflicting hardship and damage on parent and child alike.

Of course, among Christians, the damage of adultery is not limited to the family, because the effects ripple into the church. Many of us have also witnessed the tension and division created in a church on account of adultery. The body itself is convulsed as it has to deal with the effects of an affair, figuring out how to minister to both the offended and offender, and often suffering division within the body as people take sides in the matter.

Unfortunately, we live in a time where many have deified sexual pleasure and romantic love, so that everything may be sacrificed for these "gods." Movies, popular songs, and popular psychology constantly preach to us that the end-all is to find one's "soul mate" or "true love," even if it means destroying existing marriages and families. Thus, the church must take a stand to protect and support marriage, and it must help its members resist the enticements of these gods of our own time. This would include helping each other resist those things that may generate lustful desires (pornography, flirtation, etc.), which can serve as an intermediate step to acting out on those desires. Note that Jesus connects adultery and lust (Matt. 5:27–28).

In part, therefore, this means that the church must continue to emphasize Jesus' teachings against divorce. While we do not want to make divorce the unforgivable sin, we also do not want to act as though it is no big deal.[62] Again, the gods of this age say that marriage is disposable if it means getting to be with our one true love. But Jesus repeatedly pulls the ground out from under those who would see divorce as an easy way to move to one's next true love. In fact, Jesus links divorce/remarriage and adultery (Matt. 5:32, 19:9; Mark 10:11–12; Luke 16:18). While there are a number of debates about these texts, what is clear is that Jesus opposes divorce and therefore so should his disciples. Perhaps, for Israel in Jesus' day, divorce became the means to move from partner to partner on technically legal grounds while missing the intent of the marriage covenant.[63] Many in our own day look at the New Testament teachings on divorce in the same way, with the issue being less maintaining the marriage bond than asking on what grounds it can be broken. But the writer of Hebrews exhorts us, "Let marriage be held in honor among all, and let the marriage bed be undefiled, for God will judge the sexually immoral and adulterous" (Heb. 13:4).

As with Israel, our marriage covenant and our covenant with Christ and his church bear on one another. Our inability or refusal to keep one covenant is suggestive of our fidelity to the other. Our marriages become one place where we learn to exercise selfless and self-sacrificing love for another, and, in doing so, learn to imitate Christ's love for us. Likewise, our imitation of Christ teaches us how to give ourselves for our spouses (see Eph. 5:21–33).

Finally, with respect to the commandment against adultery, we should consider the witness of a community that goes against the cultural grain of sexual permissiveness and disposable marriages by working for and celebrating faithful marriages. What does it say to the world around us when we seek reconciliation in our members' marriages rather than promoting disposable marriages? We also bear witness to the power of gospel when we welcome the adulterer and divorcee in our midst, not to excuse their sin any more than our own but to show them the love of a forgiving Lord. In this light, it is important that the church not simply develop reactive measures to marriage problems but also proactively develop a healthy theology of marriage and take steps to safeguard marriages before crises arise.[64]

The Eight Commandment: Do Not Steal (5:19)

The eighth commandment protects personal property. Theft leads to loss, a sense of insecurity, and inconvenience in our day. However, this was so much more the case in a society like Israel's where there was no insurance to cover the loss or a professional police force attempting to recover what was taken. In Israel, where the number of items most people owned was far fewer that what we own today (e.g., most people would have had only one set of clothes), theft can be devastating. The commandment proscribes no penalty, but the law does elsewhere for certain cases (Exod. 22:1–4; Lev. 6:5).

The God of the Community

Stealing harms the individual victims and disrupts the very fabric of the community of God. In the first place, it demonstrates a lack of trust in God to provide, and, in many cases, a lack of appreciation for what God has already provided. Also, stealing could very well deprive the victim of the means of survival. Therefore, by extension the commandment applies to depriving anyone of the means of survival. Thus, for example, the prohibition on taking land, the primary means of livelihood in Israel, by moving boundary stones would flow out of this commandment (Deut. 19:14, 27:17; cf. Prov. 22:28, 23:10–11). Theft is also a violation against the larger community, generating fear and mistrust.

Other trajectories from this commandment in Deuteronomy would include prohibitions on charging interest on loans (Deut. 23:19–20; cf. Exod. 22:25; Lev. 25:35–37; Prov. 28:8; Ezek. 18:8, 13, 17), taking and keeping items needed for survival as pledges on loans (Deut. 24:6, 24:10–13; cf. Exod. 22:26–27), and deceitful and fraudulent business practices (Deut. 25:13–16; cf. Lev. 6:2–5, 19:35–36; Prov. 11:1, 16:11, 20:10, 23; Mic. 6:11). Deuteronomy requires an Israelite to return lost animals (22:1–4), and failing to do so would surely be counted as stealing. Keep in mind that these beasts of burden were of great significance for maintaining one's livelihood in Israel's largely agricultural setting. The law against kidnapping flows from this commandment, where a person and his or her freedom is taken (Deut.

24:7; cf. Exod. 21:16). The law against harvesting another person's field (Deut. 23:24–25) also relates to this commandment.

The commandment can lead the community to reflect on ways to prevent theft by alleviating poverty (cf. Deut. 15:1–11).[65] The community, and not simply individuals, becomes responsible for creating conditions that remove at least one motivation for stealing.

The prophet Malachi (3:8–10) suggests that Israel could also rob God by failing to give their tithes and offerings. The tithe, ten percent of one's produce and livestock, belonged to the Lord. Every two years, the Israelites were to bring it to the central sanctuary for the maintenance of the sanctuary, but every third year, it was collected in their towns to provide for the Levite, alien, orphan, and widow (Deut. 12:6, 11; 26:12). Therefore, the tithe offered to God becomes a means to provide for those in need, thus, alleviating the motivation of stealing for food. And such offerings, among other things, recognized and honored God, who had supplied his people's needs.

The Apostle Paul adds a further dimension to the prohibition on stealing, telling the thief to quit stealing and find a productive livelihood so that he or she can share with those in need (Eph. 4:28). Presumably, Paul intends to admonish those who could work but choose stealing instead. But what is especially interesting here is that Paul not only attempts to eliminate stealing; he also promotes conditions that could prevent others from stealing. Of course, the motivation that Paul provides to stop stealing is that those in Christ put off the old self and "put on the new self, created after the likeness of God in true righteousness and holiness" (Eph. 4:21–24). The shift from stealing to working so that one may provide for the poor reveals the move from the old self to the new self in Christ. As one writer notes: "The thief is to become a philanthropist, as the illegal taking of the old way of life is replaced by the generous giving of the new."[66]

Guidance for Today's Community

Stealing in our own day likewise reflects a lack of trust in God's provision or a lack of appreciation for what God has granted us. So we grasp for more. Furthermore, it demonstrates a lack of regard for our neighbor, whose property we have taken. Of course, few in our churches are so bold as to take property out of someone's house or pick someone's pocket. We choose more subtle forms, which in our minds may simply be a way of saving money but, in fact, are taking someone else's property. We may download or copy music and software without paying for it. We may steal wireless Internet service or cable television. Our justification could be that all of these come from rich companies with overpaid CEOs, and so we consider ourselves modern-day Robin Hoods, robbing from the rich and giving to the poor (ourselves). In fact, we are simply robbing from the richer to give to the rich (ourselves), not sharing a dime of our "saved" money with the poor. And it is a twisted logic that says, "Because they are rich, they can afford to lose it or even deserve to lose a little." If you have doubts about whether such practices are considered stealing, my simple advice is to call the companies first and ask if it is okay with them to take their product without paying.

Of course, some Christians consider business one thing and church another, and the two shall never meet. Thus, in their work, they feel justified misleading customers, overcharging for products or services, slipping in hidden costs, clocking hours not actually worked, or doing shoddy work for full pay. These are all means of stealing. As we have already pointed out, the people of God do not live divided lives. All of life is lived under *the priority*, God. Therefore, whatever we do in our business practices must flow out of that priority.

Finally, a couple more points can be made with respect to our hearing of the commandment against stealing. First, as we consider the witness of our community, we have to ask what it says to the world at large if we have so little regard for the property of others. Does taking what is not ours or robbing others through shifty business practices show that we have put on the new self in Christ, or does it not really show our tenacious clinging to the old self? That is, do we who claim to be in Christ look any different to the world around us? Second, we also need to consider ways to help those who might be motivated to steal to survive. Included in this would not only be our offerings for the poor in the church but also other means to empower the poor to obtain a livelihood.

The Ninth Commandment: Do Not Give False Testimony (5:20)

Though "bearing false witness," as the ninth commandment is traditionally rendered, can include lying, it goes much deeper than that. The word translated "false" here has to do with emptiness, vanity, or deceit. Its link with "testimony" suggests that on the first level, it probably has to do with false testimony in legal settings. Such testimony could be given to one's own advantage and/or to harm another person. Thus, one could make false statements in legal proceedings to fraudulently obtain or keep hold of property that rightfully belongs to another. One could make such statements to inflict punishment or even death on another by falsely accusing him or her of a crime. Keep in mind that these are the days prior to surveillance cameras, lie detectors, and C.S.I., so the bulk of the testimony came in the form of human testimony.

The outworking of such false testimony is seen, for example, in the story of Naboth's vineyard in 1 Kings 20. When Ahab cannot obtain Naboth's vineyard by legitimate negotiation, Jezebel devises a plan in which two men publicly accuse Naboth of blaspheming God and the king (cf. Exod. 22:28). Blaspheming God is a capital offense (Lev. 24:11–23). Naboth loses his life, and Ahab gains the vineyard through false witness.[67]

By extension, the commandment could apply to slandering someone and thereby undermining trust in that person or publicly shaming him or her (cf. Lev. 19:16). Thus, a husband is warned against slandering his wife, claiming she was not a virgin when they married. Such a charge shames her and her family, who entered into the marriage arrangement in good faith. This issue becomes a life-and-death matter as well, because an engaged woman who slept with another man would be subject to execution (Deut. 22:13–21; cf. 22:23–24).

To deter false witnesses, Deuteronomy 19:15–21 first calls for a thorough investigation when one person makes an accusation against another. So Israelites are not simply to take accusations at face value. Then, if it becomes evident that the witness is lying to harm the accused, he or she is to receive the punishment the accused would have received.

The God of the Community

False witness is dangerous both for the individual and for the community of God's people. False witness becomes a means of degrading an individual, of depriving him or her of a livelihood or even of life. Thus, false witness becomes an instrument to diminish or destroy a fellow human created in the image of God and sharing the common redemption of all the people of God. Furthermore, bearing false witness shows a disregard for justice and righteousness within the society, two chief characteristics of the nature of God and therefore the character expected of a God-formed community. The one who speaks falsely in this way places his or her own desires and aims above the common good of neighbor and community.

More generally, within an individual and a community, speaking the truth reflects the character of God who is truthful (Titus 1:2), and truth-telling is evidence of trust in God (cf. Zeph. 3:12–13). Deceit is the language of those who have departed from God and whose hearts are corrupted (cf. Jer. 9:1–9). Thus, God hates lies and deceit (Pss. 5:6, 50:16–22; Prov. 6:16–19).

Guidance for Today's Community

False witness can create the same havoc in communities now as then. Certainly, within our court system, a false witness can pervert justice, contributing to the unjust punishment of the innocent. False witness, particularly in the form of slander (and, in the media age, libel as well), continues to destroy reputations and lives. Within the church, false witness, especially in the form of slander, becomes a destructive force to the individual and to the well-being of the community at large. People may not kill their enemies in church, but there are those who often assassinate the character of those they oppose. In some cases, it may be publications that loosely throw around charges of "false teacher." In other cases, there are those who question the character, motives, or morality of a fellow Christian to discredit him or her or relativize his or her influence. Social media has only made it easier to demonize those with whom we disagree, and talk-show demagoguery has hardened us so that we simply draw lines between the good guys (us), who have only pure motives, and the bad guys (them), who have only sinister motives. With this dichotomy, we feel free to demonize the latter.

Christians are called to speak truthfully, no longer speaking lies and slander, because we have put off the old self and put on the new self in Christ (Eph. 4:21–31; Col. 3:8–10; James 4:11). Bear in mind that speaking truthfully does not mean simply to refrain from a lie, because, technically, truthful words can be used to create a false understanding, as can semantic quibbling. For example, "I have not told you a *single* lie" can be a sly way to cover the fact that many lies have been told. Truth is the language of the people of God, because it points to the One who is *the* Truth.

The Tenth Commandment: Do Not Covet (5:21)

Unlike the previous commandments, the tenth commandment focuses more on internal disposition. The word translated "covet," in connection with a neighbor's wife,[68] in the first part of the verse is used elsewhere in the Bible to refer to a longing for plunder (Prov. 12:12), including Achan's longing for the devoted items from Jericho (Josh. 7:21), and to lust (Prov. 6:25). It can also have positive connotations, such as a desire or longing for God's law (Ps. 19:10) and desire for a lover (Song 2:3). The word translated "desire," referring to the other things listed,[69] is often used in connection with a craving for food (e.g., Num. 11:4, 34; Deut. 12:15, 20–21; Prov. 13:4, 23:3, 6). An Israelite is told not to crave, desire, or long after what his or her neighbor has.

In some sense, this commandment moves behind the others to insist that what is in one's heart, and not simply what one does, really matters. It matters because unbridled desire can be the starting point for murder, adultery, theft, and false witness (cf. Matt. 15:19). It is also conceivable that illegitimate longings could lead one to violate the Sabbath and disobey parents. Coveting could also lead one to disregard the first three commandments in pursuit of other gods whom he or she believes can fulfill such longings.

The God of the Community

Perhaps the biggest problem with coveting is what it implies about a person's attitude toward God. Coveting, like stealing, suggests dissatisfaction with the blessings God has provided. With such dissatisfaction, how can the person who covets sincerely thank and praise God? Instead, he or she insults God like a spoiled child who is never satisfied with his or her parents' provision and gifts. Coveting is ingratitude, and the ungrateful among God's people cannot fulfill their purpose to bring praise to his name. Furthermore, if greed is a manifestation of coveting, then coveting itself can become idolatry (cf. Col. 3:5), a rejection of God as the all-sufficient provider. Coveting comes from the search to fill the voids in one's life that can only truly be filled by God; thus, this commandment circles back to the first two.

Coveting also demonstrates a lack of love for neighbor. It matters because a covetous heart, even if one does not act on the desires, leads to tension, resentment, and an inability to share joy within the community. The person who covets cannot "rejoice with those who rejoice" (Rom. 12:15). Rather, such a person is likely to rejoice in the misfortunes of others.

Guidance for Today's Community

The tenth commandment calls us to consider not only our actions but our thoughts, desires, and intentions. Evil actions begin with these. Even if we never act on these desires, they can corrupt our spiritual lives. Dwelling on what we do not have and cannot have builds resentment toward God, our fellow Christians, and our neighbors in the world at large. The solution is to learn the lesson of contentment and thankfulness (cf. Phil. 4:11–12), to learn that all of our desires and needs can only be truly met in God. With Augustine, we confess, "our hearts find no peace until they rest in you."[70]

Chapter 6

Show and Tell: Keeping the Word Alive

Read: *Deuteronomy 6; 16:1–17; 26:1–11*

Having received the general schema for ordering their lives and setting the trajectories for what that will look like in the life of the community (Deut. 5), Moses now directs Israel in how they may perpetuate a life lived in faithfulness to God's commandments, and, as a result, enjoy a long and blessed life in the land (6:1–3, 18). The key is to keep the word of God, the *Torah*, alive within Israel, both in word and deed.

But, as in the Ten Commandments, first things are first, so Israel is again reminded of the priority of God in their lives. Thus, in what in Jewish tradition is called the *Shema* (from the Hebrew word translated "hear"), Moses confesses who Israel's God is and calls Israel to love him with their entire being (6:4–5). As a quick comparison of English translations and a glance at their footnotes reveal, there is some question about the translation of verse 4.[71] At least four translations are possible:

1. "Yahweh is our God, Yahweh alone." (cf. NRSV; NAB; NLT)
2. "Yahweh our God is one Yahweh." (cf. KJV; RSV)
3. "Yahweh our God, Yahweh is one." (cf. ESV; NIV; NKJV)
4. "Yahweh is our God, Yahweh is one." (cf. NASB)

The first translation indicates exclusive loyalty to Yahweh. The second and third translations point to the singleness of Yahweh, as opposed to multiple manifestations of gods like Baal,[72] or they point to Yahweh's integrity (i.e., his "unity of will and purpose"[73]). The fourth translation captures the senses of the other three translations. Which is correct? Scholars debate the matter on various linguistic grounds, and the way Jews and Christians have understood the *Shema* has, in fact, varied over time. However, I suggest that the confession is intentionally ambiguous and is intended to cause Israel to reflect on their relationship to Yahweh (he alone is their God) and on the nature of their God (his unity and integrity, especially compared to other gods). Within the larger context of Deuteronomy, both views fit. Israel is called repeatedly to exclusive loyalty to Yahweh and later to worship him in the place he will choose (Deut. 12), which, in part, serves to limit multiple or local manifestations of Yahweh. Furthermore, as suggested earlier, Yahweh alone is all-sufficient, capable of doing what the Canaanites and others attributed to a multiplicity of gods.

Israel is called to love this unique God, who alone is their God. In Deuteronomy, when Israel is told to love God, it is in connection with their covenantal obligation to obey God's commands (cf. 10:12; 11:1, 13, 22; 13:3; 19:9; 30:16, 20), and that meaning fits the context here (cf. 6:1–3, 17–18). However, this does not rule out affection for God as well. Israel is to love God with their heart, soul, and strength. The heart, in Hebrew thought, is the seat of will and intention. The word translated "soul" refers to a person's life, the person himself or herself, or to the person's desires and emotions.[74] The word translated "might" usually means "much" or "exceedingly," but here probably suggests one's abilities and perhaps also one's possessions.[75] The point here is not three different kinds or ways of loving God, but loving God with the totality of one's being and possessions.

Having again reminded Israel of their God and their relationship to him, Moses next tells Israel how to keep "these words," and thus life, before the people. The phrase "these words" looks back to the Ten Commandments and forward to the more specific stipulations to follow. Each Israelite is to have the commands firmly in his or her own heart, which, again, is the seat of will or intention. So it is more than simply remembering or treasuring the commands; rather, the commands are to work themselves out in the behavior of each Israelite. Then he or she is to pass the commands on to the children through conversation everywhere and all day.[76] Discussing the commandments with the children indicates that the primary means of keeping *Torah* alive in the community is through one generation passing it on to the next. In addition, Israel is to manifest the continual presence of the commandments on the individual level (binding them on the head and hands), on the family level (on the doorposts), and on the community level (on the gates). This is a community saturated with hearing and doing the word of God!

The danger Moses wants to prevent is forgetfulness on Israel's part, which may occur once Israel experiences the blessing and prosperity of the land. In their prosperity, they may forget that Yahweh rescued them from slavery and that he has given them all they have in the land (6:10–12; cf. 8:10–20). In doing so, they may fool themselves into thinking they have gained what they have by their own means (cf. 8:17–18), and, having forgotten who their God is and what he has done for them, they may turn to other gods (6:13–19).

The focus on passing the commandments from generation to generation, however, does not lose sight of the fact that these commandments are not simply isolated laws or principles. They are rooted in Israel's experience of and relationship with God. Thus, when children ask about the commandments, the parents are to remind the children of the community's faith story. Yahweh brought them out of Egypt and into the land, and it is this God who calls on them to keep the commands that they may continue to enjoy his blessings in the land. The last phrase, that obedience to the commandments "will be righteousness for us," also points to the relationship between God and Israel. "Righteousness" has to do with faithfully maintaining the obligations of a relationship so that those in the relationship can enjoy the benefits of the relationship. In this case, Israel obeys the stipulations of the covenant with Yahweh and enjoys his blessings as a result.

Deuteronomy's Ways of Keeping the Word before the People

At this point, though it will cause us to break from following the order of Deuteronomy, it is worthwhile to note the many ways Deuteronomy prescribes for constantly keeping the word or *Torah* before the people.[77] Bear in mind that doing so matters because life and blessing are found in *Torah*, which shows what it means to be the people of God in relationship with God and with one another.

65

Deuteronomy presents at least seven (a nicely biblical number!) ways to keep the word before the people.

First, as already indicated above, the word is kept alive **informally in daily speech and deeds** (6:7–8). Day in and day out, the conversation of the people involves discussion of God's commands and then living out those commands.

Second, lest keeping the commands becomes simply legalistic observance, Deuteronomy calls upon the people **to tell their salvation story, what God has done on their behalf**. What this means is that Israel is to tell its story of God at work for and among them, sometimes in normal conversation and sometimes in more formal or liturgical ways. Thus, when the children ask about the commandments, the response is to tell the story of God bringing the people out of bondage in Egypt and into the land (6:20–25). Similarly, as the Israelites present the first of the harvest to the priest at the sanctuary, they are to recite their story, in this case in a specific, fixed form (Deut. 26:1–11). In this public ceremony, they begin the story with Jacob, the wandering Aramean (cf. Gen. 28:5) who goes down into Egypt with his family (Gen. 46). There Israel grew but became subject to oppression. God heard their cries and brought them out of Egypt into the rich land, a land flowing with milk and honey. And the firstfruits are an acknowledgement that they continue to live under the blessing of their God.

Third, the people are reminded of and participate anew in their stories through their **special days and festivals**. In the discussion of the fourth commandment, we have already noted how the weekly Sabbath observance draws Israel's attention to the God who has created them, redeemed them, and provides for them. Israel's attention is likewise focused on God in three annual festivals in which they appear before God at the central sanctuary (Deut. 16:1–17).[78] Passover, with the Feast of Unleavened Bread, which begins the religious calendar for Israel, celebrates the night God brought Israel out of Egypt (cf. Exod. 11:1–12:51; Lev. 23:4–8; Num. 28:16–25). The Festival of Weeks (also known as the Festival of Harvest, *Shavuot*, and Pentecost) joyfully celebrates God as the giver of the harvest (cf. Lev. 23:15–21; Num. 28:26–31).[79] This celebration takes place at the first of the harvest season. The motivation for observing the feast is God's act of bringing them out of Egypt, which suggests they are celebrating the kind of blessing they enjoy in the Promised Land but was unknown to them in Egypt. The Festival of Tabernacles (or Ingathering, Booths, or *Sukkot*), as it takes place in the land, is also a joyful festival at the end of the harvest season (16:15). However, other texts in the Law say it serves to remind Israel of God's earlier provision in the wilderness (cf. Lev. 23:33–43; Num. 29:12–38).

The festivals remind and even draw Israel into their story, reenacting past events but also showing the continuity of God's care and blessing into the present and anticipation of such care in the future. Thus, the feasts are celebrated *with joy* (16:11, 14–15). Furthermore, they are *inclusive* of the entire community, regardless of station in life or status (16:11, 14). Therefore, as with the weekly observance of the Sabbath, the festivals remind the whole community of their common redemption by God.

Fourth, Israel keeps God's word before them by **giving gifts to God and others**. In this case, the action of giving itself reminds Israel of the God who blesses them, though this is more implicit than explicit within the text. When Israel gives offerings at the festivals, they acknowledge that God has blessed them (16:16–17), and, as noted above, in offering firstfruits they are reminded of the God who redeemed them from slavery. Deuteronomy 16:16 says that Israel is not to appear before God "empty-handed" at the three major festivals. The words "empty-handed" create a verbal link with 15:13, in which Israel is commanded not to send slaves away empty-handed, a command rooted in their own freedom from slavery. Likewise, giving generously to the poor leads to God's ongoing generous blessing in the land (15:7–11), so that, in giving, Israel's attention is called not only to the one in need but also to the God who has and will make the generous giving possible. A bit more broadly, giving to God can remind Israel of the horizontal and vertical dimensions of the covenant obligations, as well as the benefits they receive from God in that relationship. However, the fact that God sets the guidelines for giving—for example, that the firstborn animals belong to him and that no defective animals are to be offered to him (15:19–23)—reminds

Israel that this is an uneven covenantal relationship; God is the suzerain and Israel is the vassal.

Fifth, Israel is to use **symbols** to keep *Torah* before them. For example, they are to make tassels for the four corners of their cloaks (Deut. 22:12).[80] The purpose of the tassels is not defined in Deuteronomy, but the parallel passage in Numbers 15:37–40 indicates that when Israel saw these tassels, they would remember God's commands and "not to follow after your own heart and your own eyes." In Deuteronomy 27:1–4, God tells the Israelite elders to erect stones on Mount Ebal that have all the words of the *Torah* written on them. They are to do this as soon as they enter the land, and the stones will remind the people of their covenant with God.

In Deuteronomy 11:29–30, God instructs Israel, when they enter the land, to have some of their number stand on Mount Gerezim and shout the blessings of the *Torah* and others to stand on Mount Ebal and shout the curses (cf. Deut. 27; Josh. 8:30–35). Though the shouting itself could be seen as symbolic action, this event would be a one-time occurrence. However, the mountains themselves stand perpetually as reminders of the blessings and the curses.

Sixth, Moses gave Israel a **song** to remind them of their covenant obligations (Deut. 31:19–22, 30; 32:1–43). More specifically, the song in Deuteronomy 32 will serve as a witness against Israel when they turn from God to pursue other gods and so experience the curses of the covenant. The song itself highlights God's faithfulness in contrast to Israel's unfaithfulness (vv. 4–18), God's judgment on Israel (vv. 19–33), God's vindication of Israel and judgment on the nations he sent against them (vv. 34–38), and God's incomparability (vv. 39–42). Thus, the song moves from God's judgment on Israel to his restoration of Israel, and praise for God brackets the song (vv. 3, 43).

Seventh, Israel is to keep the word before them through the **public reading of the Scripture**; that is, the *Torah* (Deut. 31:9–13). Every seven years, on the year of canceling debts (cf. 15:1–11), at the Festival of Tabernacles, the priests are to read the *Torah* publicly to all who have gathered for the feast at the central sanctuary. There the children who have never heard the Law being read will hear it (31:13), and the people who have heard it will be reminded and refreshed on its content and meaning. Bear in mind that no one in Israel would have had a private copy of the *Torah* (except perhaps the king; cf. 17:18–19), and few would have been sufficiently literate to read it if they had a copy. Though the seven-year intervals seem a long time to remember something that was read, oral cultures often have a better ability to retain what they hear. Also, remember that Israel is to recite the commands in their daily lives, bringing us full circle to the first way of keeping the word ever-present in Israel. It is also noteworthy that the *Torah* is read to an inclusive assembly (Israelite men, women, children, and the foreigners among them) and at a festival that reminds Israel of God's past, present, and future provision. That provision is contingent on Israel's faithfulness to *Torah*, and just as God's material provision sustains physically, so is keeping *Torah* sustains spiritually, giving life to the community (cf. 8:3).

The God of the Community

Loving God with one's entire being constantly and consistently is *the* central command for Israel, echoing the first and second commandments. It reverberates throughout the Scripture as a reminder of God's call for Israel,[81] and Jesus himself acknowledges the *Shema* as the primary or greatest commandment (Matt. 22:37; Mar. 12:29–30; Luke 10:27–28). But such love calls for intentionality.

Prosperity (even God-given prosperity) and the lure of other gods constantly compete for a share of that devotion and increase the risk of forgetting the God who truly redeems and provides. Israel's turn to idols in the period of the judges is described as forgetting God (Judg. 3:7), and the prophets often describe forsaking God and his commandments as forgetting (e.g., Isa. 17:10; Jer. 2:32, 3:21, 13:25, 18:15, 23:27; Ezek. 22:12, 23:35; Hos. 2:13, 4:6, 8:14, 13:6). Forgetting, of course, does not mean they no longer know who God is. In fact, Israel seems to continue to worship God throughout their history (but cf. Judg. 10:6), even as they worship other gods and violate God's commandments. Israel just no longer remembers the call to exclusive loyalty to God, and they do not acknowledge his sovereignty over every aspect of their lives.

Thus, as a safeguard against forgetting and as a means to be intentional about loving God, Israel is called to actively remember their God and to keep the *Torah* alive personally, in the family, and in the community. Multifaceted means are put into place that constantly call the people's attention to their God, who he is, what he has done and is doing, and what he demands of his people. The means are as diverse as God's ways of revealing himself and as diverse as the people who make up Israel, yet all the means focus on the God who is one and who is the only God for Israel. Hearing the word, seeing it enacted, singing about it, and celebrating it touch human life on many levels, creating an atmosphere in which the people of God constantly take in the richness and vitality of the word of God.

Guidance for Today's Community

As Israel was to keep the word of God in the *Torah* before them constantly, we as Christians are to keep God's fullest revelation of his word, the Word made flesh, Jesus Christ, (John 1:14) before us. Jesus is the fulfillment of the Law (Matt. 5:17; Luke 24:25–27). In him, we find our righteousness (2 Cor. 5:21), and because of his sacrifice, the righteous requirements of the Law have been fulfilled for us (Rom. 8:3–4). Jesus is the one who gives us life and in whose words are life (John 6:68, 14:6; Rom. 6:4; Col. 3:3–4). However, as with Israel, loving the Lord with our entire being is constantly challenged by the lure of present-day gods and our own prosperity. Single-hearted devotion easily slips into split loyalties and forgetting, even if we keep up the formal, ritualistic side of our religion. Therefore, the question for us is: how do we keep Jesus, the Word of life, before us and our children?

We might answer that we have to keep reading our Bible, and, of course, that is vital. However, reading the Bible is but one avenue of many provided for us to keep the Word alive in the community of faith. We must also reflect upon the fact that people learn in different ways and that we are in a postmodern world where, for many, symbols and multilevel communication have dethroned the simple written word as the primary means of communication. Bear in mind as well that the primacy of the written word, at least a written word accessible to all (because of availability and widespread literacy) is a relatively new phenomenon in world history. And, as we have noted in Deuteronomy, God put in place multiple means to keep the word before Israel, and the church can learn from these means as we strive to keep the Word of God alive from generation to generation in our communities.

First, we keep the Word before us **informally in daily speech and deeds**. Though spiritual talk seems to be unnatural for many of us, we need to cultivate the practice of talking about God and the things of God—who he is and what he has done in Jesus Christ and is doing through his Spirit. We need to do this regularly in our homes and church communities. It is fine and well to talk about the weather, news, and sports, but we need to become a people for whom speaking of our Lord and matters of discipleship becomes a natural thing. Likewise, we need to become a people for whom being disciples, living out what we say, becomes a natural thing. T-shirts and jewelry with Christian slogans, pictures and plaques in our homes with Bible verses, and crosses in our churches are fine. But if we do not wear the words in what we do, then all those other things are meaningless, and our children and neighbors will know this. On the other hand, imagine the vitality of Christian families and communities where there is no hesitancy to speak of God—Father, Son, and Spirit—daily and anywhere, and to live out the words we speak.

Second, we **tell our salvation story, what God has done and is doing on our behalf in Jesus Christ.** Of course, this means knowing the story well enough to recite it. Paul gives some nice examples of summarizing our story succinctly in Romans 1:1–4:

> Paul, a servant of Christ Jesus, called to be an apostle, set apart for the gospel of God, which he promised beforehand through his prophets in the holy Scriptures, concerning his Son, who was descended from David according to the flesh and was declared to be the Son of God in power according to the Spirit of holiness by his resurrection from the dead, Jesus Christ our Lord.

71

And in 1 Corinthians 15:3–8:

> For I delivered to you as of first importance what I also received: that Christ died for our sins in accordance with the Scriptures, that he was buried, that he was raised on the third day in accordance with the Scriptures, and that he appeared to Cephas, then to the twelve. Then he appeared to more than five hundred brothers at one time, most of whom are still alive, though some have fallen asleep. Then he appeared to James, then to all the apostles. Last of all, as to one untimely born, he appeared also to me.

A number of churches use creedal statements in worship to summarize, remind, and acknowledge the content of their faith story. Perhaps the best known is the Apostles' Creed:

> I believe in God, the Father almighty, Creator of heaven and earth, and in Jesus Christ, His only Son, our Lord.
> He was conceived by the Holy Spirit, and born of the Virgin Mary.
> He suffered under Pontius Pilate, was crucified, died and was buried.
> He descended into hell. On the third day He rose again.
> He ascended into heaven, and is seated at the right hand
> of God the Father Almighty.
> He will come again to judge the living and the dead.
> I believe in the Holy Spirit, the Holy Catholic Church,
> the communion of saints, the forgiveness of sins,
> the resurrection of the body, and life everlasting.
> Amen.

However, telling our salvation story can move beyond such recitals to include our explanations of why we do what we do, thus, contextualizing our obedience in religious practice within the story of our redemption. In this way, our obedience finds its meaning and power and is not reduced to sterile, legalistic observances. Thus, in a scenario similar to the one in Deuteronomy 6:20–25, our children may ask us, "Why do we baptize?" We can simply respond with a biblical command (e.g., Matt. 28:19–20 or Acts 2:38), which is important.[82]

But we can also, like Paul, discuss baptism in light of the gospel story: in baptism, we are buried with Christ into his death and are raised to new life, as he was (Rom. 6:3–5). When the children ask: "Why do we take the Lord's Supper?" we can respond that in Acts 20:7, the disciples met on the first day of the week, or with Paul we can tell them the story: on the night Jesus was betrayed, he took the bread saying, "this is my body" and the cup saying, "this is my blood," and that in taking the supper, we proclaim his death "until he comes" (1 Cor. 11:23–26).[83] Finally, we can cultivate the practice in our assemblies of bearing witness to one another, telling about our stories of God at work in us and how those stories find their place in the larger story of God at work through Jesus Christ.

Third, we are reminded of and participate anew in the story of our faith through **special days and festivals (or celebrations).** As with Israel's festivals, ours should be characterized by remembrance, joy, and inclusiveness. Sunday worship and observing the Lord's Supper, as discussed above, are regular such celebrations, and, in light of the resurrection, should generally be characterized by joy.[84] As with Israel's festivals, in the Lord's Supper, we do not simply recall what God has done; through the Lord's Supper, we become participants in the original story (cf. 1 Cor. 10:16). Likewise, the celebration of the religious (as opposed to the secular) significance of Christmas, Good Friday, and Easter, particularly in churches that have pageants or holiday festivals, provide a means for the community to remember together, to imaginatively participate in the events, and to share key parts of the gospel story. Fellowship meals (or potluck dinners) at church can also serve as reminders of God's provision for us and our commonality in Christ. At such meals, we invite all to the table, regardless of whether they can bring something to it.

In contrast, the community of God should avoid any observance, festival, or fellowship activity that excludes anyone on the basis of social or economic standing. This would include activities that are too expensive for some members to participate in (e.g., "fellowship" golf, ski trips, and cruises), unless the church finds a way to include everyone who wants to go without insulting their dignity. In terms of our practice and witness, we already face an uphill battle in regard to exclusiveness since our churches by and large have already divided themselves along racial, social, and economic lines.

Fourth, the church keeps the Word before it by **giving gifts to God and others**. In giving, we recognize Jesus as Lord, because one does not appear before his or her king empty-handed. And in giving, we are reminded of the good gifts God has given us. Indeed, as Paul encourages the Corinthians to give for the relief of the poor in Judea, he sets his plea within the story of Jesus: "For you know the grace of our Lord Jesus Christ, that though he was rich, yet for your sake he became poor, so that you by his poverty might become rich" (2 Cor. 8:9). In giving to others, we bear witness to the generosity of God in our lives and to his concern for others. In giving to others, we imitate our giving God.

Fifth, **symbols** become a means for us to keep the Word alive within the community. Biblical stories captured in stained glass windows, artwork, banners, and crosses in churches are all means to symbolically represent the story and call of Jesus. Of course, as already noted, participation in baptism and the Lord's Supper likewise point us to and call us within the story.

As we reflect on these means of keeping the Word alive, bear in mind again that in our postmodern world, symbols often speak louder than words (written or spoken). In this light, symbols as well as symbolic actions (participation in marches against various forms of injustice, prayer vigils, and boycotts) can also both remind us of the God who has *acted* and *is acting* in the world, and bear witness to him before the world at large. Symbols do not replace or denigrate the Word (in the Scripture or the Word made flesh in Jesus); they point to and remind of the Word.

Sixth, as in every generation of God's people, **song** is a vitally important way of keeping the Word before us (cf. Eph. 5:19–20; Col. 3:16). In songs of praise and thanksgiving, we acknowledge the Lord of our salvation and the Hope of the world. In song, we retell all or parts of our story of faith. We can use songs to admonish one another to remain faithful. Songs also allow us to express the full range of our faith, how it touches on every aspect of life, thus, reminding us that we do not live a divided life in Christ. The Psalms become an excellent resource in this regard.

Of course, if song is so significant, it is also incumbent upon us to examine the songs we sing to determine if they are faithful to the Scripture and are theologically sound. This has nothing to do with traditional versus contemporary songs, or songs that you or I prefer. Every generation's songs have both theological treasure and trash, and we may need to bid farewell to some personal favorites because they fall into the latter category. Keep in mind that the point of singing is praising God and *mutual* edification within the community, not personal preference.

Seventh, we keep the Word alive by **reading it in community,** that is, through the public reading of the Scripture.[85] In our churches, we need to hear the whole counsel of God and the whole story of our faith in the Scripture. That means that we need to move from just hearing snippets of the Scripture read here and there—as is the case in many churches—to also hearing longer readings, even whole chapters or multiple chapters. Likewise, over time, we need to incorporate all of the Scripture in our community readings and not just select favorites or texts that are immediately gratifying or that support our favorite doctrinal positions. To this end, the church in its worship services can read through books of the Bible over time or read the lectionary readings for a given Sunday. Read those parts of the Bible where the edges of the pages are still white or still have that gold gilding on them.

In doing this, the community needs to keep the significance of the practice in mind. By the Holy Spirit, God addresses us in the reading of the Scripture. So it is important that we find readers who take their task seriously in both their preparation to read and in the reading itself. It is also important that we as community recognize that when we hear the Scripture read, we are being addressed by God. Therefore, concrete actions such as standing in reverence as the Bible is read or a congregational response to the reading (e.g. "Amen," or the antiphonal "The Word of God for the people of God" and "Thanks be to God") are helpful to remind us of the significance of the event (cf. Neh. 8:1–8; Luke 4:16–20).

On a smaller scale, we can develop the discipline of reading the Scripture as families. We can set aside regular daily times to read the Bible and pray, whether it is around the table or before bedtime. We do not have to do structured lessons but rather simply let the Word be heard and discussed. Such a regular practice impresses upon our children and us the importance of the Word of God.

Reading in community does not rule out personal and individual reading, but, as indicated above, the ability to read one's own Bible is a relatively new phenomenon in the history of God's people. Furthermore, though not foolproof, reading and discerning in community can guard against idiosyncratic (or heretical) personal interpretations of the Scripture. However, as the history of Israel and the Church has repeatedly shown, the community can corrupt the teaching of the Scripture as well, bending it to maintain the status quo or to achieve wealth and power. Such readings are accompanied by forgetting or distorting the character of God and of Jesus as revealed in the Scripture. A safeguard against such readings is to constantly keep the Word before the people of God in manifold ways and asking whether the Scripture ever challenges our assumptions, beliefs, and practices.

In all of this, keep in mind that the goal is keeping the Word alive in the community so that we, our children, and their children may know God and love him heart, mind, soul, and strength; for in so loving God, there is life. Furthermore, in so loving God, there is purpose. Deuteronomy points us in the direction of understanding that raising our families in community participates in the mission of God in the world. Our children are immersed in the Word of God and in a community that lives out the call of God in that Word, so that they, too, may live out the call of God in the world.

Chapter 7

It's Not You; It's Me

Read: *Deuteronomy 7–11*

B ecause Israel is God's chosen people and because God has continually protected them and provided for them, the Israelites run the danger of thinking that they are somehow innately special compared to all other peoples. The danger can manifest itself in a number of ways, as the next few chapters of Deuteronomy will show. So Moses puts Israel in their place. They are reminded of who they are in relation to who God is, and so they lose their footing should they think they can stand on their own merits. They are reminded that it is not they who are central, but God. Therefore, they are also reminded repeatedly in these chapters to obey his commands.

Danger of Pride (7:1–26)

In Deuteronomy 7:6, Moses tells Israel that they are "a people holy to the Lord your God," his chosen people from among all of the peoples of the earth, and his "treasured possession." The descriptors of "holy people" and "chosen" indicate that God has set them apart for his purposes. Hence, God commands Israel to eradicate the Canaanites and their religious artifacts, lest Israel compromise that distinction and purpose (vv. 1–5, 16, 25–26).[86] "Treasured possession" translates a single word in Hebrew that in two places in the Bible refers to the treasure of a king (1 Chron. 29:3; Eccles. 2:8).[87] While these descriptions do indeed place a high value upon and give a significant role to Israel, they might come to believe that they have achieved the status implied by the descriptions on their own.

Therefore, Moses reminds Israel that in one sense, their fears about fighting the Canaanites are well founded. The Israelites are not the biggest, the strongest, or the best, and God did not choose Israel on these grounds. They are none of these. In fact, they were the "fewest of all peoples." Instead, God chose them because he loved them and because he is faithful to his promises to Abraham, Isaac, and Jacob. Thus, God's choice of Israel is rooted in the unexplained selection of Abraham as the one through whom God would work his redemption (cf. Gen. 12:1–3), and the Israelites are the fulfillment of the promises that began in Abraham and continued in Isaac and Jacob (cf. Gen. 15:5; 22:17–18; 26:4–5).[88]

So when Israel faces the Canaanites, they have rightly assessed that they will face nations stronger than they are (v. 17). However, their smallness is not an impediment to God's purposes or power. Moses reassures Israel that they can conquer the land, if they will only remain faithful to their covenant with God by keeping the commands (vv. 11–12). They can conquer precisely because of the God who brought them into a covenant relationship with himself, who has already shown his prowess in his deliverance of the people from the "superpower" of the day, Egypt (v. 8, 18–19). He is the God who is faithful to those who love him and so obey him. But to those who hate him—that is, those who oppose his purposes as the Canaanites do—he is a destructive force (vv. 9–10; cf. 5:9–10). On such people, he will inflict the diseases of Egypt (v. 15).

God will soften up the Canaanites by sending a "hornet" among them (v. 20; cf. Exod. 23:28; Josh. 24:12), though the text does not really explain what is meant by "hornet." It could refer to an invading army (cf. Deut. 1:44; Ps. 118:10–12; Isa. 7:18–19), or the word could also be translated "panic." If the latter, it fits well with the "confusion" God will bring upon the enemy (v. 23), since God often sends panic and confusion against human armies he fights (e.g., Josh. 10:10; 1 Sam. 7:10, 14:15). Furthermore, Israel need not fear because their "great and awesome" God is among them (v. 21). In light of the nature of the God who is on their side, no one can withstand them (v. 24).

In fact, later God seems determined to make this point. In the instructions for going to war in Deuteronomy 20:1–9, Israel is told not to fear an army greater than theirs, because their God, who has already shown his power in bringing them out of Egypt, will be with them and fight for them. The priest is to pronounce this very thing over the Israelite army prior to their going out to fight. Furthermore, God's presence among his people is later assured, as long as Israel maintains the ritual purity of the camp to prevent defilement because of nocturnal emissions of semen and by going to the bathroom outside the camp and burying the waste (Deut. 23:9–14; cf. Lev. 15:16–18; 1 Sam. 21:4). While this latter act may have also had hygienic results, there is no indication that this was the reason for the command. Rather, as the text says, the requirement has to do with the holiness of the camp.

Returning to Deuteronomy 7, in the midst of the assurances of military victory, God also extends promises for them after they are in the land. If they are faithful to the commands of God, he will bless them with many children, livestock, and crops (vv. 12–14). However, in such blessing lurks another risk, an issue addressed in the next chapter of Deuteronomy.

Danger of Prosperity (8:1–20)

In the midst of the prosperity that God has in store for Israel (vv. 7–9), a new danger may arise: Israel may forget that their prosperity is the result of God's blessing. They may grow proud and convince themselves that they obtained this prosperity on their own (vv. 10–14, 17; cf. 6:10–12).

The preventative measure against forgetting God is threefold. First, they must *remember*. Note the key words "forget" and "remember" in this chapter (vv. 2, 11, 14, 18, 19). They must remember God's commands, which constantly orient their lives on him and what it means to be his people (vv. 1, 6, 11). They must remember the discipline of the wilderness, where God led, cared for them, and taught them to trust him (vv. 2–5, 14–16). Thus, he let them experience hunger to demonstrate with the manna that their survival does not depend simply on food (bread) but more importantly on the word of their God, who provides the bread. "Word" here, in the first instance, alludes to the instructions for collecting the manna (cf. Exod. 16), but in the larger context of Deuteronomy points to the *Torah*, their true means of life (cf. v. 1). Second, they must *praise* (or bless) God when they have eaten their fill (v. 10), remembering who provided the food for them. Third,

79

they must *bear in mind that God gives the ability to produce* what they have, demonstrating his covenant faithfulness (v. 18). The danger of forgetting is spelled out for them in verses 19–20; forgetting God means Israel will become like the nations he has rooted out of the land. If that happens, God will then treat them like those nations.

Danger of Self-Righteousness (9:1–10:11)

A third danger for Israel is that they may convince themselves that they deserve the land because of their own righteousness, that God has driven out the wicked people (9:1–3) to replace them with righteous Israel (9:4a). If this is their thinking, they are half right. While the conquest of these people is definitely judgment on the Canaanites for wickedness, receiving the land has nothing to do with Israel's righteousness. Receiving the land has everything to do with the fact that God made a promise to Abraham, Isaac, and Jacob (9:4b–6). It is about God, not Israel.

Indeed, they have no grounds to claim righteousness because their walk with God is characterized by stubborn rebellion, as Moses illustrates from their own history. Moses' primary example is the idolatry with the golden calf (9:7–10:10; cf. Exod. 32–34). They had barely entered the covenant with God before they violated it. The fact that the previous generation really made and worshipped the calf image does not matter here, because the tendency to rebel is seen as characteristic of the people as a whole. Also, as we have already seen, Moses rhetorically draws Israel into their faith story by speaking to the current generation as though it were the previous one. Recognizing the earlier generation's rebellious nature in this incident, God determined to destroy them and start over with Moses, which would still fulfill the promises to Abraham, since Moses is his descendant. Moses smashed the tablets upon which God had written the commandments, symbolizing the breaking of the covenant, but he refused God's offer to start over with him. Instead, he interceded for Israel and for Aaron, who had made the calf. God listened to him and did not follow through on his intention to destroy the people. And, as if to contrast the powerless calf idol with God, who acts powerfully, Moses burned and crushed the idol, scattering the dust in a stream.

Moses briefly interrupts the golden calf story to give other examples of their rebellion (9:22–24), showing that the incident at Horeb was not an isolated one. At Teberah, Israel complained about hardship in the wilderness (see Num. 11:1–3). At Massah, Israel tested God by quarreling with Moses over lack of water (see Exod. 17:1–7; Deut. 6:16), and, at Kibroth Hattaavah, they grumbled for meat (see Num. 11:4–34). Kadesh Barnea, as we have already seen in 1:19–33, is where Israel rebelled, refusing to go into the land (cf. Num. 13–14). The common thread in all of these incidents and the golden calf debacle was a failure to trust God. So prevalent were Israel's complaints and resistance against God that Moses concludes, "You have been rebellious against the Lord from the day that I knew you" (9:24).

Returning then to the golden calf story, Moses again recounts his intercession, pleading with God to remember the ancestors and what the destruction of Israel would say to the surrounding nations (9:25–29). In all of this, Moses never appealed to any righteousness or morality within Israel. He acknowledged their wickedness. Instead, he appealed to God, who was the only one in a position to heal the broken relationship. Only God's mercy would allow Israel to be restored and stand once again in his presence. That God ordered new tablets to rewrite the commandments and then sent Israel on their way indicated that he had restored Israel to covenant relationship (10:1–11).

Summary of Obligations (10:12–11:32)

Moses sums up the covenantal obligations of Israel toward God and of God toward Israel. Most of what is in this section repeats what has been said in Deuteronomy 6:1–10:11, including the call for Israel to keep the commandments, to remember their experiences with God in the exodus and wilderness, to resist other gods, and to pass the *Torah* on to the next generation. Blessing and curse are set before Israel. If Israel is faithful, God commits himself to fight for them and establish them in the land and to bless and protect them in the land.

However, 10:14–22 does add some new elements to this summary. First, in keeping with the idea that there is nothing inherent within Israel to cause God to choose them, the absolute distance between God and Israel is highlighted, as God claims possession of earth, sky, and all that is beyond ("the heaven of heavens" [ESV] or "highest heavens" [NIV]).[89] He is not bound by the cosmos, but owns it. Yet, despite his exaltedness (the Hebrew is emphatic), he chose and loved Israel's ancestors and Israel.

So, in light of God's electing love, Israel must live as his called people by cutting away from their hearts (i.e., their wills and intentions) the stubbornness that leads to rebellion. Of course, the language of circumcising the heart also recalls the sign of the covenant, which was first established with Abraham (Gen. 17:9–14; cf. Lev. 12:3). Their call then, having circumcised their hearts, is to become imitators of God, who loves, protects, and cares for the vulnerable, as they themselves have experienced. That is, they are to so love the vulnerable as God loved them.

The God of the Community

A Transcendent and Immanent God

Yahweh, the God of Israel, is unlike anything in all his creation and is unbounded by his creation. Creation belongs to him, and he gives it commands and expects obedience. For this reason alone, he is worthy of praise. However, in contrast to the concept of gods in the surrounding culture, God enters into relationship with creation and seeks to bless rather than exploit his creation.[90] He chooses, loves, and liberates a people. He feeds them and fights for them, especially for the weak and vulnerable. Even his commands are designed to bring blessing and life, not life simply for his own people but through them to give this life to all nations.

Here then is a tension held throughout the Bible. Yahweh, the God of Israel, who manifests himself most fully in Jesus Christ, is *transcendent*. That is, he is set apart from, over, and unlike anything in all of creation. At the same time, he is *immanent*. That is, he chooses to enter relationship with human beings, to be among them, and to work for their good, which is found in relationship with him.

Psalm 113 provides a beautiful illustration of this. The psalm praises God as the high and exalted God, who stoops down to look at his creation and who gets his hands dirty to lift the needy from the ash heap and set him with princes and to provide the barren mother with children. The even more beautiful illustration, as we move into the New Testament, is that this God becomes one of us in Jesus Christ, putting on flesh, becoming a servant to his creation, even suffering and dying for it. Thus, he not only gets his hands dirty for his creations, but also bloody (see Phil. 2:6–11; Col. 1:15–20).

God's Glory Is Seen through His Use of the Weak and Unimpressive

Deuteronomy 7–11 reveals much about the nature of the relationship between God and Israel. Essentially, the call of God, his choosing a people to carry out his purposes, rests completely in God's initiative. God chooses, sets apart, and loves a particular people even though they have nothing to bring to the table to merit their selection. They are not especially impressive as a people, come as indigents who have been given all they have, and have no moral superiority over other peoples. And yet, God sets his affection on them, honoring ancient promises to Abraham, Isaac, and Jacob, who themselves are chosen by God without having anything to offer. Though Abraham will exhibit faith (Gen. 15:6; 22:15–18), there is no indication why he was initially selected. Indeed, his escapades early on in his story raise questions about his full trust in God (e.g., Gen. 12:10–20; 16:1–16; 20:1–18), and there is some suggestion that he worshipped other gods before his call (Josh. 24:2, 14–15). But both Abraham and his descendants, Israel, learned to trust God in their walk with him and were called to exhibit that trust in obedience.

God's choice of a small nation with little to commend itself makes sense in light of one of the larger theological themes of the Bible: God's use of the weak or unexpected. From Deborah and Jael (Judg. 4–5) to Gideon (Judg. 6–7) to Hannah (1 Sam. 1) to David (1 Sam. 16–17), to Mary (Luke 1:26–38), and so on, God repeatedly chooses to show his power by working through the least expected. Thus, he chooses an unlikely, often unimpressive people to carry out his purposes for all nations.

Obstacles to Fulfilling God's Call

As Israel's and the church's history have repeatedly shown, those whom God calls can frustrate the purposes God has for them. In Deuteronomy, as in the rest of the Bible, it becomes clear that God's chosen people most frequently do so by refusing to submit to their Lord. Deuteronomy 7–11 points out several ways this can occur. Fear, pride, prosperity, and self-righteousness can all play a role in frustrating the call of God. Fear prevents one from trusting that God can indeed overcome all odds. Pride inflates one's view of self and makes self the source of trust, thus, removing God from preeminence. Prosperity can lead to forgetfulness, failing to recognize the Giver of all blessings, and, again, causing one to trust in one's own power or in the wealth itself. Self-righteousness, the conviction that one stands before God on one's own merits, prevents the free and joyful reception of the gifts of God; whatever a person receives is seen as his or her due. But of course, this is also self-deception, a failure to perceive one's own true state. It is also idolatry because trust is placed in something other than God, who then merely becomes the one who delivers what is owed rather than the Sovereign Lord. Deuteronomy even recognizes the impossibility of Israelites, on their own, fulfilling the command to circumcise their hearts (10:16), so in 30:6 God says that *he* will circumcise their hearts.

The reminder that human beings do not live by bread alone but by every word that comes from God's mouth then becomes a safeguard against these obstacles. The God, whose words brought everything into existence, has given his word the *Torah* and then ultimately his Word made flesh in Jesus Christ (John 1:1–14; 6:22–59; cf. Matt. 4:4; Luke 4:4) to show his people how to live in life-giving relationship with him. To turn from him and his Word to put trust in the self or other gods means death.

Imitators of God

Israel is called to imitate, to the degree humanly possible, the character of the God they confess. Specifically in 10:19, Israel is to imitate God's care of the foreigners, because Israel had been

84

foreigners who were cared for by God. However, in light of the larger context of the *Torah*, the call extends beyond this single area. God is not partial and does not accept bribes (10:17), and Israel is to be the same way (Deut. 16:19; 27:25). God defends the cause of orphans, widows, and aliens (10:18), and Israel is to do likewise (24:17; 27:19). God feeds the needy (10:18), so Israel must also (14:28–29; 24:19–22). Elsewhere in the Law, Israel is called to be holy because God is holy (e.g. Lev. 11:44–45; 19:2; 20:7, 26).

Guidance for Today's Community

God's Transcendence and Immanence

Churches, over time, have tended to stress either God's distance and otherness (transcendence) or his nearness and involvement in life (immanence), often to the exclusion of the other. Thus, for those whose focus is his transcendence, God becomes an all-powerful but distant God who has little to do with the day-to-day activity of the world. He stands back, letting things go as they will without much direct involvement, waiting for the time when he will enact final judgment and reward. This is the god of the Deists and religious modernist, who might believe God was once more directly involved, but no more. Or the emphasis on transcendence can result in a picture of God as a micromanager of the universe who moves every piece of creation, like pieces on a game board, to accomplish his purposes. The result of this emphasis can be a Christian who obeys and respects God, but has little in the way of relationship with him or any sense of purpose from him. On the other hand, for those who focus exclusively on his immanence, God becomes a buddy or a daddy. Those with this version of God are often more interested in happiness and comfort than faithfulness. Such a God may be an object of thanksgiving but can hardly be one who is revered as Lord.

Overemphasis or exclusion in either direction leads to distortion, and the distortion can only be prevented by holding the two aspects of God in tension. God is fully transcendent and yet fully immanent among his people and all of his creation. He is God and we are not. And so, to come into his presence is a frightful and dangerous thing (cf. Deut. 5:23–27; Isa. 6:1–6). Yet, in him we live and move and have our very being (Acts 17:28), and he is our Father (Matt. 6:9; Rom. 8:15; Gal. 4:6) who knows the very number of hairs on our heads (Matt. 10:30; Luke 12:7). What allows us to come into his awesome presence in intimate relationship is his mercy. He invites us to come to him and makes the means available, ultimately and finally through his Son, Jesus Christ (John 14:6; Heb. 12:18–29). Of course, we recognize the tension as well with Jesus, who is both our friend and our Lord and God. So we enjoy the relationship but recognize the difference between him and us, and so obey (John 15:13–14).

God's Glory Is Seen through His Use of Unimpressive People

No less than in the days of Israel, God uses the weak and unimpressive in our own day to carry out his purposes. Jesus himself chooses "unschooled, ordinary" apostles (Acts 4:13). In doing so, it becomes clear that it is God at work. As Paul notes, God chooses the weak and foolish to shame the strong and wise (1 Cor. 1:27). God uses weak ministers, who are fragile like clay jars, to carry the gospel, lest the treasure chests outshine the treasure (2 Cor. 4:7). As Paul's own life illustrates, God's power is made perfect in weakness, demonstrating God's all-sufficient grace (2 Cor. 12:9).

In a time of many big churches, with big budgets, big programs, and big-name preachers, it might be worth reflecting on the fact that in the Bible, God seems to more often choose the little, weak, and unimpressive to accomplish his purposes. Not to deny that God can use such big churches. He does. But this pattern of God's use of the unlikely at least forces us to ask whether a time comes when the medium overshadows the message, when the treasure chest seemingly outshines the treasure.

On the other hand, Deuteronomy offers hope to small churches and for Christians who have nothing inherently impressive about them to recognize that these are precisely the kind of people God uses day in and out to accomplish his purposes, not necessarily with flash and a bang and immediate spectacular results, but in the sure and steady advance of his kingdom. But whether big or small, obvious or obscure, we are not about calling attention to ourselves but about bringing glory to God by bearing witness to the power of the Gospel of Jesus Christ. It is not about us.

Obstacles to Fulfilling God's Call

We are God's chosen people, royal priesthood, and holy nation (1 Pet. 2:9). That is, we are called by God. But, as with Israel, our calling has a purpose that extends beyond us. God has chosen and sanctified us to declare his praises (1 Pet. 2:9; cf. Exod. 19:5–6). Thus, our calling is not about us but about God and God's purposes to be accomplished through us. However, our own sense of importance, our prosperity, and our self-righteousness can, and often does, prevent us from fulfilling our calling. Especially for American Christians (or more broadly Western Christians), who belong to nations that command an inordinate amount of the world's power and wealth, pride in such a position can cause us to lose focus on our mission as a community. Our problem is not so much fear, as Israel had, but lack of it. Because of our size and strength as a nation, we may see no need to look to God for our protection and care. While Israel turned to gods and alliances to secure themselves instead of turning to God, we turn to our political leaders, our national resources, our financial institutions, our armed forces, our high voltage security fences, and bombs. In our prosperity, we often forget the call of God and pursue another of our gods. Jesus names the god "Mammon" or "Wealth" (Matt. 6:24) and Paul calls it "Greed" (Col. 3:5). Or we may simply believe we have what we have by our own devices. Since we do not worry about daily bread, a God who provides daily manna seems unnecessary for practical day-to-day living. Even in religious matters, we can convince ourselves that we are doing quite well on our own or with only minimal help from God. We can compare ourselves to others, especially those who are not Christians, and we look really good by contrast. From there, it is a short step to believing that we deserve what we have, because we are more righteous or morally superior.

If this becomes the case, then we will fail in our calling, because the church will become all about us instead of being about bearing witness to the God who forgives, saves, and grants life. Thus, Deuteronomy helps us understand that like Israel, everything we have comes from God, that we have no moral standing before God apart from what he has done for us in Jesus Christ, and that we do not live by bread alone but by the Word of God made flesh, Jesus the Bread of Life (John 6:32–58). Additionally, Paul again and again reminds Christians that we are saved not because of our righteousness but because of the grace of God in Jesus Christ. We are saved by grace through faith (trusting God) to fulfill the works God prepared us to do (Eph. 2:8–10; 2 Tim. 1:9).

Imitators of Christ

We, like Israel, are to imitate our Lord (Eph. 5:1). We live out the character and action of God, especially as revealed in the life, ministry, suffering, and death of Jesus. The demands of the Sermon on the Mount find their fulfillment first in Jesus, who fulfills the Law and who calls his disciples to do the same. Christ becomes not only the agent of reconciliation but the model for his people (Phil. 2:5–11). As noted earlier, our giving to the poor finds its roots in the example of Christ's self-giving (2 Cor. 8:9). When Jesus says, "Follow me," it is a call to self-denial, cross-bearing, and death, and through that resurrection (Matt. 16:24; Mark 8:34; Luke 9:23). In fact, a study of Luke's gospel and Acts together shows us that what Jesus does in Luke, the church does in Acts. For example, Jesus prays, and the church prays; Jesus provides help and healing for the poor and sick as does the church; Jesus is led by the Holy Spirit as is the church; Jesus suffers persecution as does the church. Jesus is the pattern for the life of the church.[91]

Chapter 8

A Matter of Distinction

Read: *Deuteronomy 12–14; 22:5, 9–12*

I srael was called to be holy, that is, separated by God for his purposes, and to be a witness to the nations concerning Yahweh their God. Again and again, Deuteronomy demonstrates that to fulfill their mission, Israel must be distinct from the nations to maintain their loyalty to God. In doing so, they will draw the attention of other nations. If Israel is to get noticed, and so be able to point to their distinct God, they cannot look and act entirely like the rest of the nations. Beginning in chapter 12, Deuteronomy lays out the stipulations of the covenant between God and Israel, setting them apart in matters of worship, leadership, and ethics, among others. Chapters 12–14 deal with distinctiveness in matters of worship and ritual obligations. These chapters draw out trajectories of the first three of the Ten Commandments.

Again, to emphasize the point, their uniqueness does not come from their size, wealth, or righteousness (chapters 7–9) but from their exclusive loyalty to God. Furthermore, their distinction is not self-serving or elitist but a means to glorify God.

Distinct in Where They Worship (12:1–32)

"You shall not worship the Lord your God in that way" (v. 4; also v. 31). Yahweh, not the Canaanites or Israelites, will determine where and how he is to be worshipped. Thus, the command in Deuteronomy 12 is designed to insure faithful and obedient worship of God according to his commands. Israel cannot simply borrow or adapt Canaanite ways of worship. Nor can Israel make up their own ways of worship (v. 8).[92] Thus, Israel is to destroy every vestige of the Canaanites' worship, totally eradicating any sign of the gods and thus the memory of them and their influence. God will not share the land with other gods. Their names are to be removed from places in Israel. However, God will choose a place to put his name. That is, God will select a place for his sanctuary, where he will dwell and where people may seek him (v. 5). While other nations had a central sanctuary for their primary deity and often a main sanctuary for each major deity, they would also have other shrines in their communities and homes as well as sacred sites for the many other gods they worshipped. This requirement in Deuteronomy, therefore, would set Israel apart by having only one legitimate sanctuary for their only God.[93]

This sanctuary will become the center of Israel's religious activity. To this sanctuary, they will bring their sacrifices, offerings, tithes, and payment of vows (vv. 8–14, 26–28; cf. 23:21–23). Also, here they will rejoice before Yahweh their God (v. 12), a reference to the celebrations of the three annual festivals (see 16:1–17).

The move into the land creates a new situation for Israel, however, with respect to slaughtering animals for meat. In the wilderness, the sanctuary moved with them and was set up in the midst of their camp. So all Israel had access and could bring to the tabernacle animals they wished to slaughter for meat. This was done to insure that they did not slaughter as a sacrifice to other gods and to insure that the blood was properly drained so that they would not defile themselves by eating blood (Lev. 17; cf. Gen. 9:3–4; Lev. 19:26; 1 Sam. 14:33–34).[94] However, once they spread out in the land, it would be impossible for many to travel long distances to simply slaughter an animal for meat. So a concession is made that allows people to slaughter in their towns as long as it is not a sacrifice and the blood is drained.

The chapter ends with an explanation for wiping out the names or memory of the Canaanite gods and worship practices. These can become a snare to Israel, causing them to worship in ways that are detestable to God, illustrated in the fact that Canaanite worship included child sacrifice.[95] Therefore, Israel is to obey the command regarding Canaanite worship without exception or addition.

Distinct in Whom They Worship (13:1–18)

Even if Israel removes the physical vestiges of Canaanite worship, the names of other gods would not be blotted out if Israelites promote worship of them. Thus, those Israelites who would lead their fellow Israelites to worship other gods must also be permanently removed.[96]

Deuteronomy 13 introduces three scenarios that would undermine Israel distinctiveness and loyalty to God by seducing them to follow other gods. In the first scenario (vv. 1–5), Israel is not to listen to a prophet or one who has dream visions if that prophet encourages them to follow other gods, even if he or she successfully predicts a "sign or wonder" (cf. 18:15–22). The fulfillment of such a sign or wonder will serve as a test of Israel's faithfulness to God,[97] and the prophet who uses it to entice Israel to other gods must be executed.

The second scenario (vv. 6–11) envisions a family member or close friend attempting to lure someone into serving another god. Again, the penalty is death, and familial love or pity cannot stand in the way of executing the offender. In fact, the person who is the object of the relative's or friend's efforts to lead them to other gods must throw the first stone.[98] This difficult requirement probably signifies that he or she has not given in to the enticement and so demonstrates that loyalty to God trumps even family and friendship commitments. The execution of the offender serves as a deterrent.

Finally, in the third scenario (vv. 12–18), "worthless fellows"[99] lead an entire town to follow other gods. Before any action is taken, the matter must be thoroughly investigated, lest the citizens of that town become victims of false accusations. However, if the charge is proven, then Israel is to completely destroy the town, its inhabitants, and all of the property within it. That is, because the town has become like a Canaanite city in its worship of other gods, it is to be treated like a Canaanite city. The result of purging such rebellion against God will be to experience the mercy and blessing of God.

Distinct in Mourning and Meals (14:1–29)

Israel's distinction is further highlighted in 14:1–21 in the matters of funerals and diet. With respect to the first matter, Moses tells Israel not to cut themselves or shave themselves for the dead (vv. 1–2). These are apparently mourning rites, which Israel later performed despite the prohibition (cf. Isa. 15:2; Jer. 16:6; 41:5). No explicit reason is given here for the restrictions, but the larger context suggests that these would have been Canaanite religious practices,[100] and this conclusion is supported when the text again emphasizes that Israel is chosen from among all peoples and is God's treasured possession (cf. 7:6; 26:18). Similar prohibitions in Leviticus 19:27–28 are couched in God's command for Israel to be holy (set apart, distinct) because he is holy (Lev. 19:2).

In verses 3–21, the text shifts to clean and unclean foods, moving from land creatures (vv. 4–8), to sea creatures (vv. 9–10), to flying creatures (vv. 11–20). Bear in mind that the clean and unclean represent ritual, not moral, categories. There is nothing morally wrong with the unclean animals, but eating them make Israelites ritually unclean and therefore unable to participate in worship at the sanctuary (cf. Lev. 11). *Why* certain animals are designated as clean or unclean is a matter of debate, and, in the end, it must be admitted that the Bible does not explain the difference in clean and unclean animals.[101] However, the *effect* of such a diet is obvious. It clearly sets Israel apart from the surrounding peoples (see v. 21) who would not have the same dietary restrictions. Whenever Israelites prepare and eat a meal, they are reminded of their distinctiveness and thus their covenant relationship with God.[102]

Verse 21b is one of the great mysteries of the Bible. Why is Israel prohibited from cooking a young goat in its mother's milk? Why would they ever want to? The prohibition is puzzling, and yet the prohibition is significant enough that it is cited two other times in the Law (Exod. 23:19; 34:26). Whatever it means, God was serious about Israel not doing it! Though many explanations have been given for this prohibition,[103] in light of the larger context (Deut. 12–14), this command is probably connected to maintaining Israel's distinctiveness over against the Canaanite religious culture. So it can be assumed that this was a Canaanite religious practice even if its purpose remains a mystery.

It is worth noting at this point that later in Deuteronomy, God commands Israel to do other things that seem odd from our perspective but that function in much the same way as the distinctive dietary laws. These laws have to do with prohibited mixtures. Israelite men cannot dress like women nor can women dress like men (22:5). While there is some evidence that such transvestitism was practiced in the religion of the surrounding culture and thus prohibited for Israel, it may be that the command simply calls on Israel to visibly maintain the creational distinction between men and women. Functionally, maintaining that distinction reminds them that God has called them not to mix with the surrounding culture (if the prohibition is against religious practices of other nations, it would have the same effect).[104] Likewise, the commands against planting two kinds of seed in a vineyard, yoking an ox and donkey for plowing, and wearing clothes made of mixed fabrics (22:9–11) would serve to remind Israel in daily work and life of God's call for distinction. The positive command to put tassels on the corners of their garments would do the same (22:12; cf. Num. 15:38–39).

Returning to Deuteronomy 14, the tithe (vv. 22–28; cf. Lev. 27:30–33) continues the theme of eating, but now points to celebration and inclusion rather than exclusion. Israel was to give a tithe (a tenth) of their produce and the firstborn of their livestock to God. They were to bring the tithe to the central sanctuary (12:6, 11, 17), presumably at the Festival of Tabernacles, which comes after the harvest. Note, however, that Israel gets to enjoy a portion of the tithe, eating heartily and celebrating in God's presence. The tithe recognizes God as the one who provides for Israel, and it serves to support those who serve at the sanctuary. The Levites from the various towns are also to be invited to the meal, since they have no land of their own for producing crops (cf. Num. 18:21–28). Every third year, however, the tithe stays in the town to provide for those who do not have the means, most notably land, to provide for themselves (cf. 26:12–19). Thus, they may fill their bellies, enjoying the blessing of the land, just as the rest of the Israelites do.

The God of the Community

A Distinct People for a Distinct God

Israel served a God who was unlike anything else any other people called "god." Therefore, as servants of this distinctive God, Israel was called to be a distinctive people. While their worship in many ways would look like that of other nations, the requirement to have only one sanctuary, where all sacrifice is to be done, sets them apart. Of course, one sanctuary is fitting since they have only one God to worship, which sets them apart as well. As noted above, every meal ideally reminded them of their covenant with God and their purpose. Therefore, in their worship and their meals, they would, on the one hand, maintain their religious identity over against the surrounding culture. Their common but distinctive diet and their annual celebration of the festivals at the place God would choose served to unite Israel over time as the distinctive people of God. It prevented Israel's assimilation in the larger religious culture. On the other hand, they would also draw attention to themselves, and through them to Yahweh, their God. Thus, the purpose is not to cut themselves off completely from the world around them but to draw the nations' attention and point them to an alternative, namely, the sole and exclusive worship of Yahweh, the one true God.

However, just as their eating served to distinguish, it also created an inclusive environment within the community. The Israelites who had the means share them with the Levite, the poor, the widow, the orphan, and the foreigners within the community through the tithes and at the festivals.

Worship and God's Sovereignty

God chooses where and when (at least in terms of the festivals) he will be worshiped. He is sovereign and has the right to do so. For Israel to defy his commands in this matter and worship wherever they please or to hold the festivals whenever they please is a denial of God's sovereignty. The suzerain has the right to set the terms for where and when his vassals will come with tribute for him. Such a denial of God's sovereignty in these matters is vividly illustrated in the apostasy of Jeroboam, son of Nabat, the first king of (northern) Israel after the division of the Davidic-Solomonic kingdom. Fearing his new subjects would return to the Davidic kings if they went to Jerusalem to worship, Jeroboam set up his own religious shrines with calf images in Bethel and Dan, instituted his own festival, and installed his own priests. Jeroboam claimed that these gods brought Israel out of Egypt, changing their faith story and robbing God of his special relationship with Israel (1 Kings 12:25–33).[105] Every king of Israel was critiqued for maintaining these alternative sanctuaries and leading Israelites in the north to worship at them. Ultimately, it was a primary reason for their fall (2 Kings 17:16, 21–23; cf. 1 Kings 13).

One should be careful, however, about extrapolating from the commands concerning worship that *every* aspect of Israel's worship life was prescribed. God certainly commanded that certain things be done in a certain place, at a certain time, and in a particular way. Likewise, he forbade other things that were too much like the Canaanites. But the restrictions in certain areas did not prevent some freedom in Israel's worship of God. That is, it would be a mistake to conclude that the only worship of God Israelites did was the few times a year they came to the central sanctuary. The psalms testify to the fact that worship of God pervaded all of Israel's life.[106] Even with respect to the worship during the appointed festivals at the sanctuary, exceptions could be made in light of special circumstances (Num. 9:6–13; 2 Chron. 30:17–20).

Loyalty to God Trumps All Other Loyalties

While Deuteronomy 6:6–9 emphasized wholehearted devotion to God by keeping the commands alive within the individual, the family, and the community, Deuteronomy 13 looks at the flipside of those instructions. In Deuteronomy 13, individuals, family members, and even whole communities are to be rooted out if they even attempt to entice Israel to follow other gods. Hence, loyalty to God trumps individual, familial, or civic loyalties. In a very real sense, Israelites had to love God more than friends and family members. The harshness of the command to execute those who would encourage disloyalty emphasizes the seriousness of Israel's covenant commitment to God and to one another. Since life is found only in God, and Israel is meant to draw others to that life, allowing rebellious elements to remain is akin to allowing a cancer to remain in the body untreated. To preserve the life of the body and allow it to function as intended, radical solutions are often called for. The same is true when an element within Israel threatens Israel's life as a whole.

Guidance for Today's Community

A Distinct People for a Distinct God

We Christians worship not just any god or generic god, but Yahweh, the God of Israel, who became incarnate in Jesus Christ and lived among us, and who has revealed himself to us as God the Father, Son, and Holy Spirit. Therefore, as noted previously, our God cannot be simply lumped in with or blended into whatever anyone else calls "God." Our God is distinct from notions of deity in general and particular definitions of God that do not conform to his self-revelation in the history of his people as witnessed in the Scripture. He alone is God and is not to be confused with any other(s).

This distinctive God calls us to be his distinctive people, carrying out his distinctive purposes (Matt. 5:13–16; 2 Cor. 6:14–18; 1 Pet. 2:9). Therefore, we run into the dilemma that is often summed up in the well-worn phrase "in the world but not of the world." How do we engage the world and yet maintain distinction from it, especially when we as God's people do not have a separate land and central sanctuary and when the dietary restrictions are not bound upon us (Mark 7:19; Rom. 14:14)? How do we become "all things to all people" (1 Cor. 9:22) without blending in so completely that we lose our distinctiveness? Do we become hermits, enclosing ourselves in our churches to avoid contamination? Do we come up with distinctive Christian clothes without blended fabrics? Do we throw off any behaviors that might seem exclusive or "prudish" to reach the lost? Bear in mind that the salt that loses its saltiness is worthless, as is a hidden light (Matt. 5:13, 15). Also, Paul would not embrace table fellowship on every occasion if it meant compromising one's faith or confusing one's understanding of God (1 Cor. 8–10).[107]

The following may prove helpful as we work with this dilemma. First, our engagement with the larger world arises precisely out of our faith in the one true God revealed in Jesus Christ and our call to bear witness to him. Thus, whatever we say and do must ultimately point to him. Paul's becoming "all things to all people" is for him to win them to Christ so they can be saved. Second, we remember that now we are the sanctuary of God individually (1 Cor. 6:19) and collectively (1 Cor. 3:16–17; 1 Pet. 2:4–5). God dwells within us and among us. Therefore, when others are with us, individually or collectively, they ought to experience the presence of God in some way (whether they could articulate it as such or not). Third, the New Testament repeatedly reminds us that as Christians we have put off ungodly behaviors, and, having put on Christ and having the Spirit within us, now exhibit godly behaviors. The former would include: idolatry, deceit, slander, greed, sexual immortality, rage, division, drunkenness, pride, self-seeking, and envy. The latter would include: joy, peace, patience, kindness, humility, self-control, gentleness, truth, unity, righteousness, mercy, and, of course, love (1 Cor. 6:7–11; 13:4–7; Gal. 5:13–26; Eph. 5:1–12; Col. 3:1–14; James 3:13–18). To reject the former and embrace the latter, to exhibit a lifestyle of one clothed with Christ and led by the Spirit, will guide our steps as we "are in but not of" the world. Fourth, I would argue that if what we eat (or the amount we eat) and what we wear (or the expense of and status attached to what we wear) evidences that we have indeed blended with the dominant culture and accepted its values of consumerism and materialism, then we may have to scale back to demonstrate the distinctiveness that Christ calls us to.[108]

A Worshipping Community

As God's people, we worship the God who called and redeemed us in Jesus Christ and who is present by his Spirit within us as the temple of God. As we consider our own worship, it is important to keep in mind the purposes of God's commands concerning Israel's worship. Israel's obedience in matters of worship recognized the sovereignty of God, and it prevented them from blending into the larger religious culture of their day. That is, Israel's worship served to recognize their

97

distinctive God and to maintain their distinction as the chosen people of this God. Their worship itself was a witness to their God who redeemed and called them. Likewise, our worship must recognize the sovereignty of God, and, in doing so, remind us of our redemption and our calling as God's chosen people. Our worship must bear witness to the God we serve and his transformative power in our lives. It must bear witness to our God so that when the outsider is present, he or she will proclaim, "God is really among you." (1 Cor. 14:25).

Deuteronomy also shows us that we Christians cannot simply decide for ourselves how we will approach God. We approach God in worship through Jesus, our high priest, sacrifice, and mediator (see e.g., Heb. 4:14–10:25; cf. Matt. 27:51; Mark 15:38; Luke 23:45; John 14:6). Because we live in a particular culture, our worship will—to some degree—reflect that culture. But we are not free to simply borrow elements from the larger culture without careful theological reflection in light of the witness of Scripture, especially the New Testament.[109] A close examination of our worship might reveal to us how much we have compromised ourselves to the larger culture, as too often in our worship, we pay homage to the gods of materialism, individualism, consumerism, and nationalism. Decisions on how we worship are frequently made on pragmatic bases. To borrow from the crass language of Whoopi Goldberg's character is *Sister Act*, we make decisions about worship based on "What will get butts in the seats?" Or decisions are made on the basis of individual tastes and preferences. This point has nothing to do with taking sides in the so-called "worship wars," but is a criticism of all sides since the root of such conflicts too often has more to do with tastes or pragmatism rather than faithfulness. Instead, we need to be asking constantly how our worship can faithfully bear witness to Christ and lead to our being transformed more and more into his likeness.

Our Loyalty to Christ Trumps All Other Loyalties

When Christ calls people to follow him, he demands their absolute loyalty, even when that means leaving behind family and friends. Anyone who loves family more than Jesus is not worthy of him. This is part of denying self, taking up the cross, and following

Jesus (Matt. 10:37–38; cf. Luke 14:26). In light of the biblical commands to love one's spouse (Eph. 5:21–33; Col. 3:18–19), honor one's parents (Deut. 5:16; Eph. 6:2–3), and to provide for one's family (1 Tim. 5:8), this call is not a permission to neglect familial responsibilities. But it does set a clear order of importance. Jesus' will is primary and absolute in the life of the Christian, even over familial claims on our loyalty. This is why Jesus said that the gospel would tear families apart (Matt. 10:35–36; Luke 12:53).

By the same token, loyalty to Jesus trumps civic and national loyalties. We call Jesus "Lord" and are citizens of the Kingdom of Heaven (Phil. 3:20; Eph. 2:19–20), thus, relativizing the ultimate lordship of any other authority.[110] That is why Peter and John declared that they must obey God rather than human authorities (Acts 5:29). This is why Christians do not make good patriots.[111]

Our loyalty to God over other relationships also demands that we deal with rebellion against the will of God in our churches. We are not a national entity like Israel and have neither the authority nor any command to execute such people (as much as we may be tempted to do so at times!). However, in extreme cases, Christians are told to remove such people from their midst, for example, in cases of sexual immorality, greed, business cheats, drunkards, slanderers, those who deny apostolic authority, and blasphemers (1 Cor. 5:1–13; 2 Thess. 3:14; 1 Tim. 1:20). Paul's concern in these cases is both to maintain the purity of the community (1 Cor. 5:6–8) and to ultimately restore the rebel (1 Cor. 5:5; 1 Tim. 1:20). Clearly, these texts do not have in mind those who struggle with these sins and recognize them as sins. Rather, it is the defiant and rebellious who are in view. For the church to simply tolerate their rebellion makes the church a partner in their rebellion, compromises the integrity of the body, and dissolves the church's distinctiveness, and hence witness, relative to the larger culture.

Chapter 9

Liberty and Justice for All

Read: *Deuteronomy 15:1–18; 21:10–14; 23:15–16; 24:7, 14–22*

Israel would enjoy freedom because of God's execution of justice (i.e., judgment) on Egypt. Therefore, Israel is to imitate their God by granting and guaranteeing freedom and justice. Having experienced liberation, they become liberators. Having received the life-giving blessings of God, which freed them from the fear and anxiety of day-to-day survival, they become a means of blessing for those who have little or nothing. As God granted Israel rest (i.e., security and provision) in the land, so Israel is to provide rest for one another in the land. Thus, the laws in Deuteronomy 15:1–18 flow out of the fourth commandment as an extension of the Sabbath principle.

Freedom from Debt and Poverty (15:1–11)

In Deuteronomy 15:1–11, God imposes on Israel what, to us, may sound like a most unsound fiscal policy. Every seventh year, Israelites are to cancel or forgive loans—just write them off the books.[112] The year of release occurs the same year as the reading of the *Torah* before the community (31:10–11) and therefore serves as a fitting reminder of the mutual liberation shared by Israel and the mutual obligations Israelites have toward one another as the people of God.[113] The reason Israel can afford to do so is that God will so richly bless them. If they keep the covenant, they can afford to loan and forgive debt freely (vv. 4, 6, 10). Furthermore, the familial or community bonds are stressed with the repeated use of "brother(s)" (vv. 2, 3, 7, 9, 11; more inclusively "member of your community" [NRSV]). So Israel is encouraged to lend to the poor of the community freely, not being tightfisted or calculating.[114]

To allow fellow Israelites to remain in poverty by refusing to freely lend to them is likened to oppression. If an Israelite refuses to help the poor of their community, the poor may turn to God for relief, literally "call to Yahweh against you" (v. 9). This is the same language used in 24:15 regarding those who do not pay the poor their daily wages, and it is reminiscent of the language used of the Israelites' crying out to God while enslaved in Egypt (Exod. 2:23).

Note that Israel does not have to forgive loans made to foreigners (v. 3) and that Israel will become a lender nation but will not need to borrow. The word for "foreigner" here is not the same word as the one usually translated "alien"—a non-Israelite who has attached himself or herself to the community. This is not a permission to take advantage of the foreigner, but it is recognition of a distinction between those within the covenant community and those without. However, the connection of lending to nations and ruling over them and of not borrowing and not being ruled suggests that God's blessing of his people will give them economic leverage to control other nations while avoiding being controlled by those nations.

Consider also the tension that runs through this text. On the one hand, Israel is told to lend freely to the poor, and, in fact, the poor will always be in the land (v. 11). On the other hand, verse 4 states literally that "there will be no poor among you."[115] Verse 4 sets up the expectation and ideal for life in the Israelite community: poverty will be nonexistent because God will generously bless Israel in the land. However, as is the case throughout Deuteronomy, blessing is contingent on obedience: "if only you will strictly obey…" (v. 5). While holding up and fully expecting Israel to live according to the ideal, God acknowledges the reality that this stubborn people will not do so, and poverty will exist in the land. Most likely, the poverty will result from violations of the covenant not only by general disobedience, leading to a forfeiture of blessing, but by specific acts of disobedience that cause and sustain poverty, for example, cheating in business (see 25:13–16), failing to pay wages (see 24:14–15), and corrupting the justice system (see 16:19–20; 24:17; 27:19). In light of the poverty created by such circumstances, Israel is commanded to care for the poor.[116]

Along these lines, Deuteronomy 23:19–20 also prohibits charging interest on loans to fellow Israelites, but Israelites can charge interest to foreigners. This law does not specify the type of loan, but since the law emphasizes money (literally, silver) and especially food, the law probably has in mind someone who borrows out of need, rather than someone who borrows money to make money (capital ventures). To add interest on a loan to the poor would merely compound the poor borrower's poverty and allow the one who loans to profit by another's misfortune (cf. Exod. 22:25; Lev. 25:35–37; Ezek. 22:12). Foreigners (again, as opposed to Israel's resident aliens) could be charged interest, highlighting the distinction between God's elect and others.[117] Keeping this law will lead to blessings from God.

Finally, also in keeping with the spirit of 15:1–11, Israel is not to be thorough in its harvesting of grains, olives, and grapes, so that produce will be left behind for the orphan and widow (24:19–22; cf. Lev. 19:9–10; 23:22; Ruth 2). Gleaning (collecting what is unharvested) becomes a way for the Israelites to provide for the disadvantaged among them. Rather than picking the excess and giving it to them, however, the dignity of the disadvantaged is maintained by allowing them to work for their food. Once more, the motivation to care for the disadvantaged is the memory that they were in similar dire straits in Egypt, and God delivered them. Therefore, in imitation of God, they provide means to deliver those in dire straits in Israel.

Freedom for Slaves (15:12–18) [118]

Linked by the idea of a seventh year release in 15:1–11, Israelites are also commanded to release any fellow Hebrew/Israelite[119] who has sold himself or herself to serve them (15:12–18; cf. Exod. 21:2–11[120]). Note that the person sold himself or herself. This was a voluntary arrangement, more like indentured service, probably done to pay off debt or because the slave could not support himself or herself. That is, this type of slavery provided a *temporary* means of relief or support to someone in need. The poor person is to work for six years and be released in the seventh year after entering into service.[121] The owner is also to liberally supply him or her, and, in this way, prevent a return to the conditions that led to the servitude in the first place. The motivation for doing this is the memory that the master, too, is a freed slave: freed from Egypt by God. Though the text does not spell it out explicitly, that memory surely includes the fact that God liberally supplied Israel when they plundered Egypt on the night of the exodus (Exod. 3:22; 12:35–36), that he continued to supply in the wilderness (water and manna), and that he will richly bless them in the land. Thus, the owner becomes an imitator of God in carrying out this command. Also, the owner is encouraged to recognize the value of the servant's service over the six years and to understand that blessing will result from keeping this law. That is, he will gain rather than lose in the transaction (v. 18).

However, this law also acknowledges the fact that the slave may choose to remain a slave, because he or she loves the owner and owner's family and because the slave will find a more certain livelihood in the owner's service. This scenario envisions a benevolent relationship between the slave and owner as is fitting between fellow Israelites (cf. Lev. 25:39–40). If the slave makes this decision, then his or her earlobe is to be pierced with an awl pushed through into the door.[122] The piercing is probably a way to mark the slave as one who has chosen to remain a slave to this owner for life. The fact that the decision is between freedom and provision after six years of service or being a slave for life, with no middle options, likely represents an attempt to discourage the slave from remaining in slavery.

Deuteronomy has only a few other laws dealing with slaves. In 21:10–14, Israelite men are given permission to marry women from among war captives. If a man does so and his new wife does not please him, he is forbidden from selling her into slavery. To take her as a wife and then reject her already dishonors her, a charge laid *against the husband* (v. 14); to sell her into slavery would doubly dishonor her. In 23:15–16, Israel is instructed not to return a runaway slave to his or her master. Instead, the slave becomes a free person, living wherever he or she pleases. The Israelites cannot oppress the former slave, which would negate his or her new status as a free person.[123] The law probably refers to slaves of non-Israelites, since the escaped slave is permitted to live among them.[124] Finally, in 24:7, the death penalty is imposed upon anyone who kidnaps and sells a fellow (literally, brother) Israelite as a slave. Such action is considered an evil that must be purged from the community (cf. Amos 1:6, 9). In essence, a human is undoing what God has done for Israel in freeing them from slavery.

It is worth noting that the Bible records only one instance when the Israelites released their slaves. In Jeremiah 34:8–22, as the Babylonians threatened to take their city, the people of Jerusalem released their slaves. Perhaps they did so to provide extra manpower against the Babylonians or to relieve themselves of the obligation of caring for their slaves, but verses 14–15 indicate that they did so in obedience to the law of release as an act of repentance. Their repentance was short-lived, however. They decided to take back their slaves after Nebuchadnezzar withdrew from the city, which they mistakenly thought meant the end to the Babylonian threat.[125]

The God of the Community

The God of Freedom

Deuteronomy repeatedly asserts that God freed Israel from slavery in Egypt. That claim serves as a reminder and motivation for Israel to keep the laws discussed here and throughout Deuteronomy (5:6, 15; 6:12, 21; 7:8; 8:14; 13:5, 10; 15:15; 16:12; 24:18, 22). Israel's primary foundational experience of God is that he is their liberator from slavery. Having freed Israel from slavery, he does not want them to return to conditions of bondage and servitude, whether as slaves to other humans or as slaves to debt. The land is intended as a place of rest, where Israel will be safe from oppression and want, if only they keep the covenant. The freeing of debts, generosity to the poor, and release of slaves well supplied mirrors God's gracious gift of deliverance from slavery and rest in the land. The Israelites become God's agents of rest.

Freedom here should not be understood in terms of modern notions of autonomy or democratic government. Such notions would not make sense in ancient Israel's cultural environment. Israel remains under a Lord and King, their God, Yahweh. However, unlike Pharaoh-type rulers and masters, God is benevolent and deals with his people in ways that are life-affirming and grant dignity. Israel is free of that death-dealing and degrading master, Pharaoh. God intends for Israel to remain free of whatever robs any of them of their security and dignity.[126] Israel, in turn, imitates their King through acts that provide freedom from degradation, oppression, and deprivation.

God Has Special Concern for the Vulnerable

God's special concern for the vulnerable is evident throughout Deuteronomy and the whole of the Bible, but this does not mean that he loves the widow, orphan, slave, and alien more than others. His desire is the salvation of all of his creation, which he loves. Still, God is particularly aware of those who suffer abuses at the hands of the powerful or who suffer because they are ignored and left to their fate. It is their cries that God hears. It is their cause that God takes up. It is on their behalf that God sends judgment on oppressors to deliver them. Just as he heard Israel's cries in Egypt, took up their cause, and delivered them by executing his judgment on Pharaoh and the gods of Egypt, so God continues to respond to the cries of the vulnerable.

God's ideal, and one to be taken seriously, was that there be no poor in the land. If Israel was consistent in keeping the commands, this would be the case. But their rebellious tendencies made it a sure bet that they would violate the covenant. The acknowledgement that there would always be poor in the land should not be understood as permission to maintain the status quo or to be apathetic toward the poor. In light of the ideal, the assertion that poor people would always be there should be heard as an *indictment*. Israel would not live up to its covenant obligations. But for those who loved and served God wholeheartedly, the presence of poor people in the land could also be viewed as an opportunity to do for the vulnerable of the community as God did for Israel in the exodus and in the gift of the land. This, in turn, bore witness to the larger world to the kind of God whom Israel was serving. Imagine the questions that outsiders would have raised if they had encountered an Israel where there were no poor. That certainly would have set Israel apart from nations and Israel's God apart from the gods of the nations who tended to be viewed as on the side of the powerful.

Guidance for Today's Community

The Responsibility of Freedom

In Christ, we enjoy freedom from bondage to sin, legalism, guilt, and death (Rom. 8:1–2; Gal. 4:21–5:1; Heb. 2:14–15; Rev. 1:5). We have experienced a liberation by God, so that we no longer have to live as slaves to powers that oppress, degrade, destroy, and ultimately kill (Luke 4:18–21).[127] However, the freedom we enjoy in Christ is not a freedom characterized by self-centeredness, self-indulgence, selfishness, and sin (Rom. 6:1–7; 1 Cor. 8:9; Gal. 5:13; 1 Pet. 2:16). Instead, we are freed to be the people God intended us to be: those who serve him and so enjoy his blessings, and those who serve and share the blessings with others. That is, we are freed to serve. Indeed, we are not really free at all in the sense of self-rule. Rather, we have been redeemed from harsh, death-dealing masters (sin, Satan, self) to become slaves (or servants) of Jesus Christ (Rom. 6:17–18; 1 Cor. 7:22; 9:21), who says he came not to be served but to serve (Matt. 20:28; Mark 10:45; cf. Phil. 2:7). And he calls upon us to imitate him in service to others (Matt. 20:25–27; Mark 10:42–44; cf. Phil. 2:5; Jo 13:1–17).

As with Israel, we are not talking about freedom here in the sense of political freedoms or personal autonomy. Therefore, the texts that discuss freedom cannot be used as a justification to expand political and ideological agendas even in the name of freedom. Nor will it allow us to live in isolation from the rest of the world, free to do our own thing but ignoring the plight of others. Instead, we seek ways, in the name of Christ, to free people from degrading and death-dealing situations. We uphold human dignity, since we are all made in the image of Christ, and we become agents of life to those deprived of the means of livelihood. Also, through our words and deeds, we point those outside the community of faith to the true liberator and loving king, Jesus Christ. That is, the word of liberation from Deuteronomy 15 is not merely spiritual, if by spiritual one understands it to relate only to freedom from sin and eternal death. There is a real-world, here-and-now word to us.

As Christians, we must be especially aware of those in our communities (though we need not limit ourselves to this) who find themselves in bondage of various kinds, for example, addictions, debt, depression, guilt, grief, poor health, and struggles with sin. Rather than ignoring such issues, thinking, *That's not my problem*, we need to become agents of liberation from these slaveries as well. This is not to say we ourselves are competent to fix these problems, but we can bear the burden with them (Gal. 6:2; 1 Thess. 5:14). What is more, we have to admit that some cannot be "fixed." But we can show them the God who liberates and heals.

But we must also look outwardly to the real bondage faced by others. Today, more people are enslaved in the world than in the nineteenth century prior to the various abolition movements in the West. People are forced to work in inhumane and degrading conditions for little or no pay as farmworkers, factory workers, and domestic servants. Women and girls are forced to work as sex slaves. Others, while not technically slaves, are forced to work at next to no pay in terrible and dangerous conditions. In the spirit of the God of freedom and justice, we are called to be aware and respond as we can, at least by refusing to purchase the products of companies who profit from such labor and exposing these degrading practices where we can.[128]

Care for the Poor and Vulnerable

In his ministry, Jesus repeatedly demonstrated the same concern for those who are poor and in need that God showed in the OT. Likewise, God's people today have the same obligation to care for these fellow human beings as they did in Moses' day. Jesus repeatedly taught his disciples to care for poor people (e.g., Matt. 19:21; Luke 12:33; 14:13–14; 18:22), even linking judgment to hording wealth and not helping those in need (Matt. 25:31–46; Luke 16:19–25). The early church followed the command and example of Jesus in this regard (Acts 4:34; 24:17; Gal. 2:9–10). Paul urged Christians to care for those in need, especially within the community of faith (Rom. 12:13; 2 Cor. 8–9; Gal. 6:9–10; Eph. 4:28; 1 Tim. 5:3). James rails against those who would denigrate poor Christians in favor of the rich (James 2:1–13), and his example of dead faith is one who does not aid a brother or sister in need (James 2:14–17). John argues that one demonstrates having the love of God by helping the brother or sister in need (1 John 3:16–18).

However, in our dealing with poor people within our communities and without, we, like Israel, have to bear in mind the dignity of those who are poor. They are not a problem to be solved or ignored but human beings that we care for and serve. It is easy enough to begin the blame game or to adopt a patronizing stance, treating those in need like children.[129] However, we ought instead to consider them as brothers, sisters, and neighbors whom God calls us to serve. We must remember that they, too, are people created in the image of God. While meeting immediate needs in a way that maintains the dignity of those we serve, we can also look for ways to help them overcome poverty in the long term. A friend of mine, who himself was once homeless, led a program that provided meals for homeless people in Trenton, New Jersey. He hated the phrase "feeding the homeless," because it made it sound like we were dealing with livestock. He thought such language dehumanized the people who came for a meal. So he called them "our guests." He also insisted that those who came to help in serving the meals also join the guests at the table, sharing the meal. Dignity!

And it will not do to argue that both Deuteronomy and Jesus say that the poor will always be with us (Matt. 26:11; Mark 14:7; John 12:8), if that leads us to the conclusion that we are to simply surrender to the inevitability of poverty, or worse, conclude that we are thereby not called to help and serve the poor. In Deuteronomy, the claim that there will always be poor people among them ought to be heard as an indictment for Israel's failure to keep the covenant, as well as a call to continue to help the poor. When Jesus says that there will always be poor people, alluding to Deuteronomy 15:11, he is not saying that poverty is inevitable or that it must be so. He is responding to the disciples' criticism that the woman anointing Jesus is wasting money that could have gone to the poor. His issue is timing; poverty will be here after he has gone.[130] The implication is that his disciples can and should help the poor (see Mark 14:7). Furthermore, in light of Deuteronomy 15:11, we can hear Jesus' statement as an indictment on those Jews in his own generation whose covenant failures have allowed poverty to remain in the land to his day, and it indicts Mark's

Christian readers who allow poverty to remain in their communities. It also indicts us Christians today who allow poverty to remain in the worldwide community of faith while we live in luxury. Our model and goal should rather be the description of the church in Acts 4:34: "There was not a needy person among them" (an echo of Deut. 15:4).

Imagine the witness to the world of the Christian community if it had no poor people in it, let no one fall through the cracks, and lifted up its people up instead of letting them stay down. But keep in mind that our community is not simply the people we go to church with each Sunday. We may very well look around and not see a poor person among us, which in itself is either evidence of our fulfilling our obligation to our poor brothers and sisters in our immediate communities, or, perhaps more likely, it may be evidence that we have simply removed ourselves from direct interaction with and service to the poor. What we cannot forget is that we belong to a global community of God's people. So our obligation to the poor does not stop at our church door (see, again, Paul's words in 2 Cor. 8–9). Rather, we are called to aid poor Christians throughout the world. Surely, there is enough wealth among us Christians in the West that if we did not hoard and spend extravagantly on ourselves, we could relieve much of the poverty of our brothers and sisters in Christ worldwide. What would it tell the world about our Lord if a poor Christian could not be found because we take care of our own?

Furthermore, we do not simply stop with fellow Christians, but, in our mission, we expand our service to all poor in the name of Jesus that God may be glorified. The church has done as much as anyone throughout history toward helping the poor, and that is a powerful witness. Imagine how much greater the witness if every Christian took his or her obligation to the poor seriously.[131]

Chapter 10

Who Is In Charge Here?

Read: *Deuteronomy 16:18–18:22*

A s with any community, questions and issues of leadership are bound to arise. Some will ask who is in charge, while others rush to take charge. However, in Israel, the question of who is in charge is already settled: Yahweh, Israel's God! Moses repeatedly calls Israel to obey their God (e.g., 6:3, 24–25; 12:28; 13:4). In fact, Yahweh is the king over Israel (33:5; Jeshurun = Israel).[132] The shaping of Deuteronomy in the form of a suzerain-vassal treaty points in the same direction. By extension, God's word, his *Torah*, is authoritative over all Israel, including its leaders. Furthermore, the *Torah* includes instructions concerning Israel's leaders. That is, Israel's leaders also stand under *Torah*.

Note also that no "office" in Israel has absolute power. While recognizing that some people have to serve in positions of authority or leadership, power is dispersed in Israel. No one person or group lays claim to total power. As one writer notes, "Power does not flow downward from a hierarchy; rather governing elements operate alongside one another in parallel fashion."[133] Indeed, if Israel keeps these commands, no one in Israel can claim power. Rather, God both grants and limits power.

Judges and Courts (16:18–17:13)

The people of Israel will appoint their own judges, a move already anticipated in 1:9–18. Justice alone is to guide these judges, not partiality (on social or economic grounds) or bribes, which the Bible again and again condemns (e.g., Exod. 23:8; 1 Sam. 8:3; Ps. 15:5; Prov. 17:23; 29:4; Isa. 5:23; Amos 5:12; Mic. 7:3). Bribes rig the system in favor of the rich and powerful, and Israel's judges are to have no part in that. But maintaining justice and righteousness[134] is not simply the responsibility of the judges. The demand to promote justice goes for all Israel, and verse 17 links remaining in the land to justice.

The instructions concerning judges anticipate life in the land when Moses will not be with the people anymore. So if a case proves too hard for the judges, they will take it before the priests and judge at the sanctuary (cf. 1:17). This is not an appeals court, but a means of rendering justice, and the people must act on the decisions given by the priests and judge, understanding the decision as a word from God. This may imply that the judge and priests render a decision on the basis of the *Torah*, or it could imply divine revelation of a verdict. In either case, God is instrumental in the execution of justice in Israel.

A discussion on idolatry (16:21–17:8) seems to interrupt his section on judges and courts. Perhaps it serves as a warning against inquiring of other gods in those difficult cases (cf. 18:9–14). Or it may remind Israel that justice is rooted in the just character of God, not other gods who tend to support the powerful. Or perhaps the reference to idolatry is a sample case to show the procedure these judges will use to decide cases.[135] Note the attention to "thoroughly investigating" charges (17:4) and the demand for multiple witnesses before implementing the death penalty (cf. 19:15).

The King (17:14–20)

God will allow Israel to have a king, though having one is not necessary,[136] but the king that God permits them to have will not seem like much of a king at all. First, this king does not rule by right of power or heredity. Instead, God will choose the king, and the people will appoint him.[137] Second, the king has to be an Israelite. Israel has had their experience under a foreign king, Pharaoh, and it was a brutal, oppressive experience. In contrast to kings like Pharaoh, Israel's king is not to exalt himself over his fellow Israelites. He is to be their fellow (literally, "brother") Israelite. Third, Israel's king cannot do the things other kings would do as a matter of course. He cannot build up his military might by acquiring horses. He must trust God to fight for Israel. He cannot acquire many wives. A large harem was both a sign of prestige and a means of securing foreign alliances, which become a false source of hope for security.[138] Also, with foreign wives often came their foreign gods and the potential of the king worshipping them (cf. Deut. 7:3–4; 1 Kings 11:1–8). Remember, God commanded Israel to eradicate all traces of other gods (Deut. 7:5; 12:3). Finally, Israel's king cannot amass wealth for himself. When those in power accumulate wealth, it too often occurs at the expense of the poor and weak (cf. Jer. 22:13–17; Amos 2:6–8).[139]

The one positive task of Israel's king is to read continually the *Torah,* so that he will learn to fear and obey God. In doing so, he will share with his kindred Israelites both in standing under *Torah* and recognizing that he also is a beneficiary of God's redemption. The king will then lead Israel in the practice of justice and righteousness demanded in the *Torah.*

Priests and Levites (18:1–8)

Rather than outline the duties of the priest and the larger tribe of Levi, Moses details here the community's responsibilities toward the priests and Levites.[140] God is the Levites' portion instead of a portion of the land. This means that God will provide for them. He does so by granting them a share of what is sacrificed at the altar. Levites who do not live and serve at the central sanctuary receive a portion of the tithes that remain in the towns (Deut. 26:12), though any Levite is free to move to the sanctuary and receive a share of the offerings there.

What does this have to do with power in Israel? In Deuteronomy, priestly power is limited. They do, to some extent, control access to the sanctuary and instruct the people on maintaining and regaining cultic purity, for example, with respect to lepers (i.e., those with skin diseases) in 24:8–9 (cf. Lev. 13–14). As noted above, they also have a role in some judicial procedures. Typically, however, among Israel's neighboring nations, the priests were part of the aristocracy. They had large land holdings, a source of wealth and hence power. They could also demand offerings from the people, lest the gods be angered, and such demands have the potential of abusing power and impoverishing the people. The priestly tribe, the Levites, have no allotment of territory, and their share of the offerings is

Phillip G. Camp

detailed (cf. 1 Sam. 2:12–16). Thus, compared to other priesthoods, Israel's priests are relatively powerless.[141]

The Prophets (18:9–22)

After Israel heard God's voice on the mountain, God appointed Moses as the one to speak his word to the people (5:23–29; 18:16). The problem for Israel was that Moses would not go with them into the land. Without Moses, Israel might be tempted to turn to illegitimate means of discerning divine will and activity, or they might simply seek other methods to get the word they want or to let them know the future. In any case, Moses here warns them against imitating the Canaanites' methods of discerning the future or the divine will (18:9–14). When Moses was gone, God would appoint another prophet like Moses from among the Israelites and give that prophet the words to speak to Israel. The expectation here is most likely not an individual but a series of prophets raised by God throughout Israel's history (e.g., Deborah, Samuel, Nathan, Elijah, Elisha, and the literary prophets, Isaiah through Malachi).

This office is so serious that judgment is threatened for those who do not listen to the prophet, and the death penalty is imposed on anyone who prophesies in the name of other gods (cf. 13:1–5) or who prophesies in God's name without being called by him.[142] The threat of such judgment raises the question of how Israel would know whether God had sent a particular prophet. Anyone could claim to speak for Yahweh. The test for such a prophet is twofold: he or she cannot speak in the name of any god but Yahweh, Israel's God, and his or her word must be fulfilled.[143]

God calls prophets as a check on the powerful in Israel, though they themselves rarely have individual wealth or power. Some are occasionally connected to the power structures (e.g. Samuel, Nathan, and Isaiah), but more often they tend to stand outside the official institutions (e.g., Elijah, Jeremiah, and Amos). Even those in some way linked to the authorities remain free to critique and condemn if God sends them to do so.[144]

The God of the Community

Yahweh God is Lord and Master of Israel, and Israel must conform themselves to his will and character. Indeed, God claims sovereignty over not only Israel but over all nations and all of creation (see Exod. 19:5; Deut. 10:14; Ps. 89:9–12). This fact relativizes any issues of human authority and power among God's people. Therefore, when God establishes human offices and authorities in Israel, they are not established for the sake of human power but to carry out God's purposes. In this respect, these officials exercise their authority in submission to God for the purpose of leading the community in faithfulness to God's purposes. Those purposes include justice and righteousness (16:19–20), exclusive loyalty to God (16:21–17:7), keeping *Torah* (17:18–20), and hearing and responding to the word of God (18:18–19).

In addition, God disperses human power in Israel, so that no one office or officeholder should gain or maintain absolute power. Furthermore, God appoints those in power, so that no one has an inherent claim to the power. Concentration of power tends to lead to grasping for even more power and the perks that come with power, perhaps especially wealth and prestige. As the powerful expand their power, they tend to do it on the backs of the powerless. A quick read of prophets like Isaiah, Amos, and Micah, or of the accounts of kings like Ahab (1 Kings 16–21) and Manasseh (2 Kings 21:1–18; 24:3–4) bears this out. Among God's people, however, the concept of "fellow Israelite" (literally, "brother Israelite," i.e., kinship) brings every leader back down within the community that shares in a common redemption.

This section of Deuteronomy also points us toward Jesus, who ultimately and definitively fulfills the intent of all these roles. He is the just and righteous Judge (Acts 10:42; 2 Tim. 4:1, 8; Rev. 19:11).[145] He is the great High Priest, who, rather than receiving a share from the altar, offers himself on the altar as the once-for-all sacrifice (Heb. 4:14–5:10; 7:1–10:18). He is the great King of kings, the son of David, who leads his people to love and serve God as he does (Matt. 2:1–12; 21:1–17; Rom. 1:3; Rev. 17:14; 19:16). And he is the Prophet who calls his people continually to new covenant faithfulness (Matt. 21:11;

John 6:14; 7:40), and who not only speaks the word of God but *is* the Word of God (John 1:1, 14). Thus, all of Israel's authoritative roles are placed upon Jesus, making him *the* authority for the people of God, though one who exercises that authority solely for the purposes and to the glory of God (cf. John 10:17–18; 1 Cor. 15:27–28; Phil. 2:6–11).

Guidance for Today's Community

Like Israel, the church has a Lord. He is Jesus Christ, the God of Israel incarnate. The church is his. He is the head, and we are the body (Eph. 1:22–23; 5:23). Therefore, there is no place for jockeying for position, insisting on one's own way, or exalting an individual. No one holding a leadership role or in a position of influence (e.g., because of family connections or the amount of their contribution) in the church has absolute authority, and no one can use such roles to enhance his or her own status, power, or wealth. We are all sisters and brothers in Christ, sharing in a common redemption and living as the one body of Christ. How many times has the church, the body of Christ, been ripped apart by fights over who is in charge or who will get their way? Consider the witness that gives to the world.

Jesus, our Lord, demonstrates how his followers should exercise power and influence by his own example. Instead of striving for positions of power, he calls his disciples to become great through service (Matt. 20:20–28; Mark 10:35–45; John 13:1–17). Instead of gaining and maintaining power through force, he chooses the way of self-denial and the cross, and calls his followers to do the same (Matt. 16:24; 26:51–53; Mark 8:34; Luke 9:23).

Within the larger world, seeking and maintaining power and its perks is a way of life. Some would say, "That's simply the way the world works." But that is not the case for the people of God. Rather, we must use whatever power, influence, or leadership roles (official, manager, VP, teacher, parent) we have in service to others for the glory of God. The only power we can wield freely is the power of self-giving love. Imitating our Lord, we must use our power and influence for justice, particularly, in cases where the official power structures manipulate or oppress those without power. Love of neighbor demands it. This also goes for the power we hold in our exercise of political freedoms and to the extent we participate in and have influence in the direction of our national political, economic, and military power. We cannot equate national power with moral correctness. Might does not make right, not among the people of God. The people of God lead through service and sacrifice.

Chapter 11

Those Other People

Read: *Deuteronomy 7:1–5; 20:1–20; 21:10–14; 23:1–8, 17–18; 24:14–22; 25:17–19*

How was Israel to regard those who are not Israelites? The matter in Deuteronomy gets a bit complicated. While God commands Israel to wipe out the Canaanites (7:1–5; 20:16–18), for reasons discussed earlier, this is certainly not intended as Israel's general stance toward other peoples. The Amalekites are the only other people singled out for such destruction, because of their attack on the stragglers after Israel had left Egypt (Deut. 25:17–19; cf. Exod. 17:8–16). Amalek had attacked the weak of God's people. We have already seen that God fights both for his people (1:30; 3:22; 20:4) and for the weak (10:18), so Amalek's judgment for their double-offense is not surprising. However, the more general stance of Israel toward non-Israelites, as also noted earlier, is bearing witness to God to draw others to him (4:5–8).

The Resident Alien

We have repeatedly seen God's concern for the alien, the foreigner who dwells within Israel. They must receive justice in Israel (1:16; 24:14–15, 17–18; 27:19), and the Israelites must meet their needs (10:18–19; 24:19–22; 26:12–13). It simply would not do for an Israelite to say, "Because you are not one of us, we are under no obligation to you." Their obligation to the alien, who has no official standing or power in the community, is rooted in their own experience as powerless foreigners in Egypt and God's intervention on their behalf. In this case, they are to do unto others as God has done to them.

War and the Aftermath

In warfare with non-Canaanite peoples, Israel must take steps to attempt to preserve the lives of their enemies. They must first offer terms of peace, trying to convince the enemy to surrender. If the enemy chooses to fight instead, only the men (those who would usually fight) are killed. The women and children are spared (20:1–15). Even the fruit trees are spared (20:19–20) to feed the Israelite army (v. 19), also perhaps to continue to feed those who are left behind after the battle ends, and to prevent unnecessary and wanton destruction of the environment that so often accompanies warfare (cf. 22:6–7).[146]

Israelite men can marry women captured in such battles (21:10–14). It may trouble us, given our view of marriage, that the woman has no say in the marriage. However, keep in mind that in the world of ancient Israel, all marriages were contractual matters between parents, and the couple, especially the woman, rarely had any say concerning their marriage partner.[147] What is more significant here are the limitations put on the man in 21:10–14. He must delay the marriage to allow for a set ritual and waiting period. She has to be given time to mourn for her parents. Even more, the captive becomes a wife and an Israelite, which is probably the function of the ritual of shaving her hair, trimming her nails, and changing her clothes. All these requirements prevent the man from using her merely for quick, sexual gratification.[148] Finally, if the man is not pleased with his wife, he has to let her go (i.e., divorce her; cf. Deut. 24:1), rather than profiting from either her labor or her sale into slavery. She is now an Israelite woman who is free to go, and the text places blame on the man for "dishonoring" her.

Exclusion from and Inclusion in the Assembly

The "assembly of the Lord (Yahweh)" refers to the Israelites as a whole, perhaps especially as they are involved in worship and warfare.[149] The command allowing aliens to join in the feasting around the Feasts of Week and Tabernacles and the celebration of the firstfruits (Deut. 16:9–14; 26:11) suggests an openness to the assembly, but not everyone is permitted to participate in it, as Deuteronomy 23:1–8 makes clear.

No man with damaged or severed genitalia can enter the assembly of the Lord. This may refer to any male in this condition, in which case the issue is probably symbolic, relating issues of wholeness and holiness (cf. Lev. 21:17–23).[150] Or the command may be more narrowly focused on those who are emasculated in rituals in service to other gods, so that their condition marks them as devotees of a deity other than Yahweh.[151]

In addition, no person "born of a forbidden union" ("illicit union," NRSV; "illegitimate birth," NASB; "bastard," KJV) can enter the assembly, even until the tenth generation (that is, they can never enter). Who is in view here? It is not referring simply to a child born out of wedlock, but to a child who is the product of an incestuous relationship (cf. 22:30; Lev. 18:6–20; 20:10–21), the child of a cultic prostitute (cf. 23:17–18), or to the offspring of intermarriage between an Israelite and non-Israelite (cf. 7:3).[152] To ban a child in any of these cases, since a child has no control over his or her parentage, seems unfair from our perspective. However, the exclusion likely had symbolic significance for Israel. As with the emasculated, this requirement points to wholeness and distinction. It might also serve as a warning to those who would consider the prohibited sexual unions.

Next, Moses moves to the inclusion or exclusion of particular nationalities. Ammonites and Moabites are perpetually prevented from entering the assembly of the Lord, but Edomites and Egyptians are eventually allowed in. While it may be tempting to see the exclusion of the Ammonites and Moabites in light of 23:2, given their incestuous origin as the offspring of Lot and his daughters (Gen. 19:30–38), Moses gives the explicit reason for their exclusion: They did not extend hospitality to Israel, bread and water, as Israel moved toward the Promised Land. Even worse, they hired Balaam to curse Israel, though God turned the curses into blessing (cf. Num. 22–24).[153] Israel could not take over the land God had given to these nations (2:9–23), but they were forbidden from seeking "their peace or their prosperity." God fulfilled upon Moab and Ammon his promise to Abraham to curse those who curse or dishonor Abraham's descendants (Gen. 12:3).

On the other hand, Edomites and Egyptians are permitted to the assembly in the third generation. The Edomites are a "brother" nation to Israel (Gen. 27, 33, 36).[154] In contrast to the Ammonites and the Moabites, the hospitality of the Egyptians is recalled. Presumably this refers to when they received the family of Jacob in the days that Joseph ruled in Egypt (Gen. 45–46). Admittance of the third generation of Egyptians illustrates the other part of that promise to Abraham to bless those who bless his descendants. That Edomites and Egyptians have to wait until the third generation may be a way of separating them from the idolatrous influences of their home countries.

The God of the Community

God loves all people of all nations. In carrying out his intent to redeem all of creation, he chose Israel for a special role. However, as noted earlier, that role gives Israel no grounds to claim national or moral superiority (Deut. 6–8). Graciousness and mercy should characterize their general orientation toward non-Israelites. Perhaps, ironically, even in warfare, Israel must demonstrate love of neighbor by limiting bloodshed and protecting captive women. While Israel could subject their captives to force labor, they could not, as would be expected in ancient (and often in modern!) warfare, dehumanize or brutalize their captives.[155]

Even in the choosing of Israel and later the church, there is never any doubt that God claims lordship over the entire creation, and both Israel and the church serve his purposes in the larger creation, perhaps especially in bearing witness to him (Deut. 4:5–8; Matt. 5:13–16; 28:19–20). However, Deuteronomy demonstrates a complex understanding of God's relationship to nations outside Israel. While Israel bears witness to the surrounding peoples, certain peoples are seemingly ruled out from ever really coming to God. The Canaanites and Amalekites are marked for destruction. The Moabites and Ammonites receive their territory from God, and he fought for them as for Israel, yet they are forbidden from ever becoming members of the Israelite assembly. Along with these groups, some individuals are excluded on the basis of birth or physical defect.

With respect to those individuals who are excluded, this does not reflect God's general rejection of anyone on the basis of parentage, race, or physical defect. We explored reasons above for the exclusion of certain people, usually having to do with human choices against God, but this cannot be generalized into claims about how God views these people. The exclusions are symbolic. Indeed, God's concern for those with handicaps or physical defects is evident in the fact, for example, that a curse is pronounced on any who would lead the blind astray (Deut. 27:18), and God elsewhere commands that no one curse the deaf or put a stumbling block in front of the blind (Lev. 19:14).

Likewise, the exclusion of certain nations is symbolic or representative of their response to the people of God. While some in Israel took the command to exclude Moabites and Ammonites as a command to exclude all foreigners (Neh. 13:1–2), one of the wonders of the Scripture is that it is not uniform in regard to the excluded nations, reminding us of God's larger intentions to draw all nations and peoples to himself if they will respond in trust and obedience. So, for example, Ruth the Moabite comes into the community of Israel, and even becomes an ancestor of King David and Jesus (Matt. 1:5). The same is true for Rahab, the Canaanite prostitute (Josh. 6:22–25; Matt. 1:5).

Isaiah 56:3–5 promises the perpetual inclusion in temple life of foreigners and eunuchs who ally themselves to God. The account of the Ethiopian eunuch in Acts 8 and the larger mission to the Gentiles in Acts is at least one fulfillment of that promise. Indeed, whatever barriers to participation in God's people there were, whether in the Law or because of human regulations, they are removed for those in Jesus Christ (Gal. 3:27–28). This inclusion results from the gracious invitation and gift of God, anticipated in that promise to Abraham (Gen. 12:2–3) and made possible, ultimately, through God's gift of his Son (John 3:16–17). The requirement for such inclusion, in both the Old and New Testaments, however, is faith in the Lord, expressed in accepting his sovereignty and responding in trusting obedience.

Guidance for Today's Community

How shall we regard the "outsiders" or foreigners among us? With love of neighbor, of course (Luke 10:25–37; Gal. 5:14). For God's people, this means treating the non-Christians among us, whether literally those who come into our assemblies or those we encounter day in and out, with mercy and kindness. These are people whom God so loved that he gave his one and only son. We must love and serve them as God's Son does.

On another level, we are reminded that any exclusion of particular nationalities was for a limited time and purpose. As citizens of the kingdom of God, we are not defined by ethnic or national boundaries. Therefore, we have no right to exclude anyone from the assembly of God's people on the basis of nationality or ethnicity. One of the sad legacies of much of Christianity, including many American churches, is that we have done exactly this. The legacy of that injustice continues to manifest itself in segregated churches and jingoistic rhetoric in some churches today.

Deuteronomy also reminds us that even in times of war, Christians' view toward the "enemy" cannot correspond to how others would view or treat the enemy. This is especially true since Jesus calls us to love our enemies and to do good and pray for those who persecute us (Matt. 5:43–48; Luke 6:27–28). This must cause us to seriously reflect on our participation in warfare as it is conducted, even in recent times, where some argue for the acceptability of degrading and torturing those on the "other side" and where civilian casualties are enormous, even with our so-called "smart bombs." Even more, since we are citizens of God's kingdom, and that citizenship takes precedence over all others, we cannot simply conclude that the enemies of our nation are enemies of God's kingdom and hence our enemies. Instead, we think of Jesus who forgave and died for the sake of those very people who called for and carried out his unjust execution.

Chapter 12

Family Ties

Read: *Deuteronomy 20:7; 21:15–21; 22:13–30; 24:1–5; 25:5–12; 27:20–23*

I n our discussion of the commandment to honor parents and commandment against adultery we noted the centrality of strong familial relationships for the well-being of the larger community of God. In that light, we traced some of the trajectories of those two commandments in Deuteronomy. Now, we will expand that discussion by focusing on those stipulations that have specifically to do with the wife-husband relationship and the parent-children relationship in Deuteronomy's stipulations. Israel's social and cultural world is very different than our own in many ways, but God's guidance in Deuteronomy on these matters can still speak into our family situations today.

Wives and Husbands

Before considering how the laws related to marriage may speak to us, we must first try to hear them in their own context. From our cultural perspective, many may seem unfair or unduly harsh toward the woman. However, we should at least ask how the laws might have functioned in their own time and culture in a way that would benefit the woman especially. What one finds with respect to most of the laws in Deuteronomy regarding marriage is that the man and woman are held equally responsible, as in the case of adultery (Deut. 5:18; 22:20–24) or that the man is restricted for the benefit of the woman. Since we have considered the matter of adultery in the discussion of the seventh commandment, we will focus on the other laws related to marriage.

Phillip G. Camp

Fiancés' and Newlyweds' Exclusion from War

Twice in Deuteronomy, a man is excused from military service for matters relating to marriage. If he is engaged he is excused (20:7). This law is part of a larger section in which men are excused from service for a variety of reasons (20:5–9), most having to do with sharing in the blessings of the land before he potentially meets his death in warfare.[156]

A man in his first year of marriage also does not have to go to war (24:5). The explicit reason given is "to be happy with his wife whom he has taken." Some versions indicate that the reason the man stays home is to "bring happiness" (NIV; cf. NASB) to his wife.[157] The happiness he would bring would certainly include children, who would bring honor to the woman and provide security for her later in life. However, it may also include a general concern for the wife's pleasure and well-being and aim at "laying strong foundations" in the marriage to head off future marital problems.[158]

Special Protections for Wives

In Israel's patriarchal society, the *Torah* also gave women special protections. We have already discussed the restrictions on a man who marries a captive wife and then sends her away because he is "not pleased with her." He cannot sell her as slave, and she is free to go where she wishes because the man has "dishonored" her (21:14, NIV). Two similar scenarios are also envisioned in Deuteronomy.

The first scenario (22:13–19) presents a situation in which a man decides he does not like his wife after sleeping with her. It is not clear if he is not pleased with (literally, "hates") her sexually or simply that his displeasure arises after they have consummated the marriage. In either case, rather than divorcing her, he publicly charges that she was not a virgin on the wedding night. If his charge were true, she would be subject to the death penalty as would any engaged woman who slept with another man (Deut. 22:20–21, 23–24). But this law assumes the charge is slander against the wife and not simply an accusation against her character. It is also a charge of bad faith against her parents who arranged the marriage and received the bride price.

Thus, the parents are publicly shamed as well. That is, the man is claiming that he did not get what he contracted for, a virgin.

To defend their own honor and that of their daughter, the parents would produce proof of their daughter's virginity, presumably a cloth or sheet under her on the wedding night. If she were a virgin on her wedding night, the cloth would presumably be stained with the blood of first penetration. In light of the evidence of her innocence, the husband is punished, probably public corporal punishment (cf. 25:1–3), for his bad faith in the matter. He must also pay a fine to the father. Furthermore, he can never divorce the woman.

One may ask why she would have to stay with a man who hates her and has publicly shamed her. The answer is probably this: since she was no longer a virgin, her chances at another marriage and the protections that come with it are significantly diminished. This law's requirement insures that she is cared for.

The second scenario involves a man who divorces his wife then wants to remarry her after she has remarried and become single again (24:1–4). At the outset, it should be noted that many have used this passage for various arguments in current divorce-remarriage debates, but many, if not most, of those arguments ignore the nature of this law. The law does not prescribe grounds or regulations for a divorce.[159] It assumes a divorce has already taken place. The nature of what the man finds displeasing in the woman remains unclear.[160] The process of divorce is also unclear, beyond indicating that she receives some kind of certificate acknowledging the dissolution of the marriage, which frees her to remarry.

The point of the law is to prevent the husband from taking her back if she has remarried then become widowed or divorced again. Why he would want her back is a matter of speculation. It could be that she somehow became wealthy through the intervening marriage or that he lost and wants to recover her substantial dowry. In any case, the first husband cannot remarry her under the circumstances outlined here. The text does not explain exactly how she "has been defiled" (note the passive here!),[161] but what is clear is that she is the victim and that she is now off limits to her first husband. This law aims to protect the wife from a husband who would reject and then attempt to reclaim her, as though she were property or a means to profit rather than a person. It might also have the effect of giving the husband pause before divorcing his wife in the first place.

The Seduced/Raped Woman

Deuteronomy 22:28–29 is probably, from our perspective, the most troubling marriage law in the Old Testament. Coming within a section that deals with various scenarios of sexual encounters (22:13–30), this law seems to require an unengaged woman who is raped to marry her rapist, as some translations indicate (NIV, NLT). However, other translations render it more literally, which results in the vaguer "seizes her and lies with her" (ESV; NASB, NRSV; cf. KJV; NKJV; NJB), which could suggest seduction. Commentators are also divided over whether the text indicates rape or seduction. The language of "seizing" in connection with "lies with her" suggests the former, but one cannot be dogmatic here.[162] If the former, the requirement for the man to pay the bride price, and, if her father allows, to marry her seems unthinkable to us. Even if the latter understanding is correct, the notion that a woman who "gave in" once should have to marry seems quaint or even silly. But, again, consider the limited marriage possibilities in that culture for a woman who is not a virgin. This law at least assures that a woman will not be used for sexual pleasure and then tossed aside. The man must care for her for life (cf. Exod. 22:16–17). Furthermore, such a requirement could also serve as a deterrent if a man considered such an assault on a woman. Having said all of that, the discomfort with the law from our perspective remains and should be acknowledged, and we should exercise great care in keeping context in mind when searching for the modern relevance of such texts.

Forbidden Sexual Relationships

Deuteronomy also prohibits or curses certain sexual relationships. A man cannot marry his father's wife (22:30). Presumably, this refers to a wife other than the man's own mother. If a man sleeps with his father's wife (again, probably a wife other than his own mother) he is under a curse (27:20). The text does not say whether the father is living or dead (cf. Gen. 35:22; 49:3–4). A man is cursed who has sex with an animal. Such an act would violate distinctions in the created order (cf. Gen. 2:18–24). A man is also cursed for having sex with his sister or his mother-in-law (27:21–23). Such relationships would violate the familial cohesion of the community. These prohibitions may also serve to distinguish Israel from the practices of other nations (cf. Lev. 18; 20:11–24).

Levirate (Brother-in-Law) Marriage[163]

Another stipulation, which would also serve, in part, to protect wives in Israel, has to do with a woman whose husband dies while they reside among the husband's family, and the couple had no son (Deut. 25:5–10). In such a case, one of the dead man's brothers is to marry her, and their first son will be considered the son of the dead man. The stated point of this requirement is to perpetuate the deceased man's name in Israel. The boy becomes his legacy and the heir to his property. Beyond perpetuating the dead husband's name, the law also has the effect of providing a son for the widow, giving her honor in the community and someone to care for her in her old age.

The family and community are to take this brotherly duty so seriously that they will apply social pressure to force the brother to do it, and the widow will publicly humiliate him if he refuses to do so. The exact meaning of the ritual with the sandal is a matter of speculation. Given that "feet" sometimes have sexual overtones in the Old Testament, it might relate to the refusal to procreate for the dead brother. Or it could deny the brother any claim on the dead man's property and free the woman to marry outside the family. Or it could have to do with declaring the woman free of the brother's authority (particularly conjugal rights) while permitting her to continue as a full member of the family, with the associated rights and protections.[164] In any case, the shame attaches to the brother who refuses and to his family through the label "Family of the Unsandaled" (NIV).

Limits of a Wife Rescuing Her Husband

The law in Deuteronomy 25:11–12 deals with a woman who attempts to rescue her husband in a fight by grabbing the genitalia of her husband's opponent. If she does so, perhaps with implication that she causes permanent damage to the man, the community shall cut off her hand. This is the only law in the OT that specifically calls for mutilation, which suggests the severity of the offense.[165] The purpose, however, is to deter such action and protect a man so that his name might continue in Israel (cf. 25:6).

Parents and Children

We have discussed the primary basis for the parent-child relationship with respect to the fifth commandment, "Honor your father and your mother." There we saw that the commandment applies to all children, including adults, in their relationships with their parents, and it affects several aspects of that relationship. Two other stipulations in Deuteronomy also bear on that relationship: one dealing with a father's obligation toward one of his sons, and the other dealing with a child's responsibility toward his parents.

The law in 21:15–17 envisions a situation in which a man has two wives, one loved and one unloved (literally, hated). Since neither the Law nor custom prohibit polygamy, that in itself is not the problem. However, if the unloved wife has a son by him and later the loved wife does as well, the man must resist the inclination to show favor to the younger son in matters of inheritance. The older son, the son of the unloved woman, gets the firstborn's share. This requirement means that if these remain the only two sons, the estate would be divided into thirds, and the older son would receive two-thirds while the younger son one third. The older son's position in the family is honored, even when his mother is not, though she might enjoy honor through her son. And this law prevents her and her son from being left without resources once the father has died. Here the *Torah* places an obligation on a father toward his children and demands that he acts justly within his family.[166]

In 21:18–21, which we touched upon briefly in the context of the fifth commandment, the death penalty is employed for a rebellious son. This is not a case of a child throwing temper tantrums. This case involves a perpetually rebellious son who continues in behaviors that bring shame upon his parents and the family, and who may endanger members of the larger community as well. Such behavior continues despite the parents' attempts to discipline him. In this case, the issue ceases to be simply a family matter and becomes a community matter, because of the detrimental ripple effect it can have on all levels of authority—ultimately, including God's authority.[167] The parents become the two witnesses (Deut. 17:6; 19:15) against their son as the entire community executes him. In this way, the community itself halts the detrimental effects, and the severity of the punishment should deter others from imitating this son's behavior. Perhaps, the mere presence of such a requirement, before it has to be carried out, would have a deterrent effect.

The God of the Community

What the texts above reveal about God dovetails with the theological reflections given previously on the fifth and seventh commandments, so you may want to return there to read again on what the commandments to honor one's parents and against adultery say about God and to God's community.

However, a few other reflections arise here. First, the family is important to God, not just certain members. The whole family matters to God, and so the *Torah* includes laws dealing with behaviors that can disrupt or even destroy families, including certain sexual prohibitions, parents' responsibilities to their children, and children's duties to parents. The married life, and, by extension, the family, becomes the place to model the love of God for the weak, those who might otherwise be tossed aside, and those who disappoint in some way. This love does not arise so much from affection, though it certainly can include that, as from covenant commitment, especially in less than ideal circumstances.

Also, reflecting the character of God, this committed love places a check on unrestrained, arbitrary, and selfish use of power, as seen in the restrictions on husbands, and instead calls for justice and righteousness within the family. God certainly has power, but he

131

exercises it for the sake of the other and in the name of justice. He calls those in position of power within the family to do the same. We see this characteristic of God, especially in his self-giving love through Jesus Christ, who surrendered himself for the sake of others. Note that in one instance, Paul uses such a view of marriage to talk about Christ and the nature of Christ to guide Christians in marriage (Eph. 5:21–33). These families that reflect God's character then model that character to the larger faith community that, in turn, models it to the world around them.

On the other hand, families cannot become idols. No one can place loyalty to family above loyalty to God and obedience to him (cf. 13:6–11); the first and second commandments as well as the Shema will not allow it. Look again at the picture of family life following the Shema in 6:4–8. The individual, family, and community are all marked by immersion in the *Torah*, the reflection of God's character and purposes. Selfish refusal to honor one's own marriage covenant, the sanctity of others' marriages, justice for one's children, and even discipline of one's children tears at the very fabric of the witnessing community God has created.

Finally, these laws recognize the full humanity, worth, and right to justice of all. No man may use a woman as an object of sexual pleasure and then toss her aside. Provisions are in place to insure the woman's well-being and security. No father can fail to recognize the rights of his children. The weak and the unfavored have a right to have their needs met. Likewise, this recognition of one's full humanity demands that one accept personal responsibility for decision, actions, and commitments, including the penalties for certain decisions.

Guidance for Today's Community

There is much in these laws in Deuteronomy that is not repeatable in our own culture, because the understanding and conduct of marriage has changed. Marriage in our culture is not a contractual arrangement between parents, in which, especially, the bride has little say, and most families are not structured along patriarchal lines. Women in our time can find security and provision apart from men, whether fathers or husbands. Thus, many of those strange or even disturbing laws no longer make sense in our time, at least in terms of any literal application.

Still, we are reminded that we cannot use people, including our marriage partners, simply for personal gratification, and that our concern must be for their welfare. Noncommittal sex, or hooking up, has no more place within the Christian community than it did within Israel. These laws force us to look at the humanity of the other and to respond in a way that assures the dignity and well-being of the other. They also call us to honor our marriage commitments while respecting other couples' commitments by not becoming a source of conflict or infidelity.

We also see a call for harmony and justice within the family. Children are not pawns in parental conflicts, nor are they conduits for parents' self-glorification. With respect to the latter, you might sit among parents at their children's sporting events sometime and see how, for many parents, the issue is not so much their child as how the parents find their own validation (or not) through their children. Though parents must certainly discipline their children, they must also treat them justly, with the child's best interests (as opposed to the parent's wishes) in mind. This concept becomes more difficult in our day, since parents rarely exercise the same control over their adult children that parents did in ancient Israel. Still, parents can give moral and spiritual guidance that seeks the well-being of their children.

These stipulations also remind us of the role of the larger community in family matters. These laws move the community to help couples maintain their marriage commitments. They call on the community to help parents raise and discipline their children. We might resist the notion that others would discipline our children, but assuming a loving community that looks out for one another's best interest, we should welcome such help. It takes a church to raise a child, at least a Christian one.

Finally, as in Israel, parent-child and husband-wife conflicts reverberate throughout the entire church and can affect its well-being. One hopes that the church would first deal with such issues pastorally, seeking reconciliation. Of course, unlike ancient Israel, the church community has no authority to execute adulterers or rebellious children (thankfully!). Still, at times, the community must take drastic steps against individuals to insure the well-being of the whole. Note, for example, Paul's admonition to expel certain members for the sake of the larger church body—including, in keeping with our texts, the sexually immoral and drunkards (1 Cor. 5:9–13).[168] Beyond protecting the well-being of the church, however, Paul suggests that the ultimate goal is to make the person realize his or her sin, repent, and be restored to the body (1 Cor. 5:5; cf. 2 Thess. 3:14–15).

Chapter 13

Choose Life

Read: *Deuteronomy 27:1–32:47*

The last few chapters of Deuteronomy look both to Israel's present and future responses to Moses' call to live in covenant relationship with God. To choose to continue in obedient relationship with God is to choose blessing and life, but to reject this relationship is to choose curse and death as a people. These chapters clearly anticipate that Israel will choose against God, and yet they also point to God's fidelity to the covenant relationship even when Israel forsakes it. That is, God opens a way to return from death to life, a resurrection of the community, if you will.

Curses, Blessings, and Curses (Deut. 27–28)

Chapters 27–28, the blessings and curses, actually provide a conclusion to the stipulations and a motivation for keeping them, [169] but we will examine them here because they segue into the expectations concerning Israel's future in the subsequent chapters.

However, before examining the blessings and curses, note what precedes them in 27:1–10, a section bracketed with the admonition to keep/obey the word of God. As Israel enters the land to take it, their first act as a community involves both memory and worship as ways to keep the people faithful to the *Torah* of God. [170] Memory and worship are tied together as Moses tells Israel to set up monuments with the entire *Torah* written on them and to build an altar for burnt offerings and fellowship offerings. [171] After the conquest of Jericho and Ai, Joshua will carry out these instructions (Josh. 8:30–35).

That Israel will build the altar on Mount Ebal, the mountain of curse (v. 13) is somewhat surprising. Perhaps it will remind them that in choosing to enter covenant with God, they also accept the consequences for violating that covenant.[172] Such acceptance and the general call to obey make sense for a people who are now declared to be the people of God (v. 9). Note, however, that the declaration that they are God's people precedes their assent and obedience. God acts first, and Israel responds to his gracious initiative.

In 27:11–26, Moses commands a one-time ceremony that will further demonstrate the current generation's commitment to the covenant. Already anticipated in 11:29,[173] six tribes will stand on Mount Gerizim to bless the people and six tribes will stand on Mount Ebal to pronounce curses.[174] However, rather than spelling out that ceremony, Moses next instructs the Levites (not the six tribes on Ebal) to recite a series of curses, twelve total, before all the people. Some of these curses echo the Ten Commandments, and all echo either Deuteronomy's concern for wholehearted devotion to God or for the right treatment of one's neighbor.[175] One of the most noticeable things about the cursed actions is that one could do most of these, if not all, undetected. That is, these are things people can get away with. So these pronouncements remind Israel that even if no human sees the acts and no human court will render justice, God does see and will respond. The final curse (v. 26) leaves no wiggle room, as it points to upholding the *Torah* in its entirety. With each curse, the people will signal agreement and their acceptance of the consequences with "Amen."

The Blessings (28:1–14)

"Blessing" refers to "benevolent power, health-creating power," in this case God's power, and "blessing" is an effective word, bringing life, prosperity, and security to his people as a whole.[176] That is, blessings are communal. Rather than a checklist of individual blessings, these verses should be viewed as a composite picture of the kind of life Israel will enjoy if they obey God, as they are reminded at both the start and finish of the blessings (vv. 1, 13b–14). The major concerns of provision and protection are covered. Israelites will enjoy these blessings everywhere ("in the city and…in the country," v. 3) and all the time ("when you come in, and…when you go out," v. 6). Yahweh, the God of Israel, not any other god or gods, will make human wombs, animal wombs, and crops fruitful (vv. 4, 5, 8, 11, 12a). Israel's enemies will be routed (v. 7), and those who might be enemies will be intimidated (vv. 9–10). Indeed, Israel will rise above the nations, who will defer to them (vv. 12b–13a). In this way, they will also find themselves in a position to bear witness to the nations concerning God. Overall, this is a picture of well-being (*shalom*) and rest. This is the gift of God in the land, if they are willing to trust God enough to submit to his commands.

The Curses (28:15–68)

"Curse" can refer simply to the absence of blessing, but the curses are not simply forces that rush in to fill the vacuum left by the absence of blessings. Rather, God inflicts the curses (see vv. 20, 25, 36, 49, 59, 61, 64). Thus, understood more actively, a "curse" is an effective pronouncement that creates a "zone" of disaster or danger.[177] Such a situation arises when Israel refuses to trust God and submit to his *Torah*. In a sense then, Israel chooses curses. As indicated by the conditional "if" in verses 15 and 58, the curses are not fated. The curses are communal punishments for the accumulated sin of the people over time. As with the blessings, the list of curses does not present a checklist of curses to come, but rather a composite picture of curse. However, the curses do intensify as this section progresses, culminating in the ultimate curse of exile—banishment from the land (vv. 64–68). It is also hard to miss the disparity between the lengths of the lists of blessings and curses. The longer list of curses may serve to emphasize the tragedy of not keeping the covenant and to offer a strong warning of the dangers of failing to trust and obey God.

The first few verses in this section (vv. 16–19) mirror and reverse the initial section of blessings (vv. 3–6). Like the blessings, the curses will come upon Israel everywhere (v. 16; cf. v. 3) and all the time (v. 19; cf. v. 6). As the curses continue, they mirror the blessings in that the curses will also affect Israel in their areas of primary concern: provision and protection. The curses will undo Israel's peace and rest in the land. Human, animal, and agricultural fertility will fail (vv. 17–18, 23–24, 38–42). Famine, disease, and pestilence will come upon them (vv. 20–24), which are all consequences of agricultural failure. Enemies will invade and rout Israel, plundering and destroying (vv. 25–37). The death will be so great that bodies will be left unburied (v. 26), a final, tremendous disgrace. Israel's plan and work will come to nothing, as others take their fiancées, homes, and vineyards (v. 30).[178] Taking homes and vineyards that one did not work for is part of the promise of God *to* Israel back in 6:10–12. But now, God fights against rather than for Israel. Eventually, the curses culminate in exile, banishment from the Promised Land (vv. 36, 47–68) and the associated blessings.[179] So foreigners will dominate Israel instead of the other way around (cf. vv. 12b–13a). In all this, Israel will remain a witness, but now a negative witness to what rejection of God looks like (v. 37). What it will look like is that Israel will become a nation like all others, subject to invasion and destruction by more powerful nations.

The description of exile, in verses 58–68, represents a reversal of the exodus. Plagues and the "diseases of Egypt" will now fall on Israel (cf. 7:15). No longer will they be "as numerous as the stars in the sky" (cf. Gen 15:5; 22:17; 26:4; Exod. 1:7, 12). God will scatter Israel among the nations rather than gathering them in the land of Canaan. There, in a sense, Israel will get what it pursues in its rejection of God: now they will be able to worship other gods in those gods' home territories (see also v. 36).[180] Israel will find no rest even though rest had been the promise of the land (cf. Deut. 3:20; 12:9–10). Finally, they will return to Egypt, which here probably is symbolic for any powerful nation that will deport Israelites in fulfillment of the curses.[181] The mention of return to Egypt by ship may be a way of imaging a return across the Red Sea, but this time into slavery and without the miracle of God parting the sea so they can cross.

Warnings and Promises Concerning the Covenant (Deut. 29–30)

In Deuteronomy 29, Moses summons the new generation of Israelites to enter the covenant, or, some might say, to renew the covenant with God. He begins with reminders from Israel's distant and recent past. These again emphasize the faithfulness of God, who delivered Israel from Egypt, cared for them in the wilderness, defeated their enemies, and has already begun to give some tribes their territory.

Still, a certain spiritual dullness lingers that prevents them from understanding the magnitude of God's faithfulness and what that calls them to as his people.[182]

Moses enjoins obedience to the covenant on all levels of Israelite society (vv. 10–11), and upon future generations (v. 15). Thus, Israel will have the responsibility of passing on the *Torah* to each new generation (cf. Deut. 6). The major area of concern is turning from God to other gods. Apart from wholehearted devotion to God, the covenant is meaningless, and Israel cannot fulfill its mission in the world. Furthermore, persistent or stubborn rebellion against God will not allow for the possibility of forgiveness, because it is a rejection of God.[183] This is not simply a matter of committing sins. This is a matter of spitting in God's face and declaring, "I don't care what you say!" (whether verbalized, or more likely, revealed in what they do). It will lead to the unleashing of all the curses, and the destruction will be akin to that of Sodom and its neighbors (see Gen. 19).[184] Israel's condition in light of these curses will serve as a negative witness both to later generations of Israel (which indicates that the nation as a whole will not be wiped out) and to foreigners. Israel may not know all of the mysteries of God, but his reaction to their serving other gods and his expectations for them as his people are no secret. The *Torah* clearly reveals these things (v. 29).

However, as chapter 30 demonstrates, curse or judgment is not God's last word; restoration is! For God to restore them, they must first return to him. That is, they must turn around or reorient themselves on him, which is the basic understanding of repentance in the Old Testament. If they turn back to God, he will turn toward them and return them to the land.[185] Not only will he bring them back to the land, he will make them more prosperous than before. Furthermore, he will empower them to do what he had earlier simply commanded them to do—circumcise their hearts (v. 6; cf. Deut. 10:16). God will remove from them that stubbornness of heart (of will and intention) that prevents them from keeping the covenant, if only they turn back to him. Then they can fulfill the call to love him with their entire being (Deut. 6:4–5) and live. God will again take care of their concerns for provision and security.

139

And so, Moses lays a choice before the people: "life and good" or "death and evil" (or with the NIV, "life and prosperity, death and destruction").[186] The path to such life is no great mystery for Israel. It is both accessible, in the *Torah*, and feasible, if only they remain oriented on, or reorient themselves upon, God who will circumcise their hearts.[187] To choose God is to choose life, "for he is your life and length of days" (v. 20).

Preserving and Passing on Torah (Deut. 31–32)

Moses knows he is about to pass from the scene. He can no longer lead them, not because he is too old (cf. Deut. 34:7) but because God had told him he would not enter the land (1:37–38; 3:23–29; 4:21; 32:48–52). So, in 31:1–29, Moses encourages both Israel and Joshua, as Joshua prepares to assume leadership over Israel and take them into the land. They need not fear, because God will be with them. However, they are not left to their own devices. God's word to Moses in the *Torah* will continue as the authoritative word among the people. Thus, Moses writes down the *Torah* and gives it to the priests who will read it to the people every seven years. The *Torah* will also stand as a witness against them, testifying to their violation of the covenant, which God fully expects, given their stubborn nature. As an additional witness, God commands Moses to teach Israel the song in 31:30–32:43.

Both the public reading of the *Torah* and the Song of Moses as ways of keeping God's word alive are discussed in Chapter 6 of this book. But the content of the song is worth noting briefly. The first verse calls upon abiding witnesses, heaven and earth, who will affirm the justice of God (cf. 30:19; also 17:6; 19:15). The next two verses note the teaching purpose of the song and then move to praise of God, exalting him, as is fitting in recognition of his position relative to Israel's and all creation's.

Verses 4–18 then contrast Yahweh, the God of Israel, and Israel itself. Yahweh is "the Rock," the "God of faithfulness, whose "work is perfect," and who is "just and upright" (v. 4). In fact, "rock" becomes a keyword in the song to point to Yahweh's reliability and steadfastness, especially over against other gods (vv. 4, 15, 18, 30, 31, 37). He is Israel's Creator and imaged as Israel's father (vv. 6–9), as well as sustainer and mother (vv. 10–14, 18). Israel, on the other hand, is corrupt, "crooked and twisted," "foolish and senseless" (vv. 5–6). Israel grew fat and turned to other gods (vv. 15–18; cf. Deut. 6:10–15; 8:10–20). Thus, Yahweh has proven to be a faithful covenant partner to Israel, but Israel has not reciprocated. Therefore, Israel cannot attach blame to Yahweh for violating the covenant. The fault lay with them, and their punishment is just.

In verses 19–27, God deliberates Israel's punishment, using various poetic images to portray the realization of the curses, but "curse" is not the last word. Aware that the nations might take credit for what is his own work (keep in mind that the nations are a means of God's judgment), God refuses to totally destroy his people. In this light, in verses 28–43, the song highlights the foolishness of trusting impotent gods of the nations and turns to judgment on the nations that God has used against Israel. He will vindicate, shelter, and heal Israel.[188] The song highlights God's incomparability, because he is the only true God. Thus, in its movement from Israel's judgment to restoration, the song mirrors the movement from judgment to restoration in chapters 29–30. Israel will be restored, not because they have a right to be but because of their incomparable God.

The God of the Community

God's Sovereignty and Power

The God of Israel, our God, has the authority and power to move nature and nations, and does so, whether in the exercise of blessing or curse. Nothing and no one is beyond his reach or power. Therefore, whatever anyone else might turn to, whatever "rock" they may trust in, the power of Israel's Rock reveals those things to be powerless, empty, and vain sources of hope and security.

God's Judgment

God sends curses on his people. It is hard to read this section and escape that conclusion. But to what end does he do so? While certainly there is an aspect of just punishment for wickedness, within the larger sweep of this section, curse or judgment appears ultimately designed to get Israel to turn back to God that he may restore blessing to them once again. That is, on one level, the curses are disciplinary or remedial to remind Israel, corporately, that there is no life and blessing apart from God. This aspect of the curses is more obvious in Leviticus 26, where the curses escalate if Israel refuses to listen to God (vv. 18, 21, 27). Furthermore, the curses operate in connection to Israel's mission as witnesses to the nature and purposes of their God. The infliction of the curses serves as a negative witness if Israel refuses to obey. However, God will restore them to their intended role as positive witnesses when they turn back to him.

God's Faithfulness

Whether Israel chooses blessings or curses, life or death, this section demonstrates that God is a faithful covenant partner. God is and will be innocent of wrongdoing against Israel. The violation of the covenant comes on Israel's part if and when they refuse to obey the God's commands. When Israel turns back to God, he will again demonstrate his faithfulness, first to Israel in restoring them, and then to their ancestors to whom he made promises about the nation.

Taken from another angle, God's faithfulness is also demonstrated in the giving of the *Torah*. He provides Israel with the accessible and feasible means of living in relationship with him. There are no hidden clauses or incomprehensible fine print. Also, he is not an unpredictable God, whose worshippers have no idea what pleases or angers him. They know the terms of the covenant and have agreed to them. If they obey, God is faithful in blessing them according to the covenant. If they disobey, God faithfully keeps the covenant by doing what he said he would do: send curses.

God's Desire to Bless

Despite the seeming preponderance of curses in this section of Deuteronomy, the overall movement and call is from curse and death to blessing and life. God is not the caricatured wrathful and vindictive "Old Testament God." He is the same God, who, throughout the Bible, Old and New Testaments, is the gracious, compassionate, and merciful

God (e.g., Exod. 34:6–7; 2 Chron. 30:9; Pss. 86:15; 111:4; 145:8; Jonah 4:2; Luke 6:36; James 5:11). Though it might be hard to see from Israel's perspective, this is true even when he sends curses. Again, these serve to turn Israel back to God, the source of blessing, and to have them fulfill their role so that all nations might receive blessing through them. The fact that God warns them up front of the consequences of rebellion and calls upon them to choose life emphasizes that he desires blessing for them.

God further demonstrates his desire to bless them when he says he will enable Israel to obey by circumcising their hearts. They are continually stubborn, spiritually blind, and spiritually deaf even to the great acts of God. Still, he determines to work within them to create a change, at least among those who attempt to orient themselves toward him. Along these lines, God elsewhere speaks of writing the law on their hearts (Jer. 31:33) and replacing unresponsive stone hearts with responsive hearts of flesh (Ezek. 36:26–27).

Guidance for Today's Community

God's Sovereignty and Power

As the people of God today, we continue to recognize the sovereignty of God over all of creation. Thus, in whatever circumstances we find ourselves, good or bad, whether of our own making or not, we will never be beyond the reach and care of the one who is over all (Rom. 8:31–39). Therefore, we do not put our trust in any "rock" (whether the nation, the economy, the military, family, self, or even religion) other than the "Rock of Ages." There we find our security and hope. There we find life. A constant and repeated theme of not just Deuteronomy but of the Bible as a whole is that the Lord is the only unmovable and unfailing source of provision, security, deliverance, and hope.

God's Judgment

Certainly, the church is subject to God's judgment when we turn from him by disobeying either the call to love God with our whole being or to love our neighbor as ourselves. The New Testament points to the possibility of such judgment (e.g., Acts 5:1–11; 1 Cor. 10:1–13; 11:27–32). What that curse or judgment might look like in our own day is not clear. Some might say sickness or death, though there is nothing in the Old or New Testament to suggest that every or even most instances of sickness and death are God's curse (cf. Job; John 9:2–3). Indeed, keep in mind that both blessings and curses are corporate in nature, and so cannot be correlated to individual good deeds or sins.

I suspect that judgment looks more like churches full of people with broken, empty lives as they go through the motions but seek their security in other "rocks." I suspect it looks like constantly bickering and splitting churches and churches that have so accommodated to the larger culture that they no longer have a discernable voice. While any given disaster that affects a church may not be the result of God's curse, such disasters might invite the church to introspection to discern if something is amiss in its relationship with God. However, we should understand such judgments as ways of God to discipline his people and to draw them back to his purposes for them (see Acts 5:11; 1 Cor. 11:32). Furthermore, keep in mind God's promise to those who trust him in light of his work in Jesus Christ: "There is therefore now no condemnation for those who are in Christ Jesus" (Rom. 8:1).

God's Faithfulness and Desire to Bless

We have entered the new covenant with God through the blood of Jesus Christ. We believe that God's covenant faithfulness to us is as strong as his faithfulness to Israel. Thus, on the one hand, any violation of the covenant relationship arises on our side, not God's. On the other hand, no sin (communal or individual) puts us beyond the reach of God's forgiveness and grace, as long as we continually orient ourselves on him (1 John 1:5–10).[189] This ongoing orientation (or reorientation) is greatly aided by using those means that God has given us to constantly remind ourselves that we are in covenant relationship with him (Scripture, worship, symbols, song, community accountability, etc.).

Additionally, given our fallen human nature, even the accessibility and feasibility of God's requirements for his people do not prevent us from turning from him. We need divine help—grace—

to be the people God has called us to be. God's grace is not simply a matter of us becoming his people—getting in, so to speak. It is also the divinely given power to *live* as his people. Thus, we sing not only, "Amazing grace! How sweet the sound; That saved a wretch like me! I once was lost but now I'm found; Was blind but now I see." We also sing, "Through many dangers, toils and snares, I have already come. 'Tis grace has brought me safe thus far, and grace will lead me home."[190] And we recognize, in the words of another hymn, "O to grace how great a debtor daily I'm constrained to be! Let Thy goodness like a fetter bind my wand'ring heart to Thee. Never let me wander from Thee, never leave the God I love; Here's my heart, O take and seal it, seal it for Thy courts above."[191]

All of this points us to Jesus Christ, who is the Life (John 14:6) and who came to give us life to the fullest (John 10:10). Through him, God dealt decisively with the curse of the Law by having him become a curse for us (Gal. 3:13). In him, we move from death to life through baptism, joining him in his death that we may be raised to new life (Rom. 6:3–4). By his grace, and apart from our own efforts, God in Christ Jesus saved us and created (or recreated) us for good works (Eph. 2:8–10). In Jesus, we receive what God desires for all his creation: blessing (Rom. 10:11–13; Eph. 1:3–14) and eternal life with him (John 3:15–16; 5:25; 17:2–3; Rom. 6:22–23; Titus 3:3–7). And bear in mind that "eternal life" with God is not simply in the "sweet by and by." It is life now, and it is a life of joy, peace, blessing, and faithful witness to the God who gives these.

Chapter 14

The Beginning

Read: *Deuteronomy 33–34*

One could construe the last couple of chapters of Deuteronomy as an ending. Moses blesses the tribes, which is often a prelude to death in the Old Testament (cf. Gen. 27, 49). Then he does, in fact, go off to die, fulfilling an expectation that has been present throughout the book (e.g., 4:22; 31:27; 32:48–52). However, even as these chapters close the story of the life of Moses, they point forward to future chapters in the ongoing story of God's work among his people Israel. Deuteronomy has already prepared us for the next chapter in this great story as it anticipates the conquest of the Promised Land under the leadership of Joshua. Moses' presence will continue in the story as well in the form of the *Torah* of God that he has delivered. In Joshua through 2 Kings, this *Torah* in Deuteronomy will serve as the basis for assessing Israel's history in relation to God's purposes for them.

Moses Blesses the Tribes (Deut. 33)

Moses' last spoken words, in Deuteronomy 33, are words of blessing on Israel's tribes.[192] Be sure to get that: the last words are blessing! The book ends on a gracious note toward the people, despite the expectation of future rebellion. God will indeed do as he has said when the people enter the land: he will bless them. The blessings themselves are spoken in the evocative and imaginative language of poetry.

Moses begins the blessings, not with Israel but with God, the one who will bless Israel (vv. 2–5). God approaches them because of his love for them (cf. 7:8), and they respond in reverence and reception of God's instructions given through Moses. Again, God initiates and Israel responds, at least ideally. The name Jeshurun, "the upright one," (also in 32:15; 33:5, 26; Isa. 44:2) expresses this ideal for Israel in relation to their king, God.

147

The blessings proper then begin in 33:6. In keeping with the book as a whole, the major themes that surface in the blessings are protection from or overcoming enemies, fruitfulness (human or agricultural), and abundance. Thus, Reuben's blessing deals with the concern for human fertility, while Judah's points to protection from enemies.[193] Levi receives more attention because this tribe will teach the *Torah* (cf. 31:9–13) and will offer Israel's sacrifices. Also, the Levites distinguished themselves as the tribe whose zeal for God trumped even familial and national loyalties (Exod. 32:25–29; cf. Matt. 10:37). For them, Moses invokes God's blessings as they carry out their duties as well as calling for their protection. Likewise, the blessing on Benjamin calls for protection. Joseph's lengthy blessing points to both agricultural abundance and victory over enemies. Moses blesses Zebulun and Issachar together. It appears that they will take the lead in calling Israel to worship. However, the references to the mountain and to "right sacrifices" (ESV; "sacrifices of righteousness," NIV) could indicate that they will lead Israel in keeping the *Torah*, which Israel originally received on Mount Horeb (Sinai). Gad is blessed with abundant good land. That he carries out God's commandments and justice (or judgments) may represent the ideal of *Torah*-keeping. What is said of Dan is more a description than a blessing, but it also points to protection. Naphtali's blessing points generally to abundance. The blessing on Asher, whose name in Hebrew comes from a synonym for the word "blessed" in verse 24, brings together the themes of lavish provision and protection.

The conclusion of the blessing returns to God, so that the blessings on the tribes are couched beginning and end in the source of those blessings. Like the ending of the song of Moses in Deuteronomy 32, the blessings conclude by stressing God's incomparability. He alone can and will provide for and protect Israel. Indeed, the language of God as one who "rides through the heavens" may intend to echo Baal myths, where Baal is called "cloud rider." But neither that so-called god nor any other can do these things for Israel. Furthermore, receiving salvation and blessing from God will make Israel unlike any other nation. This distinction then brings us back to Israel's role as a witness to the nations concerning Israel's incomparable God, Yahweh (cf. 4:5–8). In light of the fear that the previous Israelite generation showed with respect to taking the land (cf. 1:26–40), Moses surely intends to embolden Israel's faith with the description of God as a "shield," "helper," and "sword," along with the image of enemies cowering before them.

The Death of Moses (Deut. 34)

Deuteronomy has hinted at and plainly stated that Moses' death was coming, and the final chapter gives us a remarkably brief account of his death, given the length of time (forty years!) that he has spent leading God's people. As promised (32:48–52), God graciously gives Moses a view of the land from Mount Nebo before he dies. He sees all that God promised to Abraham, Isaac, and Jacob long ago. Though he will not enter it himself, Moses can die with confidence that God will hand over the land to the new generation. The reference to Mount Nebo, being situated across the Jordan River from Jericho, points us ahead to the first step in God's delivering of the land to Israel (Josh. 6).

Moses dies at 120 years old, and God buries him. The general vicinity of his burial is known but not the exact location, possibly to prevent his grave from becoming a shrine. Israel's great leader is mourned, and they recognize Joshua as their new leader. Through the laying on of Moses' hands, Joshua had received the "spirit of wisdom", that is, divine skill and empowerment for his task. Therefore, Joshua is fully equipped to assume leadership.[194]

Alert readers will note that earlier, in 18:15, it said that God would raise up a prophet like Moses, but here, in 34:10, it says that no prophet like Moses has arisen before or after him. While this appears contradictory, 34:10–12 explains the distinction between Moses and other prophets. No other prophet knew God face-to-face (as close and personally) as Moses did, and no other prophet performed the same kinds of signs and wonders that Moses did in Egypt. The statement in 34:10–12 functions within Deuteronomy to claim that the words of all other prophets must be tested against Moses' words in the *Torah*. Not only that, the *Torah* becomes the authoritative word of God for all of Israel's life now that Moses has moved off the scene. While Joshua will lead Israel, he will not simply lead them in battle. Joshua will also lead them in keeping the Word of God: "So the people of Israel obeyed him *and did as the LORD had commanded Moses"* (v. 9b).

The God of the Community

This final chapter of Deuteronomy once again highlights the ongoing theme of God's faithfulness. Both on the small-scale—in granting Moses a glimpse of the land—and on the large-scale anticipation of the conquest, God has kept his promises. God is also faithful in giving Israel the *Torah* through Moses, so that after Moses is gone, Israel will know how to live a blessed life in relationship with God and with one another, and how to return to God when they have turned from him. Thus, one might say that this book is about "grace in the end."[195]

In the end, Deuteronomy points the reader to God. Neither this book, nor the larger story of Moses (beginning in Exodus 2) has ever really been about Moses. It has been about who God is and what God is doing. To be sure, he used Moses in a mighty way. But that is the point. *God* used Moses to his ends and purposes. It is not that God did not care for Moses as a person. We have seen the close relationship between God and Moses (34:10; cf. Exod. 33:11). But Moses had fulfilled his role in the divine story, including serving as an example of the consequences of breaking faith with God and not upholding his holiness before the community. Indeed, what abides of Moses is the word of God through Moses.

Guidance for Today's Community

Deuteronomy invites us into the great story of God, looking back to God's faithfulness to his creation and his people and looking forward to what God will do. With respect to the latter, Deuteronomy ends on an open note. Like Moses looking into the Promised Land, it sets our sights to the horizon and even beyond to see what God will do and is doing through his people. It points us toward a future that will be realized, in part, in the conquest of Canaan but pushes our gaze even further. It looks ahead to life in the land, a life of blessing and rest, but also a life of stubborn rebellion. It looks ahead to exile and return. It holds up an ideal and expectation of a community fully and singly faithful to the Lord in every aspect of life. Flowing from that faith commitment, it likewise envisions a faithful community of God, imitating the character of God by seeking justice, righteousness, and peace for those inside and outside the community. Deuteronomy opens the expectation that God will, in fact, enable his people to live such faithful lives, so that we bear witness to the world concerning the God we confess. It opens expectations for a King who fully embodies *Torah*-faithfulness and to a Prophet who will speak and enact the Word of God within the community of faith—indeed, one who is the Word of God (John 1:1–4, 14). That is, Deuteronomy ultimately points us to Jesus Christ and the kingdom life he has called us to and empowered us to live through his Spirit. Deuteronomy also calls us to imitate his character, the very character of God, as we continue to live under blessing as the community of God.

However, we must remember that this is God's story. It is about him and not about us. God has called us, and he will certainly use us to his glory. However, like Moses, we may never see the final result of our service to God. In our ends-oriented, assessment-driven culture that equates success or victory with tangible outcomes, this may be hard to swallow. We want to see the results of our labors, and we get frustrated if we do not. We may wonder whether all that we have done has come to nothing. Yet it is precisely because we are a part of God's story that what we do matters even if we cannot see how from our limited perspective. God is at work through his people. Our responsibility is not to measure our outcomes and successes, but to trust that God is at work and will accomplish his purposes whether we see "results" or not. We are called to live as the community of God, bearing witness to God in the world and leaving the outcome in his mighty hands.

History is full of Moses-like examples. Consider Martin Luther King Jr. with respect to responding to God's call in the way we have been discussing. He was a Christian (imperfect, to be sure, like Moses and the rest of us) who reluctantly, but in faith, responded to his sense of God's calling for his life, namely, to lead others in the often painful fight against racial injustice in the United States.[196] He did much to draw America's attention to these injustices and to begin the process of change. Yet he died a relatively young man without seeing the long-term results of his and his coworkers' labor, including the passage of

151

the 1968 Civil Rights Act (signed a week after his death), the dismantling of legalized segregation, the appointment of two African-American secretaries of state, Colin Powell and Condoleezza Rice, and the election of Barack Obama as the United States' first African-American president. In light of our study, it is all the more interesting that on the night before he was assassinated, somewhat prophetically, King delivered a sermon that ended with an allusion to the last chapter of Deuteronomy. He said:

> Well, I don't know what will happen to me now. We've got some difficult days ahead. But it doesn't matter with me now. Because I've been to the mountaintop. And I don't mind. Like anybody, I would like to live a long life. Longevity has its place. But I'm not concerned about that now. I just want to do God's will. And He's allowed me to go up to the mountain. And I've looked over. And I've seen the promised land. I may not get there with you. But I want you to know tonight, that we, as a people will get to the promised land. And I'm happy, tonight. I'm not worried about anything. I'm not fearing any man. Mine eyes have seen the glory of the coming of the Lord.[197]

So we walk by faith with the glimpses of God's promises before us. We, as the community of God in Jesus Christ, by God's grace, live out our calling to serve him alone and imitate his character in our relation to others inside and outside the community. We do so, trusting that the one who is our Rock, the only Rock, is at work and has been and is faithful to his promises and purposes. We do so, knowing that in him alone are blessing and life.

Excursus on Slavery in the Bible

I t is without dispute that some Israelites and early Christians owned slaves, and this situation is reflected in the Old and New Testaments. This fact was at one time used as a justification for the continued enslavement and mistreatment of slaves by Christians, as is well established in the history of American slavery. Furthermore, some would point to Genesis 9:20–27 to argue that God intended the descendants of Ham, identified in these arguments as Africans, to be slaves of those of European descent (identified with Japheth's descendants). Occasionally, one still hears this line of argument today to justify seeing people of African descent as inferior in our society today.

African-American preacher and theologian Howard Thurman tells how he used to read the Bible to his grandmother, a former slave. He would often read to her from such books as Psalms, Isaiah, and the Gospels, but she would not let him read to her from Paul's letters, except very rarely 1 Corinthians 13. She explained that it was because, when she was a slave, the master would send white preachers to preach to the slaves occasionally. The sermons frequently drew on Paul's admonition for slaves to submit to their masters. Thurman, citing his grandmother, says, "Then he [the white preacher] would go on to show how it was God's will that we were slaves and how, if we were good and happy slaves, God would bless us. I promised my Maker that if I ever learned to read and if freedom ever came, I would not read that part of the Bible."[198]

Even today, Christians sometimes point out that the Bible never calls for the release of slaves or abolition of the institution. In fact, Paul tells slaves to be good, obedient slaves. Any honest reading of the Bible would have to acknowledge that this is the case. The question is whether such an observation justifies any and all slavery. Is more going on in the Bible's treatment of slavery?[199]

Beyond the issue of racist uses of the slavery texts, there is also the evangelistic issue. In light of the Bible's seeming support of slavery, or at least acceptance of slavery, some may question the moral value of the Bible in ethical matters. That is, if the Bible condones or permits slavery, which is morally repugnant in our day, can it be trusted in general on moral and ethical issues. What are we to make of the God of the Bible, who legitimates or, again, at least permits the practice? One can argue that he freed Israel, but what about the other slaves in the world at that time (and since) who were not freed? What about the fact that Israel is allowed to enslave? Is this, in principle, any different than Europeans and Americans enslaving Africans on the basis of race?

We will briefly explore what the Bible says about slavery and the theological issues and trajectories. The Old Testament and the New Testament each use a single term (`*ebed* and *doulos*, respectively) to denote various types of people who owe service to a superior in some way, but our interest here is when the words mean one person is owned by another.

As noted above, both Israel and Christians have as a primary experience of God the gift of freedom from bondage, whether from literal masters or from forces such as sin and death. Therefore, our experience as freed slaves ought to affect how we view the issue of slavery. Already, this experience suggests that it will not do to simply think, "Lucky for us, but too bad for you." As we have said, freedom from slavery becomes a motivation for how Israel treats the slaves among them. Likewise, I think, for Christians, the freedom we have experienced in Christ becomes a motivation to become agents of freedom.

In addition, recall that in the discussion of Deuteronomy 15, it was pointed out that freedom in the sense of personal autonomy or of individual rights is foreign to the Bible and the world of the Bible. Indeed, the Bible itself indicates that both Israel's deliverance from Egyptian bondage and Christians' deliverance from slavery to sin and death are not liberation in general. Israel was freed to serve God, and Christians are likewise freed to serve God. That is, we become slaves of God (e.g., Lev. 25:55; Rom. 6:15–23). To be sure, there is a freedom in serving the Lord, but it is a freedom to live out and fulfill God's purposes and to enjoy his blessings. Also, the merciful and loving nature of the Master ought to inform our own view of slavery.[200]

Slavery in the Old Testament[201]

The institution of slavery was a part of the ancient Near Eastern world, and Israel participated in this institution, both as slaves and, at least for some, as slave owners. For example, Abraham received slaves from Abimelech (Gen. 20:14), and both Abraham and Jacob were told by their wives to sleep with female slaves belonging to them to produce offspring (Gen. 16:1–2; Gen. 30:3, 9). The law itself recognizes the right of Israel to own slaves and to discipline their slaves in a way that certainly seems harsh by our standards, because the slaves were the property of their owners (Exod. 21:20–21). Israel was to get their slaves from other nations or the aliens among them (Lev. 25:44–46; cf. 1 Kings 5:13–18; 9:20–23), and they could enslave the inhabitants of conquered cities outside Canaan as spoils of war (Deut. 20:10–11, 14). The value of a slave over against an Israelite also seems relative. If an ox gores a man, woman, son, or daughter to death, the owner can avoid the death penalty by paying "whatever is imposed on him." However, if a slave is killed in the same way, the ransom price is set at thirty shekels of silver, payable to the master, not the slave's family (Exod. 21:28–32).

At the same time, limits were put on the Israelites' participation in the institution that in some ways set them apart from the larger ancient Near East. In the larger culture, slaves were *merely* property and without much in the way of rights or protection. If someone permanently injured his or her own slave, the slave in most cases had no recourse. If someone harmed another person's slave, compensation had to be made,[202] which is akin to the situation in Exodus 21:32. But in Israel, even though there was a distinction between Israelite and non-Israelite slaves, whose release was not mandated after six years of service, both types of slaves were afforded personal protections. A master could not kill his slave and was punished if a beating led to the slave's death (Exod. 21:20), possibly incurring the death penalty.[203] Exodus 21:26–27 calls for the release of a slave if the owner strikes him or her so as to destroy an eye or knock out a tooth. Furthermore, Israel was to harbor refugee slaves (Deut. 23:15–16). Given Israel's repeated disobedience to the *Torah* in general, one can ask whether or how often they were obedient in matters regarding slaves, but the demand for and ideal of more humane treatment were there.

Furthermore, the two versions of the Sabbath commandment also put a new perspective on Israelites' relationship with their slaves in such a way that the dehumanization that often accompanied the institution was relativized. Both versions of the commandment require that the Israelites include their slaves in the Sabbath rest (Exod. 20:10; Deut. 5:14–15). The Exodus version of the commandment is rooted in the Creation account (Exod. 20:11). Therefore, Sabbath observance according to the Exodus version should remind Israelites of their commonality with their servants in two respects: as creatures created by God and as those created in the image of God. Slave and master share a common creatureliness but also a common dignity rooted in their bearing the image of God. The Deuteronomy account roots Sabbath in Israel's liberation from slavery in Egypt. Therefore, there is a weekly reminder that they once were slaves, and this is the motivation not only for their enjoying rest but also providing it to their slaves. This commonality and the memory of the Egyptian oppression should lead them toward more humane treatment of their slaves.

Something should also be said about the curse of Ham, since this has been used to justify the enslavement of Africans, and, in some quarters even today, remains justification for racist attitudes toward Africans. After the flood, Noah's son Ham sees his drunken father naked, while his brothers honor their father by covering him without looking (Gen. 9:20–23). Whatever the exact nature of Ham's offense,[204] Noah curses Ham's son Canaan, saying he will be a slave to his brothers, that is, to Ham's brothers, Shem and Japheth (vv. 26–27).[205] Note then, that *it is not actually Ham that is cursed, but his son Canaan.* Therefore, reference to the "curse of Ham" is incorrect, and already any notion that all of Ham's descendants are identified with Africans is misplaced. In fact, if you check a map for the nations that are named for Ham's descendants, not all of them are in Africa. With respect to Canaan, the point is not the enslavement of the man himself, but of his descendants to the descendants of Shem and Japheth, as most interpreters recognize. Within the larger biblical context, this curse (not command or permission!) points to the future relationship, particularly between Israel (descendants of Shem) and the Canaanite nations (see Josh. 9:16–27; 1 Kings 9:20–23). There are no legitimate interpretative grounds for using the curse on Canaan to define racial relationships or to justify the enslavement of Africans by Western nations in previous centuries.[206]

Slavery in the New Testament

As in the Old Testament world, slavery was a regular and largely unquestioned part of the Greco-Roman world in which the New Testament was written.[207] Whatever Jesus and Paul intended by "freedom" in their proclamations of the gospel, it clearly did not involve an immediate, general liberation of slaves. Paul seems to have seen freedom as preferable to slavery, but he did not press the matter (1 Cor. 7:21–23). Of course, neither Jesus, the man in Palestine, nor Paul, the apostle and Roman citizen, had the political authority or power to make and enforce such a general emancipation. It is true as well that neither Jesus nor Paul directly condemned slavery.[208] In whatever way the liberating message of the gospel was to work for slaves, it would have to work from within the well-established system.

The New Testament consistently calls for slaves to submit, obey their masters, and serve well. In Ephesians 6:5–8, slaves are told to obey their masters as if serving the Lord, knowing that *the Lord* will reward their good work. The similar passage in Colossians 3:22–23 likewise calls upon slaves to work for their earthly masters as for the Lord, fearing him, and to do so consistently, not just when the master is looking. Again, Paul mentions reward. In 1 Timothy 6:1, Paul gives a more "evangelistic" motive for slaves to honor their masters. They are to do that so that neither God's name nor the apostle's teaching will be misrepresented as disruptive, and, in this way, hinder the spread of the gospel. These texts do not specify whether the masters are Christian or not, though in most cases, they probably were not. Still, Paul's concern is that the gospel not be hindered as it spreads, which could be the case if the larger society somehow saw Christianity as undermining the social structure.[209]

It should also be noted, as was also the case in the Old Testament (Exod. 21:5; Deut. 15:16), that not all slaves would see freedom as desirable, and many may have preferred the protection of their master's household. If so, with Christian masters at least, Christian slaves could not take advantage of the fact that they were fellow Christians with their masters and so not fulfill their obligations. If the masters were not Christian, then the Christian slaves could not expect special treatment but were told, nonetheless, to bear witness for Christ in their present situation. In all of this, bear in mind that these are instructions to slaves, not masters. They are intended to address slaves in *their* situation, not to serve as a club by which the Christian masters could belittle slaves or justify mistreating them.

But Paul also addressed Christian masters. In Ephesians 6:9, which follows his instructions to slaves, Paul begins his instructions to masters with "do the same to them." The same? Does this mean masters are to serve their slaves? Perhaps. Or perhaps, as the rest of the verse spells out, they are to remember that they and their slaves have a common master, the Lord. So, as ones living under the call and authority of the Lord, they must treat their slaves with the same mercy and love as the Lord.[210] In either case, Paul says that masters are not to use threats. Thus, they are not to create a fearful environment for their slaves. Furthermore, from Colossians 4:1, the masters are to treat their slaves "justly and fairly." Paul rules out capricious, cruel, and abusive practices.

In addition, Paul's remarkable letter to Philemon, concerning his escaped slaved Onesimus, suggests that the relationship between a Christian slave and Christian master is not the same as the master-slave relationship in the society at large.[211] The slave can no longer be regarded as simply property but as one who should now receive from his master forgiveness and mercy, and whom the master should receive as a brother or sister (vv. 12–17).[212] Thus, the basis of the social relationship between the slave and master is transformed, if not eradicated, when both are Christians. Even if only the master is a

Christian, his way of dealing with those under his authority is transformed.

Within the church, slaves were full and equal members, and so like all other members in their call, redemption, and service to Christ (Gal. 3:28; Col. 3:11). Even if such recognition could not be pulled off within the larger society, Christians were to recognize it within the body, and the Lord's supper especially became a regular reminder of that commonness in Christ (cf. 1 Cor. 11:17–34[213]). This was a remarkable denial, on one level, of the world as it was and an anticipation of the world as it ought to be. The distinctions are broken down in Christ. Each is to see the other as a brother or sister. Each is to become the servant of the other (Matt. 20:26–27; Mark 9:35). Each is to recognize that they all have a common master in Christ. Thus, where Christians were involved, the relationships within the institution of slavery were transformed.

Slaves whose masters were not Christians were reminded that any innocent suffering on their part was not in vain. God was aware of their plight and would make things right in due time. In the meantime, however, their responsibility was to serve and endure, and, in doing so, to imitate Christ, who came to serve and who suffered on their behalf (1 Pet. 2:18–24). It seems a small comfort, perhaps. But it reminds the slave that he or she is not alone, not forgotten, and will be vindicated. Indeed, the Christian slaves' true master suffered unjustly, too, and so shares in the suffering of his servants.

Conclusion

While both the OT and NT recognize and accept slavery as a given, both also transform the relationship from the side of those who serve and fear God. For the community of God, human beings can no longer be treated as expendable objects, as "human resources" in the worst sense of the concept. They are humans created by God whom God intends to redeem. If the slaves and masters are both members of the community, the relationship is drastically altered even if the formal structures remain in place. These people are no longer slave and master, except on paper. They are now brother and sister and mutual servants of Jesus Christ. They now also serve one another as they carry out Jesus' purposes in the world. To use these texts to justify modern slavery with its abuses is to ignore the transformative and ultimately undermining effect of the Bible's teaching on slavery.

It is probably no accident that the slave trade and then slavery itself was first officially abolished in the modern world by so-called Christian nations. It is also a shame that some of these nations, while considering themselves Christian, maintained a brutal and dehumanizing form of the institution as long as they did, and that we are still feeling the effects of that, particularly on Sundays in our race-segregated churches. Thus, in light of the gospel of freedom and reconciliation, there is still work to be done. There are still people who need to know literal freedom[214] and the freedom of Christ, and there is still healing to be done among those affected by slavery.

And though Jesus did not overthrow slavery, we will do well to remember his announcement of the nature and goal of his own mission and participate with him in that mission from Luke 4:18–19 (citing Isa. 61:1–2; 58:6):

> The Spirit of the Lord is upon me,
> because he has anointed me
> to proclaim good news to the poor.
> He has sent me to proclaim liberty to the captives
> and recovering of sight to the blind,
> to set at liberty those who are oppressed,
> to proclaim the year of the Lord's favor.

Excursus on the Ban

T he commandment against killing raises the issue of the ban,[215] where Israel is commanded to kill all of the members of the several nations within Canaan, including the women and children (Deut. 20:16–18; see also 2:32–35; 3:3–7; 7:1–5, 16; 25:17–19). Joshua 11:12–15 reports that Israel carried out the commandment during the conquest. However, because Israel later makes covenants with the inhabitants of the land (Judg. 2:1–5), disobeying God's command, the ban is not fully carried out. Still, the fact that they were commanded to do so does not sit right with most of us in our day because of our sense of the "rules" of warfare in which combatants and noncombatants are distinguished. Moreover, the command may become more troubling for us, because the Bible constantly refers to God as gracious and compassionate (e.g., Exod. 34:6; Ps. 86:15; Pss. 103:8, 111:4, 145:8; Joel 2:13; John 4:2; James 5:11) and in light of Jesus' command to love our enemies (Matt. 5:44; Luke 6:27, 35). To say that Israel stopped short of carrying the ban out fully does not really resolve the situation, since that comes as a result of disobedience to the command of God.

How then are we to understand this unsettling command, especially in light of the sixth commandment: Do not kill? Some explanations are inadequate. It will not do, as has already been suggested in the Introduction, to separate the God of the Old Testament from the God of the New Testament. Nor will it do to say that the aim of this command is to keep Israel from profiting from warfare so that Israel loses a primary motivation for warfare. In most cases, the ban does not cover property and possessions but only the people. Israel is usually allowed to keep the plunder (cf. Deut. 2:32–35; 3:3–7; 6:10–11).[216] To make the ban symbolic or spiritualized (e.g., saying that this is really about removing spiritual impediments), or to deny it ever actually happened also does not sufficiently resolve the problem.[217] Certainly, there is a spiritual aspect to the command, but even if it did not literally happen, there would still be the problem of Israel *claiming* that their God commanded them to do this and recording in their history the fact that they carried it out at times in obedience to that command.

Scholars have also noted that similar language of total destruction appears in other ancient Near Eastern texts.[218] For example, in the Mesha Stele (aka the Moabite Stone), a ninth century B.C. inscription by a Moabite king, the king claims that his god (Chemosh) told him to take the Israelite city of Nebo. Mesha says, "I took it and slew all in it, seven thousand men and women, both natives and aliens, and female slaves; for I had devoted it to Ashtar-Chemosh. I took from thence the vessels of YHWH and dragged them before Chemosh."[219] The word translated "devoted" in this text is the Moabite cognate of the word translated as "ban" in the Old Testament. This usage suggests that the practice was not unique to Israel. Other nations carried out the ban as well, though Israel does seem unique in seeing the ban as a means to prevent worship of other gods. While "they did it, too" is not a satisfying response, especially when Israel is at odds with the nations in many other ways, it does contextualize the practice in a certain time and place.

But maybe "they did it, too" is not quite right either. Some scholars who examine the rhetoric of ancient Near Eastern warfare argue that the "all" language is hyperbolic. That is, the totality of the language is not literal but an over-the-top expression to suggest total victory. Furthermore, in light of the ancient Near Eastern parallels, it may be that phrases such as "men and women" or "young and old" were not meant literally but were stereotypical ways of talking about the people of a town. In practice, however, it was the leaders and soldiers, in fortresses and military installations, who were targeted. The original readers would have caught onto such idiomatic usages, where we as modern readers miss them and so read them literally.[220]

Though they will not resolve the theological dilemma completely, the following considerations should also be kept in mind. First, the basis for this command is theological rather than social, ethnic, or political. The command is given so that these people will not lead Israel into worship of their gods and thus into violating the first two commandments (Deut. 7:16; 20:17–18). God is making the land a holy space where he will dwell among his people. So the land must be free from influences that would draw the Israelites to other gods and so contaminate the space, preventing them from living out God's purposes for them. Therefore, the command does not arise from a claim of ethnic or moral superiority; in fact, Deuteronomy expressly denies that Israel receives the land because it is more righteous than the nations already in the land (9:4–6). Indeed, God tells Israel that if any of their towns become like the Canaanite nations by serving their gods, the ban will be directed against those Israelite towns (Deut. 13:12–18).

Second, the Bible makes it clear that the inhabitants of the land are being judged for their own wickedness (Gen. 15:16; Lev.18:1–27; 20:1–24; Deut. 9:5; 12:29–31). As with many other nations in the Bible, including Israel, judgment takes the form of conquest. The fact that women perish in the conquest would then be understood as judgment upon them as well for participation in the larger societal wickedness. This does not, however, resolve the issue of the killing of children, whom we tend to assume—at least at some early age—could not be accountable for evil deeds. The problem is mitigated somewhat when we recall that in the ancient world, identity (and thus responsibility and culpability) was viewed more corporately than individually. And the problem is mitigated if, indeed, the totality language is hyperbolic in keeping with ancient Near Eastern practice.

Third, the ban applies to a particular people (the Canaanite nations), in a particular time (the period of the conquest), and a particular place (within the boundaries of the land given to Israel).[221] Thus, there is no "go and do likewise." Even within Israel, there was no general "go and do likewise" as indicated in the discussion of Deuteronomy 20:10–15, where terms of peace are offered and where women and children are spared when Israel fights cities outside Canaan.[222] Therefore, the ban cannot be used to justify attacks on "pagans," such as the crusaders' attacks on Muslims or American settlers' attacks on native Americans, or in a war on terror against Islamic extremists (though in these cases this misguided biblical justification can serve as religious cover for ulterior motives, such as gaining plunder, taking land, or accomplishing political and ideological ends). Furthermore, since the people of God today, the church, are dispersed among the nations and not geographically bounded as Israel was, the ban no longer serves the function of creating sacred space. And since God has nowhere designated the location for a Christian nation, no nation can use the ban as justification for war, conquest, or genocide.

Fourth, Israel's willingness to kill even women and children in obedience to their God, when they obey God in this regard, demonstrates their level of commitment to their covenant with God. That someone would go this far seems fanatical to us, but it may reveal our own lack of seriousness about our covenant with God—that there are certain things we simply would not do if God commanded us to do so. Of course, our level of covenant commitment normally dissolves at a much lower threshold. And while we, from our "enlightened" and "civilized" standpoint, may critique Israel for their brutality in the name of their God, we so-called Christian nations have killed and brutalized the innocent for far lesser gods: political ideology, greed, territory, security, etc. Indeed, in the twentieth and twenty-first centuries, we have devised means to kill on a scale never imagined prior, and have relegated the noncombatant women and children who die to the sterile-sounding realm of "collateral damage."

Fifth, the biblical text itself implies that Canaanites who submit themselves to the God of Israel could be spared the ban. Rahab, who knows the Lord's reputation and hides the spies from Israel, is the prime example. She and her family are spared in the conquest of Jericho (Josh. 2:8–21; 6:22–25). The Gibeonites provide another example. They deceive the Israelites into thinking they are from a distant land, because they have heard about what Israel did at Jericho and Ai and what God had done in Egypt. Israel is critiqued for not inquiring of God before entering a covenant with the Gibeonites, but once they enter that covenant, they are bound to protect them (Judg. 9–10; cf. 2 Sam. 21). One wonders what would have happened had other Canaanites shown humility toward and faith in Yahweh.

Sixth, again, the idea of "all"—meaning, every single person, including all women and children—has to be heard against the backdrop of the ancient Near Eastern context. If the use of such language is conventional and hyperbolic—that is, not intended as literal—then the extent of the dilemma is lessened.

Admittedly, all of these explanations cannot completely undo our discomfort with the ban, especially with the idea or claim of the killing of children. If, in fact, children were put to death, our faith that the little children belong to God and that the innocent are ultimately eternally safe with God may provide comfort as well. Still, perhaps at this point, the best we can do is to admit our discomfort and accept in faith what we cannot bear in thought: that God did, indeed, command this for purposes that the Bible somewhat explains even if not to our total satisfaction. Also, we bear in mind that the overwhelming testimony of the Scripture is that God is merciful and compassionate, as is especially shown in the giving of his own Son on behalf of all peoples and nations. Finally, it is worth remembering as well that we do not get to shape God into our image or ideal (which is idolatry!) even when we find biblical portrayals of him troubling.

Citations of Deuteronomy in the New Testament

Deuteronomy is one of the most quoted Old Testament books in the New Testament. When comparing the New Testament citations to Deuteronomy, bear in mind that the New Testament writers often cited Greek translations of the Old Testament (the Septuagint) or cited texts from memory. Therefore, the wording between Deuteronomy and the New Testament texts may not always match precisely.

Matthew	Deuteronomy	New Testament citation (ESV)
4:4	8:3	Man shall not live by bread alone, but by every word that comes from the mouth of God.
4:7	6:16	You shall not put the Lord your God to the test.
4:10	6:13	You shall worship the Lord your God and him only shall you serve.
5:31	24:1	Whoever divorces his wife, let him give her a certificate of divorce.
18:16	19:15	Every charge may be established by the evidence of two or three witnesses.
22:37	6:5	You shall love the Lord your God with all your heart and with all your soul and with all your mind.

Mark		
12:29–30	6:4–5	Hear, O Israel: The Lord our God, the Lord is one. And you shall love the Lord your God with all your heart and with all your soul and with

all your mind and with all your strength.

Luke

4:4	8:3	Man shall not live by bread alone.
4:8	6:13	You shall worship the Lord your God, and him only shall you serve.
4:12	6:16	You shall not put the Lord your God to the test.
10:27	6:5	You shall love the Lord your God with all your heart and with all your soul and with all your strength and with all your mind.

Acts

3:22–23	18:15, 18–19	The Lord God will raise up for you a prophet like me from your brothers. You shall listen to him in whatever he tells you. And it shall be that every soul who does not listen to that prophet shall be destroyed from the people.
7:37	18:15	God will raise up for you a prophet like me from your brothers.

Romans

10:6	30:12	Do not say in your heart, 'Who will ascend into heaven?'
10:7	30:13	Who will descend into the abyss?
10:8	30:14	The word is near you, in your mouth and in your heart.
10:19	32:21	I will make you jealous of those who are not a nation; with a foolish nation I will make you angry.

11:8	29:4	Eyes that would not see and ears that would not hear, down to this very day.
12:19	32:35	Vengeance is mine, I will repay.
15:10	32:43	Rejoice, O Gentiles, with his people.

1 Corinthians

| 5:13 | 13:5; 17:7; 19:19; 21:21; 22:21, 24; 24:7 | Purge the evil person from among you. |
| 9:9 | 25:4 | You shall not muzzle an ox when it treads out the grain. |

2 Corinthians

| 13:1 | 19:15 | Every charge must be established by the evidence of two or three witnesses. |

Galatians

| 3:10 | 27:26 | Cursed be everyone who does not abide by all things written in the Book of the Law, and do them. |
| 3:13 | 21:23 | Cursed is everyone who is hanged on a tree. |

Ephesians

| 6:2–3 | 5:16 | Honor your father and mother … that it may go well with you and that you may live long in the land. |

1 Timothy

| 5:18 | 25:4 | You shall not muzzle an ox when it treads out the grain. |

Hebrews

1:6	32:43	Let all God's angels worship him.
10:30	32:35	Vengeance is mine; I will repay.
12:21	9:19	I tremble with fear.
12:29	4:24	God is a consuming fire.
13:5	31:6	I will never leave you nor forsake you.

Questions for Class Discussions

Chapter 1: Are We There Yet? (Deuteronomy 1:1–2:1)

1. As you read this section, what do you see as the causes for Israel's failure to trust God?

2. Why is sin and rebellion against God's will such a waste and tragedy in the lives of God's people?

3. According to Deuteronomy 1:1–2:1, in what ways has God shown himself faithful to his people?

4. What steps can we take for ourselves and our children to continue to build trust in God?

Chapter 2: Give and Take (Deuteronomy 2:2–3:29)

1. What is the relationship between *receiving* the promises of God and *taking* the promises of God?

2. Given all that Moses had done in obedience to God, do you think his exclusion from the land is just? Why or why not? What does his exclusion suggest about those who lead God's people?

3. What does this section teach us about God's relationship to those who are not his chosen people?

4. In what ways do we enjoy "rest" now? In what ways is "rest" still not a full reality?

Chapter 3: What's Going on Here? (Deuteronomy 4:1–43)

1. For Israel, how did keeping the commands of God bear witness to the nations?

2. In Deuteronomy 4, what makes Yahweh, Israel's God, distinct from the gods of the nations?

3. What is the relationship between keeping God's commands and "life"? What is the relationship between God's jealousy and judgment, on one hand, and his mercy on the other?

4. What should the world today see in Christians that would draw them to Jesus Christ? What often stands in the way of what they should see?

Chapter 4: Ordering Life, Part 1: Devotion to God (Deuteronomy 4:44–5:11)

1. How does keeping the "vertical commandments" (commandments 1–3) relate to keeping the "horizontal commandments" (commandments 4–10) and vice versa?

2. Why is it important to see the commandments in the context of a covenantal relationship with God, rather than simply as abstract principles?

3. What does it mean to make God *the* priority of your life, rather than *a* priority (even if top priority among others)?

4. Where can we see idolatry in our lives today? Where can we see it in the church?

5. How can we who wear the name of Christ avoid taking that name in vain by what we say and do?

**Chapter 5: Ordering Life, Part 2: Devotion to Neighbors
(Deuteronomy 5:12–33)**

1. What values and virtues are implied in the fourth through tenth commandments?

2. For the negatively stated commandments ("You shall not..."), how might we phrase these in a positive way that still gets at the heart of the commandment ("You shall...")?

3. How do the fourth through tenth commandments reveal God's concern for the community? How do they reveal God's character?

4. How would observing the fourth through tenth commandments build community among God's people and further our witness today?

5. Give specific examples of how we can apply each of these commandments today.

**Chapter 6: Show and Tell: Keeping the Word Alive
(Deuteronomy 6; 16:1–17; 26:1–11)**

1. What does it mean to love God with one's entire being (heart, soul, and strength)?

2. With respect to obeying God's commands, why might it be more helpful to connect the commands to the story of God, rather than simply to talk about them in the abstract?

3. How can we become more comfortable making spiritual talk a more regular part of our lives?

4. What are some specific means we can employ to keep the faith alive and pass it on to the next generation as: (a) individuals, (b) families, (c) churches?

Chapter 7: It's Not You; It's Me (Deuteronomy 7–11)

1. What are the ways that Israel might "forget" God, and what can help them "remember"?

2. What does "we do not live on bread alone but every word that comes from God's mouth" mean? In what ways can we understand "word"?

3. What are the dangers of emphasizing either God's transcendence or immanence? What is the value in fully affirming each?

4. What characteristics of God are evident in Deuteronomy 7–11? What are ones we can and should imitate?

5. In what ways do we find pride, trust in prosperity, and self-righteousness in the church today? How does this section of Deuteronomy help us respond?

Chapter 8: A Matter of Distinction (Deuteronomy 12–14; 22:5, 9–12)

1. Why would a single place of worship, chosen by God, be important for Israel?

2. What is the relationship between family and community loyalties and loyalty to God for the community of faith (then and now)?

3. For the church, how do meals properly become both a place to distinguish ourselves from the larger culture and a place to bear witness to God?

4. What are specific steps the church can take to maintain distinctiveness from the world while, at the same time, welcoming others into the fellowship of Jesus Christ?

**Chapter 9: Liberty and Justice for All
(Deuteronomy 15:1–18; 21:10–14; 23:15–16; 24:7, 14–22)**

1. What kinds of slavery and oppression threaten the freedom God gave Israel by delivering them from Egypt, and how was Israel to prevent such slaveries?

2. How does the modern view of freedom differ from the biblical view?

3. Why is the reminder that God brought Israel out of slavery in Egypt a primary motivation for Israel's ethics? Why or how is freedom in Christ a primary motivation for our ethics?

4. How can we become God's agents of liberation today to those under oppression and slaveries of various sorts in our contexts?

5. What does Deuteronomy teach us about our own ministry to the poor, and what practical steps can we take to help those in need?

Chapter 10: Who Is in Charge Here? (Deuteronomy 16:18–18:22)

1. How do the various leadership roles (priest, judge, king, and prophet) compare and contrast with those roles in the larger world around ancient Israel?

2. Why does power become seductive and often abusive? What are some biblical examples of this tendency for those with power, and what are some biblical examples of proper use of power?

3. Why is it important to recognize that God was Lord and King over Israel and that God in Christ is Lord and King over the church?

4. When we find ourselves in positions of power or influence over others (e.g., as managers, parents, officers, etc.), how should we exercise our power in keeping with the picture in Deuteronomy 16:18–18:22 and with the picture of how Jesus exercises his power?

Chapter 11: Those Other People (Deuteronomy 7:1–5; 20:1–20; 21:10–14; 23:1–8, 17–18; 24:14–22; 25:17–19)

1. How do we make sense of Deuteronomy's exclusions of certain people in light of the larger biblical picture of God's acceptance of others? What explains the exclusions in Deuteronomy?

2. How did Israelite warfare (ideally) differ from ancient warfare in general? In what ways is mercy demonstrated?

3. How do we reconcile God's call to love enemies in the New Testament with Israel's involvement in warfare in the Old Testament?

4. How should we regard and treat those who are not Christians? What is our role in relation to them as God's people?

5. As God's people, how should we regard our own nation and national citizenship, particularly with respect to people of other nations?

Chapter 12: Family Ties (Deuteronomy 20:7; 21:15–21; 22:13–30; 24:1–5; 25:5–12; 27:20–23)

1. Why is concern for family relationships so important for community life in Israel and for their witness to the nations?

2. Why is it important to keep historical and cultural context in mind when dealing with laws on family in Deuteronomy (and the Bible in general)?

3. Why is God concerned about proper family relationships?

4. How can the family model God's commitment to covenant and justice?

5. What concrete steps can Christian families take to insure they are God-honoring in their relationships and that they are offering a positive witness to the larger world?

Chapter 13: Choose Life (Deuteronomy 27–32)

1. How do the blessings and curses relate to God's covenant and purposes for Israel?

2. What, in these chapters, indicates that God's ultimate purpose is the blessing and restoration of his people?

3. Why does God give his people a choice between life and death, blessing and curse?

4. How can we hear these promises and warnings, blessing and curses, as a word to God's people today? How does God's work in Christ inform our understanding of these?

Chapter 14: The Beginning (Deuteronomy 33–34)

1. Why is it significant that Deuteronomy ends on blessing?

2. In what ways is Moses unlike the prophets after him?

3. What does Moses' death outside the land teach us about God and God's use of individuals?

4. How does Deuteronomy ending on an "open note" inform our own faith journeys? How does the ending point us to Christ?

Notes

Introduction

[1] The title "Deuteronomy" comes from the Greek Old Testament's translation of "a copy of this law" in 17:18 as "second law" (*Deuteronomion*, which, in the ancient Latin version called the Vulgate, becomes *Deuteronomium*), an unfortunate translation since this is not an additional law to the one given at Sinai/Horeb but a rehearsing and reapplication of the Sinai covenant, with updating to be sure, for a new generation of Israelites. The title in Hebrew, drawn from the first line of the book, is "These Are the Words," which helpfully reminds the reader that what follows is Moses' address from God to the people of Israel.

[2] For discussions of various views on the Christian's relationship to the Old Testament Law, see Greg L. Bahnsen, et al. *Five Views on the Law and Gospel* (Grand Rapids: Zondervan, 1996). Though I depart from them to an extent, my reflections here are indebted to Gordon D. Fee and Douglas Stuart, *How to Read the Bible for All Its Worth*, third ed. (Grand Rapids: Zondervan, 2003), 165–169.

[3] See, for example, Matthew's portrayal of Jesus in Matthew 1–7, which has often been interpreted as Jesus representing Israel's ideal obedience. Jesus is miraculously conceived and born as a child of promise, escapes the clutches of a king bent on killing the young boys, goes into Egypt and is brought out, passes through the waters in his baptism, then goes into the wilderness. In the wilderness, he meets temptations similar to those faced by Israel (over bread, testing God, and worshipping something other than God), yet, unlike Israel, Jesus does not succumb to the temptations. He then goes to a mountain, not to receive a law, but to expound upon the true intent of Moses' law.

[4] One common misunderstanding among certain segments of Christianity, based on Colossians 2:14, is that the Old Testament or Old Testament Law was "nailed to the cross." But the word translated "written code" (NIV) or "handwriting of ordinances" (KJV), often understood as a reference to the Old Testament Law, is better translated with the ESV's "record of debt." That is, the record of debt (or I.O.U.) created by our sins is forgiven through the sacrifice of Jesus.

[5] The following questions are adapted from Christopher Wright's series of questions designed to get at the objective of a particular law. All of his questions are helpful in exploring the significance of a given law: "What kind of situation was this law

179

designed to promote, or to prevent? Whose interests did it protect—that is, who would have benefited from it? Whose power was controlled or restricted by it? What social ideals are expressed or implicit in it? What effect would the functioning of this law have had on the social shape and ethos of Israel?" See Wright's *Deuteronomy*, Understanding the Bible Commentary Series (Grand Rapids: Baker, 1996), 14.

[6] In fact, Deuteronomy is structured as a series of speeches by Moses, each beginning with "these are..." or "this is...." The speeches are: 1:1–4:43 ("These are the words..."); 4:44–5:33 ("This is the law..."); 6:1–11:32 ("Now this is the commandment..."); 12:1–28:68 ("These are the statutes and rules..."); 29:1–32:52 ("These are the words of the covenant..."); 33:1–29 ("This is the blessing..."). Chapter 34 serves as the epilogue.

[7] In the Jewish canon, Joshua, Judges, 1 and 2 Samuel, and 1 and 2 Kings, make up the section known as the Former Prophets (Ruth is found in the section called the Writings). In modern scholarly circles, these books are referred to as the Deuteronomistic History because of the theory that these books comprise a single work whose theology is rooted in Deuteronomy. For a discussion of the theory and variations on it, see Richard D. Nelson, *The Historical Books* (Nashville: Abingdon, 1998), 67–77.

[8] The correspondences are not exact, however. Also, scholars debate whether Deuteronomy most resembles treaties by a people called the Hittites in the second millennium (before 1,000) B.C. or Assyrian treaties from the first millennium (after 1,000) B.C. Most good, up-to-date OT introductions and commentaries on Deuteronomy will present the arguments for and against each position as well as other arguments for early and late dating for Deuteronomy.

[9] Yahweh is a best guess at the pronunciation of the Hebrew consonants transliterated YHWH, often referred to as the tetragrammaton. The practice arose in Judaism of not pronouncing God's proper name, lest one accidentally take the name in vain. So the Hebrew word for "lord" was pronounced in its place, a tradition carried over into English translations that use LORD to translate YHWH.

[10] This understanding of Deuteronomy is argued by S. Dean McBride, "Polity of the Covenant People," *Interpretation* 41 (1987): 229–244.

[11] This understanding of Deuteronomy comes from Dennis T. Olson, *Deuteronomy and the Death of Moses: A Theological Reading* (Eugene, Ore.: Wipf and Stock, 1994), 7–14.

Chapter 1: Are We There Yet?

[12] In this account of the appointing of leaders, Jethro's role is omitted (cf. Exod. 18:13–27). It may be that there were differing traditions concerning this matter, or it could simply be that Moses simply recounts his enactment of his father-in-law's advice.

[13] The fact that Moses would hear and decide cases for them suggests that the phrase "for the judgment is God's" (v. 17) means that God's authority lies behind their office, not that their decisions come to them directly from God.

[14] The discrepancies between the account of the sending of the spies here and Numbers 13 are well-known. In Numbers 13:1, God instructs Moses to send the spies into the land. While varying traditions may explain the difference, one could also understand God's command in Numbers 13:1 as representing his agreement with or condescension to the people's desire to explore the land before entering.

[15] The Anakites appear several times in Deuteronomy (1:28; 2:10, 11, 21; 9:2–3). Numbers 13:33 links them with the Nephilim (see Gen. 6:4). In Numbers 13:33, the spies liken themselves to grasshoppers in comparison to the Nephilim/Anakim. The Septuagint, the ancient Greek translation of the Old Testament, has in Deuteronomy 1:28 "sons of giants," which is perhaps overly interpretative. Whatever their background, in Deuteronomy they represent a fearful obstacle that stands in the way of Israel trusting God with respect to taking the land. For an extended discussion on the Anakites, see Patrick D. Miller, *Deuteronomy, Interpretation, A Bible Commentary for Preaching and Teaching*, (Louisville: John Knox Press, 1990), 34–36.

[16] The fact that God threatens to destroy Israel and start over with Moses (Exod. 32:10) in no way negates this assertion. The promise to the ancestors would have remained in effect had God started over with Moses, because Moses descended from Abraham, Isaac, and Jacob.

Chapter 2: Give and Take

[17] According to Deuteronomy 2:8, Edom descends from Esau, who is the brother of Jacob (cf. Gen. 36), and according to Deuteronomy 2:9, 19, Moab and Ammon descend from Lot, the nephew of Abraham (cf. Gen. 19:36–38). Any good Bible dictionary will provide details on these three "kin" nations to Israel. See also Deuteronomy 23:3–8 for more on these nations.

[18] Cf. Gen. 15:18; 1 Kings 4:21.

[19] In the period of the judges, the Ammonites will protest that Israel did encroach upon their territory, and they will fight Israel to regain it (see Judg. 11:13–28).

[20] Cf. Exod. 3:8, 17; 13:5; 23:23; 33:2; 34:11; Num. 13:29; Josh. 3:10; 24:11.

[21] Cf. Num. 21:21–35; Josh. 12:2–6.

[22] Compare Moses' claim in 2:28–29 that Edom and Moab allowed Israel to pass through their territories and pay for their food and water with Numbers 20:14-21, which says Edom denied Israel passage even though Israel offered to pay for water. Is Moses using deceit here? Merrill allows for this possibility but argues that, if so, the culpability for deceit falls on Moses and not God, and the biblical text merely gives an account of what happened. Eugene H. Merrill, *Deuteronomy*, The New American Commentary (Nashville: Broadman and Holman, 1994), 101. McConville suggests that Moses' false claim "May be simply the rhetoric of war, aiming to bring pressure to bear." J. G. McConville, *Deuteronomy*, Apollos Old Testament Commentary, (Downers Grove, Ill.: InterVarsity Press, 2002), 87.

[23] It is noteworthy that the same Hebrew word is also used to describe Israel's obstinacy against God in Exodus 32:9; 33:3, 5; Deuteronomy 9:6, 13; 10:16, *et al.*

[24] The picture in the book of Joshua is of all Israel participating in the general conquest of the land, while both Joshua and Judges indicate that individual tribes would have to root out pockets of resistance once the general conquest was complete.

[25] Moses' death casts a shadow over the entire book, beginning in 1:37–38. Other references to his impending death occur in 4:21–22; 31:1–2, 27; 32:48–52. For a thorough treatment of this theme, see Olson, *Deuteronomy and the Death of Moses*.

[26] For an excellent discussion of Deuteronomy's theology of the land, see Miller, *Deuteronomy*, 44–52.

[27] My own study came up with 79 instances of the command in the Old Testament. Of those instances of the command, 42 are spoken by God and 27 from someone else (e.g., a human or angel) to an individual or group in which the speaker highlights what God will do. Thus, in 69 instances, the command has a theological motivation. It refers to humans merely encouraging each other only 10 times. If the New Testament occurrences are added, I found the command 20 times (24 if one counts parallel texts in the gospels), 12 times from Jesus, 6 times from an angel, and twice in citations of the Old Testament. In all of these cases, the command is couched in the promise, presence, purposes, or power of the Father, Son, or Spirit. That is, it is couched theologically. Thus, 89 of the 99 times the command occurs in the Bible, it is theologically rooted.

For those who want to further explore the matter on their own, I have listed the texts for you. Bear in mind that if you are using a translation, synonyms for "fear" may be used. Also, you may have to read the larger context to see who is speaking or the theological motivation. OT texts in which God gives the command: Gen. 15:1; 26:24; 46:3; Num. 21:34; Deut. 1:21; 3:2; 20:1; Josh. 8:1; 10:8; 11:6; Judg. 6:23; 2 Kings 19:6; 2 Chron. 20:15; Isa. 7:4; 8:12; 10:24; 35:4; 37:6; 41:10, 13, 14; 43:1, 5; 44:2; 51:7; 54:4; Jer. 1:8 10:5; 30:10; 42:11 (2 times); 46:27, 28; Lam. 3:57; Ezek. 2:6; 3:9; Joel 2:21, 22; Hag. 2:5; Zech. 8:13, 15. Texts in which another gives the command but couches it theologically are: Gen. 21:17; 43:23; 50:19; 50:21; Exod. 14:13; 20:20; Num. 14:9; Deut. 20:3; 31:6, 8; Josh. 10:25; 1 Sam. 12:20; 23:17; 1 Kings 17:13; 2 Kings 1:15; 6:16; 1 Chron. 22:13; 28:20; 2 Chron. 32:7; Neh. 4:14; Job 5:22; Ps. 49:16; Prov. 3:25; Isa. 40:9; Dan. 10:12, 19. The command for the sake of others without the theological couching occurs in: Gen. 35:17; Judg. 4:18; Ruth 3:11; 1 Sam. 4:20; 22:23; 28:13; 2 Sam. 9:7; 13:28; 2 Kings 25:24; Jer. 40:9. In the NT, Jesus gives the command (*mei* or *ou* with an imperative form of *phobeo*) in: Matt. 10:26, 28 (with parallel in Luke 12:4); 10:31 (with parallel in Luke 12:7); 14:27 (with parallels in Mark 6:50 and John 6:20); 17:7; 28:10; Mark 5:36; Luke 5:10; 8:50; 12:32; Acts 18:9; Rev. 1:17. An angel gives the command in: Matt. 1:20; 28:5; Luke 1:13, 30; 2:10; Acts 27:24. The two Old Testament citations in the New Testament with this command are John 12:15 (citing Zech. 9:9) and 1 Pet. 3:14 (citing Isa. 8:12).

[28] For a discussion of the Israelite understanding of rest and its connection with the temple in light of the larger ancient Near Eastern context, see John H. Walton, *Ancient Near Eastern Thought and the Old Testament* (Grand Rapids: Baker, 2006), 157–158, 196–199. According to Walton, neither the concept of rest nor seeing rest as a precondition to temple-building is unique to Israel. The difference, of course, is that Israel attributes the rest to Yahweh, their God.

Chapter 3: What's Going on Here?

[29] Wright's commentary consistently draws out the missional themes of Deuteronomy. For his initial discussion of this theme, see his *Deuteronomy*, 8–17. For his treatment of the theme through the whole Old Testament and into the New Testament, and for an argument for a missional hermeneutic, see his *The Mission of God: Unlocking the Bible's Grand Narrative* (Downers Grove, Ill.: InterVarsity, 2006).

[30] The ESV's "rules" is an unfortunate translation, because it can mean that the essence of keeping *Torah* is simply keeping a bunch of rules. Rather than a checklist approach, however, the "rules" ("ordinances," NRSV) that Israel was to keep were ones that guided and shaped Israel's life in keeping with God's purposes.

[31] My former student Trey Gwinn added Tyre to the picture for me.

[32] These aspects of the community will be fleshed out in subsequent chapters.

[33] Wright argues that this aspect of hearing is the primary difference highlighted here between Yahweh and other gods (*Deuteronomy*, 50).

[34] Scholars debate the extent to which Israel was monotheistic, and if or when they became so. Certainly, the biblical text itself indicates that Israel rarely lived as though they were monotheistic. And perhaps there lies the issue. Whatever they thought about the possible existence of other gods, for Israel there was only one God whom they were to trust, obey, and worship. Along these lines, see Walton, *Ancient Near Eastern Thought*, 156.

Chapter 4: Ordering Life, Part 1: Devotion to God

[35] Deuteronomy regularly uses Horeb to refer to the mountain where Moses received the Law, while Exodus through Numbers uses Sinai to refer to the same place. Deuteronomy 33:2, however, uses "Sinai." Exodus 3:1 and 33:6 use "Horeb."

[36] This relational understanding of the Ten Commandments should inform our discussion of debates about the posting of the Ten Commandments. The Commandments now, as then, are meaningless apart from a relationship with God. To reduce (yes, reduce!) them to timeless principles or historical precedents robs them of their real power and purpose, which come only from a committed, covenantal relationship with God. For a brief, thoughtful treatment of this issue, see the op-ed piece "Hang Ten? Thou Shalt Avoid Ten Commandments Tokenism" in *Christianity Today* 44:3 (Mar. 6, 2000), 36. The article is available online at http://www.christianitytoday.com/ct/2000/march6/28.36.html (accessed Dec. 17, 2013). For a longer discussion see, Nancy J. Duff, "Should the Ten Commandments Be Posted in the Public Realm? Why the Bible and the Constitution Say, 'No'" in *The Ten Commandments: The Reciprocity of Faithfulness*, ed. William P. Brown (Louisville: Westminster John Knox, 2004), 159–170.

[37] "Decalogue" means "ten words," a literal great translation of the Hebrew in Exodus 34:28; Deuteronomy 4:13; 10:4. Different religious traditions reckon the numbering of the Ten Commandments differently. Most Protestants number the commands as follows: (1) no other gods; (2) no images; (3) do not misuse the Lord's name; (4) observe the Sabbath; (5) honor parents; (6) do not kill; (7) do not commit adultery; (8) do not steal; (9) do not give false witness; (10) do not covet.

Roman Catholics and Lutherans divide them in this way: (1) no other gods and no images; (2) do not misuse the Lord's name; (3) observe the Sabbath; (4) honor parents; (5) do not kill; (6) do not commit adultery; (7) do not steal; (8) do not give false witness; (9) do not covet your neighbors wife; (10) do not covet your neighbor's possessions.

Jewish tradition, understanding these are "ten words," divides them as follows: (1) "I am the Lord your God who brought you up... (Exod. 20:2; Deut. 5:6); (2) no other gods and no images; (3) do not misuse the Lord's name; (4) observe the Sabbath; (5) honor parents; (6) do not kill; (7) do not commit adultery; (8) do not steal; (9) do not give false witness; (10) do not covet.

[38] There is no scholarly consensus on whether the stipulations that follow the Ten Commandments can be divided into distinct sections that correspond to each of the Commandments. Those who do see such divisions do not always agree on the details. For two suggestions, see Andrew E. Hill and John H. Walton, *A Survey of the Old Testament*, third ed. (Grand Rapids: Zondervan, 2009), 168–174; Olson, *Deuteronomy and the Death of Moses*, 63–65.

[39] The Ten Commandments have been thoroughly studied throughout the centuries, and a great deal has been written on them. Therefore, the discussion here can merely scratch the surface. A useful recent resource on the Ten Commandments is William P. Brown, ed., *The Ten Commandments: The Reciprocity of Faithfulness* (Louisville: Westminster John Knox, 2004). This volume includes examples of historical interpretations of the Commandments and contemporary essays on the Ten Commandments as a whole and individually. See also Patrick D. Miller, *The Ten Commandments*, Interpretation Resources for Use in the Church, (Louisville: Westminster John Knox, 2009).

[40] Wright, *Deuteronomy*, 65–66.

[41] McConville, *Deuteronomy*, 125–126.

[42] It should also be noted that the law in Deuteronomy 24:16, which prohibits executing children for the crimes of their parents, does not contradict the second commandment. Deuteronomy 24:16 refers to a sentence of execution in a judicial setting—that is, punishment inflicted by humans, while the punishment in the second commandment comes from God.

[43] McConville, *Deuteronomy*, 127. Weinfeld says that "to the third and fourth generation" represents the average lifespan of a person (cf. Job 42:16) and thus the punishment comes upon the parents' household during their lifetime. Moshe Weinfeld, *Deuteronomy 1–11*, Anchor Bible 5 (New York: Doubleday, 1991), 296.

[44] Walton argues that the emphasis of the command is that Yahweh "works alone" in contrast to the conception of gods in the world around Israel, where each god has jurisdiction over or a certain aspect of the cosmos. In Israel, Yahweh controls all of those aspects, leaving no place for other gods. The command does not specifically

deny the existence of other gods, he argues; it simply renders them useless. *Ancient Near Eastern Thought*, 155–56.

[45] With respect to manipulative or magical views of prayer, Bruce Wilkinson's *The Prayer of Jabez: Breaking Through to the Blessed Life* (Sisters, Ore.: Multnomah, 2000), which was very popular a few years ago, comes to mind. Wilkinson treats this prayer from 1 Chronicles 4:9–10 as a formulaic prayer that God answers without fail.

Chapter 5: Ordering Life, Part 2: Devotion to Neighbors

[46] For this chapter, I will depart from the usual format. Instead of waiting until I have discussed all of the remaining commandments and then what they say about God ("The God of the Community") and to the church ("Guidance for Today's Community"), I will discuss these after each commandment.

[47] "Sabbath" comes from a Hebrew root word meaning "to cease or rest."

[48] Cf. Exodus 20:11, where the motivation to keep the Sabbath is: God rested from his work of creating on that day. The two motivations are not mutually exclusive, and it is God the Creator who unleashed the forces of his creation against the Egyptians to liberate and provide rest for Israel.

[49] In Exodus 20:11, they become imitators of God by resting from their work as God rested from his in Creation.

[50] This second means of providing rests to servers was suggested to me by my former student, Kate Watkins.

[51] One of my former students, Andy Irvine, made a connection between Sabbath and the Lord's Supper in a class on Deuteronomy, and his insight stimulated my thinking on the theological relationships between the two observances. For a full treatment of the connections, see my article "The Lord's Supper as Sabbath Observance," *Restoration Quarterly* 51:2 (2009): 81–92.

[52] For a discussion of the socioeconomic aspects of the Lord's Supper, see, e.g., Gordon D. Fee, *The First Epistle to the Corinthians*, New International Commentary on the New Testament, (Grand Rapids: Eerdmans, 1987), 531–569.

[53] The same word is used in Deuteronomy 25:3 with respect to preventing the "degrading" of a fellow Israelite through excessive corporal punishment.

⁵⁴ Admittedly, those who seek power for themselves have abused the idea of God-ordained authority, which no doubt has created suspicion regarding authority claims. But misuses of authority by some does not relieve us of the responsibility to submit to proper authority, though we will have to be discerning with respect to illegitimate and legitimate authority.

⁵⁵ Note that all of the cases where it refers to unintentional killing are in the context of instructions for the cities of refuge in Israel. In every case, except Proverbs 22:13, it has to do with people killing people.

⁵⁶ Wright says, "The presumption is always that killing is wrong unless compelling reasons indicate otherwise," (*Deuteronomy*, 78).

⁵⁷ Ibid., 79. Wright argues that the notion of the sanctity of life in connection with this commandment cannot be broadened to consider the killing of any other life-form as equal to the killing of a human being. Human beings are set apart from other life-forms in that they are created in the image of God. Wright's observation should not be taken to mean that humans have the right to destroy nonhuman life wantonly. Humans were charged with the care of creation, rather than its exploitation and degradation.

⁵⁸ The insistence on parents and children being punished for their own crimes can be contrasted with certain examples of justice from elsewhere in the ancient Near East (e.g., the Law of Hammurabi calls for the execution of a builder's son if a house constructed by the builder collapses and kills the homeowner's son (LH 230)).

⁵⁹ Clearly, this text does not satisfy our modern sensibilities about women and children in war since Israel could take them as plunder, probably as slaves. But in their context, the law prevented the wanton killing of noncombatants. Also, we can ask whether the modern methods of warfare are actually always more humane or morally superior. In modern warfare, women and children are far more likely to become casualities, because our methods are so much less precise (even with "smart bombs"!) than the mostly hand-to-hand fighting of the ancient world. Also, taking captives as slaves would mean that these women and children would be cared for, as opposed to the refugee crises we often see in modern warfare. It should also be noted that the rules of warfare in Deuteronomy 20:10–15 apply only to cities outside the Promised Land. The cities within the land are subject to the ban, which includes the killing of women and children. See the "Excursus on the Ban."

⁶⁰ The literature on Christians' use or rejection of violence is immense. For Christian nonviolence and pacifism, see, e.g., John H. Yoder, *The Politics of Jesus*, second ed. (Eerdmans, 1994); Richard B. Hayes, *The Moral Vision of the New Testament: A*

Contemporary Introduction to New Testament Ethics (New York: HarperCollins, 1996), 317–346. For a Christian defense of "just war," see, e.g., J. Daryl Charles, *Between Pacifism and Jihad: Just War and the Christian Tradition* (Downers Grove, Ill.: InterVarsity, 2005); Daniel M. Bell, *Just War as Christian Discipleship: Recentering the Tradition in the Church rather than the State* (Grand Rapids: Brazos, 2009).

[61] The cultural situation in ancient Israel demands that Yahweh always be portrayed as the husband and Israel and/or Judah as the wives, because husbands could have more than one wife, but a wife could have only one husband.

[62] I fully realize the complicated nature and multiple interpretations of the Bible's teachings on divorce. I also realize that in cases of spousal and child abuse, divorce may be necessary for protection. Much has been written on the Bible's teaching on divorce, but here are a few resources representing different points of view to begin a more in depth study of the subject. Elizabeth Achtemeier, *The Committed Marriage* (Philadelphia: Westminster, 1977); Hays, *Moral Vision*, 347–378; Rubel Shelly, *Divorce and Remarriage: A Redemptive Theology* (Abilene, Tex.: Leafwood, 2007).

[63] This certainly seems to be at least one way people in Jesus' day treated divorce. The law in Deuteronomy 24:1–4 is employed in a technical and legalistic way to excuse divorce (see Matt. 5:31; 19:7; Mark 10:4). However, such an interpretation of Deuteronomy 24:1–4 is mistaken. This text is discussed in more detail in Chapter 12.

[64] In this regard, see Daniel F. Camp, *The Marriage-Friendly Church* (Nashville: 21st Century Christian, 2013).

[65] The issue of poverty will be discussed further in Chapter 9 of this book. Though stealing is not condoned, at least one place in the Bible recognizes that one's need to survive might motivate a person to steal (Prov. 6:30–31).

[66] Andrew T. Lincoln, *Ephesians*, Word Biblical Commentary 42 (Dallas: Word Books, 1990), 304.

[67] This story is interesting for the way that Jezebel manipulates the law, drumming up a capital offense using two witnesses (Deut. 17:6). 2 Kings 9:26 indicates that his sons were also killed, which would directly violate the law (Deut. 24:16). Of course, divine retribution plays out for Ahab and Jezebel (1 Kings 21; 2 Kings 9).

[68] The inclusion of "his wife" is not evidence that the Israelites thought of the wife as the man's property, on par with his house, land, donkey, etc., anymore than "his wife" would have that implication if someone said it today (Wright, *Deuteronomy*, 89).

[69] The shift in vocabulary from "covet" to "desire" is not found in the Exodus version of the commandment (20:17), which uses only the former term. McConville says that the use of the two verbs probably intend to separate "adulterous desire as a different kind" of coveting, in keeping with Deuteronomy's "tendency to show concern for the standing and the rights of women" (*Deuteronomy*, 130–131).

[70] Augustine, *Confessions*, Book I, 1. Cited according to the edition *Saint Augustine Confessions*, R. S. Pine-Coffin, trans. (New York: Viking Penguin, 1961; reprint 1987), 21.

Chapter 6: Show and Tell: Keeping the Word Alive

[71] Very literally translated, it is "Hear Israel Yahweh our God Yahweh one."

[72] E.g., Baal of Peor (Num. 25:3–5; Deut. 4:3; Ps. 106:28); Baal-berith (Judg. 8:33; 9:4); Baal-zebub of Ekron (2 Kings 1:2–16).

[73] Wright, *Deuteronomy*, 96.

[74] The translation "soul" is unfortunate, because it conjures up dualistic notions that separate the material body from an immaterial soul. This notion is not biblical but derives from ancient Greek philosophers. Such a view can and has led Christians to both denigrate God's material creation and to ignore the physical needs of other people by concentrating on "saving souls."

[75] McConville, *Deuteronomy*, 142. One of my students, trying to translate the sense of this word as "muchness" or "exceeding" did not offer a word but an enthusiastic grunt, "and with all your *oomf*!" I like this understanding, though it is hard to convey here her body language and facial expression that accompanied and gave emphasis to her translation.

[76] The meaning of the Hebrew word translated "impress" in the ESV (and NIV) and "recite" in the NRSV is debated. One possibility is that it comes from a root meaning "to sharpen, whet, or pierce." In this case, the meaning would be to insert or incise it in the hearts of the children. Another possibility is that it comes from a root meaning "to repeat or recite" (so NRSV; NLT; NJB).

[77] This observation about Deuteronomy and its relevance for the church comes from Duane L. Christensen, *Deuteronomy 21:10–34:12*, Word Biblical Commentary 6B, (Nashville: Thomas Nelson, 2002), 655. I have significantly expanded upon his observations in what follows.

[78] According to Deuteronomy 16:16 (cf. Exod. 23:17; 34:23) the men of Israel must appear at the three major festivals. That women would be exempted at times makes sense in light of issues such as pregnancy and nursing small children that would make travel more difficult for them.

[79] In later Jewish tradition, the Festival of Weeks became associated with Yahweh giving Israel the Law at Mount Horeb/Sinai. This understanding may have been present by the time of Jesus.

[80] The cloak was a square piece of cloth—hence, four corners—used as an outer garment that was either wrapped around the body or worn like a toga. It could also serve as a cover at night (cf. Deut. 24:10–13). Philip J. King and Lawrence E. Stager, *Life in Biblical Israel* (Louisville: Westminster John Knox, 2001), 268–269.

[81] The Shema is cited or alluded to in at least the following: Deut. 4:29; 11:13, 18; 26:16; 30:2, 6, 10; Josh. 22:5; 1 Kings 2:4; 8:48; 2 Kings 23:3, 25; 2 Chron. 6:38; 15:12; 34:31; Jer. 32:41; Zech. 14:9; Matt. 22:37; Mark 12:30; Luke 10:27; and in the Apocrypha, Tobit 13:6.

[82] Even the commands in these texts are contextualized within our story of faith. Matthew 28:19–20 comes only at the end of Matthew's account of Jesus life, death, and resurrection. Likewise, Peter first tells the story of Jesus (Acts 2:22–36), which elicits the crowd's question about what they should do (2:37), to which Peter responds, "Repent and be baptized…" (2:38).

[83] The phrase "until he comes" suggests that our telling of the story should also include the resurrection.

[84] See John Mark Hicks, *Come to the Table: Revisioning the Lord's Supper* (Orange, Calif.: New Leaf Books, 2002). I say the worship assembly should generally be characterized by joy, because there are times for lament services, though the resurrection should always be kept in view.

[85] Reading in the community does not rule out personal and individual reading, but, as indicated above, the ability to read one's own Bible is a relatively new phenomenon in the history of God's people. Furthermore, though not foolproof, reading and discerning in community can guard against idiosyncratic (or heretical) personal interpretations of the Scripture. However, as the history of Israel and the Church has repeatedly shown, the community can corrupt the teaching of the Scripture as well, bending it to maintain the status quo or to achieve wealth and power. Such readings are accompanied by forgetting or distorting the character of

God and of Jesus as revealed in the Scripture. A safeguard against such readings is to constantly keep the Word before the people of God in manifold ways.

Chapter 7: It Is Not You; It Is Me

[86] For a discussion on the command to wipe out the Canaanites, see the "Excursus on the Ban."

[87] See also Deut. 14:2; 26:18; Exod. 19:5; Mal. 3:17.

[88] The promises that the descendants of Abraham, Isaac, and Jacob would be "as numerous as the sands on the seashore" or as many as the "stars in the heavens" stand in some tension with Deuteronomy 7:7, where their smallness is emphasized. Deuteronomy 7:7 also stands in tension with Numbers 26:51, which says the number of Israelite men of fighting age after the forty years of wandering was 601,730. Of course, hyperbole is in play in the promises to Abraham, Isaac, and Jacob to emphasize the growth from a single man, his son, and grandson into a nation of people. The number of Israelite men in Numbers 26:51 is probably best explained as either a translational issue (the word translated "thousand" can also refer to a military unit or tribal division) or hyperbole, given that this many men would have constituted, by far, the largest army in the ancient Near East at that time.

[89] Such a description of highest heavens, heaven, and earth reflects the ancient view of the cosmos in which there is the earth, then above that are the heavens, or what we would call the sky, which includes the sun, moon, and stars. "Sky," however, is a bit misleading, since they would understand the sky (or firmament) as the solid stratum above heavens that held the upper waters in place. Then above the heavens were the highest heavens where God (or gods) dwelled. For a full discussion, see Walton, *Ancient Near Eastern Thought*, 165–178.

[90] Ancient Near Eastern creation myths, such as the *Enuma Elish* and the *Atrahasis Epic*, portray the gods creating human beings to serve them, essentially as slaves. Israel also believed that humans were created to serve God, but as priests in his cosmic temple (i.e., his creation). Human beings are granted far more dignity in the biblical creation account than they are in other ANE accounts of human origins. See Walton, *Ancient Near Eastern Thought*, 214–215.

[91] For a popular treatment of this theme, see Mark C. Black, *Luke*, College Press NIV Commentary (Joplin, Mo.: College Press, 1996), 22–26.

Chapter 8: A Matter of Distinction

[92] This is not to deny commonalities between Israelite and Canaanite worship, or, more broadly, ancient Near Eastern worship, which also includes temples, sacrifices, a priesthood, etc. One would expect commonalities. But where overlap exists, it is supposed to be because God has commanded Israel to worship in that way.

[93] Ideally, Israel would have only one sanctuary and one God. But both the Bible and archaeology confirm that this was, in fact, rarely the case in Israel. See, e.g., King and Stager, *Life in Biblical Israel*, 319–353. The Bible twice notes centralization efforts by kings of Judah to reverse the multiplication of shrines and to centralize worship in Jerusalem in keeping with this law in the reigns of Hezekiah (2 Kings 18:1–4) and Josiah (2 Kings 23:1–25). Many scholars insist that Deuteronomy, with its centralization mandate, was written in the time of Josiah as justification for, not the cause of, his reforms (cf. 2 Kings 22). In this view, Jerusalem is the "place" Deuteronomy has in mind, but, to avoid anachronism, Deuteronomy does not name the city. Other scholars, however, argue against this view, noting that God's sanctuary was in other places before Jerusalem, at the very least in Shiloh (Judg. 18:31; 1 Sam. 1:3, 24; Jer. 7:12–14). One can find a discussion of these issues in many of the good Old Testament introductions and commentaries on Deuteronomy.

[94] Blood was seen to contain the life of the animal (v. 23) and thus belonged to God. From the ancients' perspective, that the blood contained the life of the animal makes sense. When the blood drains out of an animal, it dies.

[95] Israelites would later imitate this practice in worship of God or other gods. Cf. 2 Kings 16:3; 21:6; 23:10; Jer. 7:31; 19:5; 32:35; Ezek. 16:20–21; 20:26, 31; 23:37, 39. Note that in all three texts from Jeremiah listed, God says that he never commanded such a practice, nor did it enter his mind.

[96] This section finds parallels in the vassal treaties of Assyrian king Esarhaddon, which demanded that vassals report to him any hint of disloyalty or treason from anyone, including family members or prophets. Those who failed to do so were cursed in the name of various Assyrian gods.

[97] That God uses the fulfilled sign as a test may suggest that God himself fulfills the sign, which makes sense in light of Deuteronomy's refusal to attribute significance or power to other gods (4:28; 32:37–39). On the general subject of God testing his people, see, e.g., Gen. 22:1; Exod. 15:25; 16:4; Deut. 8:2, 16; Judg. 2:22; 3:4. However, elsewhere in the Bible, such "miraculous" deeds do not seem to be reserved only for true prophets and servants of God. Jesus says that false messiahs and false prophets will come performing signs and miracles in an attempt to deceive the elect (Matt. 24:24; Mark 13:22).

[98] Stoning was a communal form of execution. Having so many hands involved in an execution served to declare the community's adherence to the law of God and repudiation of the offense. By this means, the community removed evil from its midst.

[99] The term used for these "worthless fellows" (wicked men [NIV]; scoundrels [NRSV]) is "sons of *belial*," which suggest worthless or corrupted people. E.g., it is used in Judg. 19:22 of the men who want to sexually assault the Levite and who do assault his concubine. It is used for the sons of Eli the priest, who have no regard for the Lord (1 Sam. 2:12) and of Nabal, who rudely and foolishly refuses hospitality to David and his men (1 Sam. 25:17). In 1 Kings 21:10, 13, Naboth's false accusers are called this. In Proverbs, *belial* is used for a person with corrupted speech (6:12), one who plots evil (16:27), and a witness who perverts justice (19:28).

[100] The practices are attested in the Baal myths and the ancient Aqhat epic, and they have been associated with ancestor worship. See John H. Walton, Victor H. Matthews, and Mark W. Chavalas, *IVP Bible Background Commentary: Old Testament* (Downers Grove, Ill.: InterVarsity, 2000), 184.

[101] One explanation often given is that the food laws have to do with hygiene, claiming that the unclean animals are more likely to carry disease. See, e.g., Fee and Stuart, *How to Read the Bible*, 177–178. This is an anachronistic reading, projecting modern understandings of hygiene onto an ancient culture. Most scholars rightly reject this explanation. One popular explanation among scholars is rooted in anthropological studies and argues that each of the clean animals represents "wholeness and completeness" within given categories of animals, conditions related to the concept of holiness. The seminal essay in this regard is Mary Douglas's "The Abominations of Leviticus," in *Anthropological Approaches to the Old Testament*, ed. Bernhard Lang, (Philadelphia: Fortress, 1985), 100–116. For a detailed discussion of the dietary regulations in Israel, see Jacob Milgrom, *Leviticus 1–16*, The Anchor Bible (New York: Doubleday, 1991), 718–736.

[102] Wright, *Deuteronomy*, 182. Observing the food laws was one of the ways the Jewish exiles in Babylon were able to avoid assimilation into the larger culture (cf. Dan. 1), as well as enabling them to maintain their distinctiveness under Persia, Greece, Rome, and every empire and nation Jews have found themselves in to this day.

[103] Among the explanations given for this prohibition are: (1) a humanitarian concern, preventing cruelty to the animal; (2) the ancient Israelites wanted to avoid consuming what they believed was blood in the milk, a mistake that could be made because the mother goat's colostrum could have a red tint; (3) an ethical objection in some way that violates the mother-offspring relationship. For an extended

discussion, see Milgrom, *Leviticus 1–16*, 737–742. Jeffrey H. Tigay discusses rabbinic tradition with its requirement to keep all meat and milk products separate. This practice continues until this day in some branches of Judaism. See his *Deuteronomy: The Traditional Hebrew Text with the New JPS Translation* (Philadelphia: Jewish Publication Society of America, 1996), 140.

[104] McConville argues that the law is aimed against homosexual practice or participation in foreign religious practices (*Deuteronomy*, 337). Miller sees the focus of the command more in terms of maintaining creational distinctiveness, which then points to purity and holiness (*Deuteronomy*, 162–163). Since culture determines what is the appropriate dress for men and women, and since those conventions change over time, this text can hardly be used to make blanket statements about what kind of clothes are masculine and what kind are feminine.

[105] It is common among biblical scholars to claim that Jeroboam's calves were not images of other gods but pedestals for Yahweh, akin to the Ark of the Covenant. Some archaeological evidence has been cited as proof of this claim. The biblical claims that the shrines were idolatrous are then seen as a polemical distortion by those in Judah who opposed any sanctuary other than the one in Jerusalem. See, e.g., Patrick D. Miller, *The Religion of Ancient Israel* (Louisville: Westminster John Knox, 2000), 93–94; Mordechai Cogan, *1 Kings: A New Translation with Introduction and Commentary*, The Anchor Bible (New York: Doubleday, 2000), 358. See also the extended discussion of this text in relation to Exodus 32 in William H. Propp, *Exodus 19–40: A New Translation with Introduction and Commentary*, The Anchor Bible (New York: Doubleday, 2006), 574–578. However, one should note that the biblical text itself claims that Jeroboam's images were, in fact, other gods in place of Yahweh: "Here are your *gods* who brought (plural verb) you out of Egypt" (1 Kings 12:28; cf. 1 Kings 14:8–9). Note also the association with these images and general idolatry in 2 Kings 17:7–23.

[106] While the psalms were used in the temple worship at the festivals, and some seem to have been written specifically for that purpose, many of the psalms appear to have their origins in individuals' and the community's experiences of and reflections upon God, even if these psalms were later incorporated in the official worship at the sanctuary.

[107] Keep in mind that Paul gives up his freedom in Christ in order not to hinder the gospel of Christ (1 Cor. 9:1, 15), and that the entire discussion of freedom and becoming "all things to all people" in 1 Corinthians 9 is set within a discussion of whether Christians may eat food sacrificed to idols (1 Cor. 8–10). For a discussion of these chapters, see Fee, *Corinthians*, 357–491.

[108] On the discipline of simplicity, see Richard J. Foster, *Celebration of Discipline*, rev. ed. (San Francisco: Harper San Francisco, 1988), 79–95.

[109] This does not imply that there is a set New Testament "pattern" of worship, as some would claim the Old Testament has for Jews (a claim that is also hard to sustain if all of the texts dealing with worship are laid side by side and an attempt is made to systematize them). Certainly, if there is a set and discernable pattern for Christian worship, the larger Christian community has not been able to discern it to everyone's agreement. Clearly, there is no one text that simply lists all the elements of Christian worship, so any such list must be cobbled together from a variety of texts.

[110] Even Romans 13:1–7, which calls for submission to governing authorities, relativizes the authority of human governments by insisting that their authority is *derived from* or *granted* by God. This is consistent with the Old Testament view of nations and governments as raised and used by God but also subject to his judgment.

[111] See Lee Camp's insightful discussion of the issue of Christians and their relationship to their home countries in his *Mere Discipleship: Radical Christianity in a Rebellious World* (Grand Rapids: Brazos, 2003), 137–149.

Chapter 9: Liberty and Justice for All

[112] Some suggest that what is cancelled, literally "released," is the security held against the loan, most likely land. Others think the loan is not forgiven but that payments are suspended in the seventh year. See Wright's discussion, *Deuteronomy*, 188, 196. However, the prohibition against refusing a loan because the year of release is near (v. 9) indicates the debt itself was forgiven as well.

[113] The land itself is to get a rest every seventh year (Exod. 23:10; Lev. 25:17; 2 Chron. 36:21). In this light, the seventh year release of debt would be especially important, because the poor Israelites would have no crops with which to pay off loans in the year the land remains fallow. See McConville, *Deuteronomy*, 259.

[114] In Hebrew, the commands are literally "Do not close your hand" and "You shall indeed open your hand." The latter command is emphatic in Hebrew.

[115] Other translations that relieve the tension are possible; for example, "there should be no poor among you" (NIV; NAB), though such a translation may be seen as an intentional move to alleviate the tension.

[116] Note Nelson's comments on this tension: "Verses 4–6 portray the world as it should be, a society without poverty, while v. 11 admits how things really are. Verse

4 is the expected norm; v. 11 the temporary exception. The recurring problem of poverty is not due to some systemic fault in Yahweh's blessing or bestowed land, but is episodic and implicitly assumes a lack of obedience to laws such as this one. The reality of poverty provides an opportunity for obedient generosity, but does not undermine the sufficiency and goodness of Yahweh's gifts." Richard D. Nelson, *Deuteronomy*, Old Testament Library (Louisville: Westminster John Knox, 2002), 193–194.

[117] It may be that commercial loans in the conduct of international trade are in mind with respect to foreigners, since it would be less likely that a poor person from another country would come to Israel seeking a relief loan.

[118] For a further discussion on slavery, see the "Excursus on Slavery in the Bible."

[119] In verse 12, the slave is more literally described as, "Your brother, a Hebrew male or Hebrew female." The term "Hebrew" is usually used in contexts where foreigners are interacting with Abraham and his descendants. Here the use of the term may intend to recall Israel's common experience of slavery in Egypt (see Exod. 1:15, 16, 19; 2:6, 7, 11, 13; 3:18; 5:3; 7:16; 9:1, 13; 10:3). The origins and meaning of the term are debated. For a brief discussion, see Nahum Sarna, *Exploring Exodus: The Origins of Biblical Israel* (New York: Schocken Books, 1986, 1996), 54–55. What is important to note in verse 12, however, is the familial aspect: these slaves are kindred, fellow Israelites. Wright, however, argues that "brother" means a member of the community, and "Hebrew" here has a broader meaning in this context (and in Exod. 21:2–6)—a "nonethnic Israelite, landless people who were dependent on land-owning Israelite households for their employment and survival" (*Deuteronomy*, 192, 197). He overstates the case when he says there is general agreement on this meaning of the word "Hebrew" in Exodus 21:1–6. There may be a general agreement that this is the meaning of the term (*habiru*) from which "Hebrew" may have derived, but not that this is the meaning in Exodus 21:2. Several commentators say the term refers to Israelite slaves in Exodus 21:2. See, e.g., John I. Durham, *Exodus*, Word Biblical Commentary, (Waco: Word, 1987), 320–321; Propp, *Exodus 19–40*, 186–188.

[120] The differences between the versions of this law in Exodus and Deuteronomy are well recognized in scholarship. Some see Deuteronomy's version as a drastic rewriting of the earlier version in Exodus (or, more precisely, the Covenant Code in Exodus 20:22–23:33). For a discussion of the differences from this perspective, see Nelson, *Deuteronomy*, 197–199. The matter is further complicated by Leviticus 25:39–42, which says a poor Israelite who sells himself into slavery to a fellow Israelite is to be released in the year of Jubilee. Since the context of this latter law is the Jubilee, it surely intends a special release of any Israelite enslaved at this time.

Since property reverts to its original owners and debts are forgiven, such slaves would again have means of livelihood.

[121] The release of debt slaves was not unique to Israel. Hammurabi's law (117) calls for the release of a wife, son, or daughter, who has been sold as a debt slave, after three years of service.

[122] Whether the door is the door of the owner's house or the door of the sanctuary is not clear. Exodus 21:6 may suggest the latter and indicates that the piercing was done publicly, which would insure that remaining a slave was, indeed, the choice of the slave.

[123] Nelson suggests that "oppress" here could imply "reduce to slavery" again (*Deuteronomy*, 280).

[124] Ancient Near Eastern treaties often stipulate the return of runaway slaves. Also, note the following from Hammurabi's Code (LH 16): "If a man should harbor a fugitive slave or a slave woman either of the palace or of a commoner in his house and not bring him out at the herald's public proclamation, that house holder shall be killed." Trans. from Martha T. Roth, *Law Collections from Mesopotamia and Asia Minor*, second ed, SBL Writings from the Ancient World Series 6 (Atlanta: Scholars Press, 1997), 84.

[125] Nebuchadnezzar withdrew from Jerusalem temporarily to fight King Hophra (Apries) of Egypt, who was invading Palestine. After defeating Hophra, Nebuchadnezzar again laid siege to Jerusalem and took the city in 586 B.C.

[126] An excellent work that brings out this death-dealing and degrading nature of empires, such as Pharaoh's, is Walter Brueggemann's *Prophetic Imagination*, second ed. (Augsburg Fortress, 2001).

[127] This is not to imply that Israel's bondage in Egypt or that experienced by others who were enslaved were the result of their own sin.

[128] One ministry that works relentlessly to combat such injustices is the international justice mission. Their website offers a great deal of information on these injustices and ways to respond. http://www.ijm.org/.

[129] This is not to deny that some who are poor have caused or contributed to their situation (cf. Prov. 24:33–34; 28:19). However, the situation is far more complex than simply telling someone to get a job or to stop wasting money. Poverty arises from any number of factors or combination of factors, including laziness, poor

judgment, greed, theft, injustice, lack of opportunities and education, natural disasters, place of birth, and so on. That is, a person can experience poverty of his or her own making (and should we not be merciful to them as well?), but more often, poverty is systemic and cyclical, making escape without help nearly impossible. To borrow from Shane Claiborne's comments in his *The Irresistible Revolution* (Grand Rapids: Zondervan, 2006, 150–151), the matter is not simply giving a fish versus teaching to fish (to use a well-worn analogy), though both can be good things to do. One must also ask who owns the pond, who put a fence around it, and who polluted it.

[130] M. Eugene Boring, *Mark*, New Testament Library (Louisville: Westminster John Knox, 2006), 383–384.

[131] Some excellent, practical, and challenging studies on Christians' use of wealth and their obligation to the poor are: Craig L. Blomberg, *Neither Poverty nor Riches: A Biblical Theology of Material Possessions* (Grand Rapids: Eerdmans, 1999); Ronald J. Sider, *Rich Christians in an Age of Hunger: Moving from Affluence to Generosity* (Dallas: Word, 1997); Brian Fikkert and Steve Corbett, *When Helping Hurts: Alleviating Poverty without Hurting the Poor ... and Yourself* (Chicago: Moody, 2009).

Chapter 10: Who Is In Charge Here?

[132] "Yahweh" does not occur in 33:5, and this leads some scholars to claim that a human king is in view. However, the context for verse 5 is the introduction to Moses' blessings on the tribes of Israel and v. 2 seems to indicate that Yahweh is understood as the king. The reference in v. 5 to the assembled leaders and tribes of Israel probably intends the assembly before Mount Horeb when Israel heard their God and King speak (5:1–27).

[133] Nelson, *Deuteronomy*, 215.

[134] Despite the impression left in numerous English translations (e.g., KJV, NKJV, NIV, RSV, NRSV, NAB, NJB, NLT), the words translated "justice" in verses 19 and 20 are not from the same word in Hebrew. The word in verse 19 is *mishpat*, which is usually translated "justice," and in verse 20 it is *zedek*, usually translated "righteousness." The concepts are certainly related and overlap, and both have to do with restoring and maintaining peaceful relationships within the community. Justice may point more to the restoring, while righteousness to the maintaining, though the lines are not strict.

[135] Wright, *Deuteronomy*, 205.

[136] One may ask: why then was Israel's request for a king like the nations view as a rejection of God as king (1 Sam. 8) if Deuteronomy 17:14 says they can have such a king. The problem with the request at that time was that when Israel asked for a king, they did so because they did not trust God to deliver them from their enemies. They wanted a king, rather than God, to fight their battles, even though God repeatedly demonstrated his power to overcome Israel's enemies (1 Sam. 8:20; 12:6–25).

[137] Note how God, through his prophets, both selects and rejects Israel's kings (1 Sam. 9–10, 16; 1 Kings 11:26–34; 14:6–14; 16:1–4; 21:20–24; 2 Kings 9:1–10; 10:30). The situation in Judah differs a bit after the Israelite kingdom split, because God chose David's line as kings over Judah (2 Sam. 7; 1 Kings 11:12–13).

[138] See the graphic portrayals of the sin of trusting foreign allies in Ezekiel 16 and 23.

[139] Commentators have often noted that the limitations placed on kingship in Deuteronomy 17:16–17 contrast to the description of Solomon's reign. Solomon amassed great wealth, imported horses from Egypt and other places, and had many wives (1 Kings 10:14–11:8). Some would argue that Deuteronomy 17:16–17 was written in response to Solomon. However, the author of 1 Kings only explicitly censures him for his many wives, who led him to worship other gods. According to 1 Kings, his wealth comes from God as a blessing for Solomon's request for wisdom (1 Kings 3:4–15).

[140] On God's setting apart the tribe of Levi, see Exodus 32:25–29 and Deuteronomy 10:8–9. The duties of the Levites are given elsewhere in the Pentateuch. See, especially, Num. 1:49–54, 8:5–26; Deut. 10:8. On the distinction between priests and Levites, see Num. 8.

[141] Wright, *Deuteronomy*, 215.

[142] Unlike NT Greek, which has a word for "false prophet" (*pseudoprophetes*; Matt. 7:15; 24:11, 24; Mark 13:22; Luke 6:26; Acts 13:6; 2 Pet. 2:1; 1 John 4:1; Rev. 16:13, 19:20, 20:10), the Hebrew Old Testament does not. It simply uses the same word, and the reader determines by context whether God has sent the prophet or not. The concept of a "false prophet" is certainly there (cf. Jer. 14:14, 23:9–40; Ezek. 13:8–9). Some people would assume the title "prophet" and serve basically as yes-men and women for the king (see 1 Kings 22; Jer. 23), but these would also be considered false prophets, since God did not call them.

[143] This criterion of fulfillment has become a notorious problem in discerning true and false prophecy. This means of testing a prophet's words requires insight into the prophet to know whether he or she was truly called. It also requires hindsight,

because one does not know whether to obey the prophet's words until fulfillment occurs, which may be too late. Perhaps this text means the prophet has a track record of fulfilled prophecies and thus establishes his or her prophetic credentials. On this criterion, see Peter C. Craigie, *The Book of Deuteronomy*, New International Commentary on the Old Testament (Grand Rapids: Eerdmans, 1976), 263. In some cases, prophets offer more immediate signs, which, when fulfilled, serve to guarantee prophecies dealing with the more distant future (see, e.g., 1 Sam. 10:1–7; 1 Kings 13:1–5 with 2 Kings 23:15–20; 1 Kings 14:12–13, 17–18). Another test to verify the prophet's words would be to ask whether that word conforms to the *Torah* of Moses. For a recent work that seeks to help clarify how to discern God's prophetic word, then and now, see R. W. L. Moberly, *Prophecy and Discernment* (Cambridge: Cambridge University Press, 2006).

[144] For example, note Samuel's critique of Saul (1 Sam. 15:16–29), both Nathan's pronouncement of judgment on David (2 Sam. 12:1–14), and Isaiah's rebuke of Hezekiah (2 Kings 20:12–20).

[145] Other texts imply Jesus' role as judge. For example, Luke Timothy Johnson notes several passages in Luke's Gospel that point to the concept of Jesus as Judge: Luke 9:26; 10:13–16; 11:29–32; 12:41–48; 17:25–37; 18:8; 22:69. Luke T. Johnson, *The Acts of the Apostles*, Sacra Pagina (Collegeville, Minn.: The Liturgical Press, 1992), 193.

Chapter 11: Those Other People

[146] Wright says the law calls for "ecological restraint in the conduct of war." He notes that though the ancients were certainly responsible for gross ecological destruction in warfare, such a command even more serves as a "poignant protest against atrocities like the defoliation of Vietnam or the pollution of the [Persian] Gulf, to mention only two of the most recent ecological war crimes of our day" (*Deuteronomy*, 230).

[147] On marriage in ancient Israel, see King and Stager, *Life in Biblical Israel*, 54–56.

[148] Nelson says that the woman "sheds her former life and captive status, represented by her clothes, hair, and nails" (*Deuteronomy*, 259). He, however, denies that it is a humane law or that it prevents having sex with a captive woman apart from marriage. He sees this law as addressing a special case in which an Israelite man chooses to marry a captive (pp. 258–260). Wright, however, says the law is humanitarian, restricting the man and benefiting the woman. Thus, consistent with Deuteronomy as a whole, the person in a position of weakness is protected (*Deuteronomy*, 234–235).

[149] McConville, *Deuteronomy*, 347–348. McConville notes that "assembly" in Deuteronomy usually refers to all the people of Israel gathered at Mount Horeb (5:22; 9:10; 10:4; 18:16). For other uses of the phrase "assembly of the Lord," see Num. 16:3, 22; 20:4; Josh. 22:16; 1 Chron. 28:8; Mic. 2:5. The OT usage of "assembly" in reference to Israel, apart from the "qualifier of the Lord," frequently points to occasions when Israel is involved in matters of worship or is in the presence of Yahweh. See also, Walton, et al., *IVP Bible Background Commentary: OT*, 196; A. D. H. Mayes, *Deuteronomy*, New Century Bible Commentary (Grand Rapids: Eerdmans, 1979), 315.

[150] See Wright, *Deuteronomy*, 247. If one compares the case of the priests in Leviticus 21:17–21, it becomes clear that those who are so damaged by accident or birth are not totally excluded from the priesthood or community. Such a priest may still eat food from the altar, but he cannot participate in performing the rituals (Lev. 21:22–23).

[151] Craigie, *Deuteronomy*, 296–297; McConville, *Deuteronomy*, 348; J. A. Thompson, *Deuteronomy: An Introduction and Commentary*, Tyndale Old Testament Commentaries (Downers Grove, Ill.:1974), 239.

[152] For the options, see McConville, *Deuteronomy*, 348; Craigie, *Deuteronomy*, 297.

[153] According to Numbers 31:16, Balaam led the Israelites to sleep with Moabite and Midianite women and to worship their god, Baal of Peor (Num. 25; Deut. 4:3). The Israelites eventually executed Balaam (Num. 31:8; Josh. 13:22), though he remained a symbol of enticement to rebellion against God in Israel and the early church (Mic. 6:5; 2 Pet. 2:15–16; Rev. 2:14).

[154] The brotherhood of Israel and Edom arises frequently in the OT and will later become a basis for judgment against Edom. In the Bible, the relationship between the nations is more often than not hostile. Cf. Gen. 27:38–41; Amos 1:11; Ps.137:7–9; Obadiah.

[155] Wright, *Deuteronomy*, 225, 230. Wright compares the restriction upon Israel to the brutality portrayed by the Assyrians in their own treatment of captives where some are impaled and others are linked by chains connected to hooks through the prisoners' noses. He also notes the judgment on nations for their "excesses" in Amos 1:3, 6, 9, 13.

Chapter 12: Family Ties

[156] Those who are afraid are also excused from service, and, in that case, the reason is to prevent the fearful from demoralizing the rest of the troops. One could argue

that without the other exceptions, the army might have men who are not focused on the battle but on matters at home. However, more likely, the point is to allow them to enjoy the blessings of the land. In fact, if a man died in battle without enjoying these things, some might consider him under God's curse (cf. Deut. 28:30; Amos 5:11; Mic. 6:13–15).

[157] Either translation is possible. The difference has to do with what pointing (vowels) go with the Hebrew consonants. In either case, it is important to note that the woman's happiness is taken into consideration.

[158] McConville, *Deuteronomy*, 360.

[159] Jesus appears to make this point when he responds to traditions and questions on divorce (Matt. 5:31–32, 19:1–12; Mark 10:2–12).

[160] The word translated "indecency" in the ESV ("objectionable" in the NRSV), usually refers to nakedness, often with illicit sexual connotations (e.g., Lev. 18:6–19; 20:17–21), but, in Deuteronomy 23:14, it is used in connection with burying excrement. A sexual sin is probably not what is in view here, since such offences would normally require the death penalty. Thus, the exact nature of the "indecency" is not described but is probably serious, at least in the eyes of the husband. For the classic rabbinic debate between Hillel and Shammai on the nature of this indecency, a debate may stand behind the questions raised to Jesus on divorce (Matt. 19:3–12); see most any detailed commentary on Matthew 19.

[161] Wright suggests that from the perspective of the original marriage, the intervening marriage would be considered adulterous, resulting in defilement, so the law prevents that situation from occurring (*Deuteronomy*, 255). McConville understands the defilement more in terms of the victimization and shaming of the woman who is driven into a second marriage (*Deuteronomy*, 359–360).

[162] Similar, but not identical, language is used elsewhere in the Old Testament, though English translations may blur the differences (Gen. 34; 2 Sam. 13; cf. Judg. 21:20–23). The differences mean that one must be cautious in equating the offence in Deuteronomy 22:28–29 with those texts, but the parallels are suggestive.

[163] "Levirate" comes from the Latin word for brother-in-law (*levir*). The story of Tamar and Judah in Genesis 38 portrays levirate marriage, though the account occurs before Israel receives the Law, which suggests it was first a cultural expectation. Some similarities exist between the levirate law and the story of Ruth and Boaz (Ruth 3–4). The situation in Ruth, however, may not reflect levirate marriage, since the issue between Boaz and the closer relative of Ruth's dead husband focuses

primarily on a piece of property and no shame attaches to the relative who refuses to redeem the property and marry Ruth. Note also that the Sadducees bring up the levirate marriage law to challenge Jesus on the matter of the resurrection of the dead (Matt. 22:23–33).

[164] On the various possible meanings, see, e.g., Wright, *Deuteronomy*, 266, 269; McConville, *Deuteronomy*, 370.

[165] McConville, *Deuteronomy, 371.*

[166] This law calls to mind two stories in Genesis, though neither is precisely parallel and neither would be subject to this law, since the stories occur before the giving of the Law. In Genesis 25:27–34, the older son of Isaac, Esau, trades his birthright (the double portion of the inheritance) for food. In this case, the brothers make a deal apart from their father. Genesis 37:3–4 illustrate Jacob's preferential treatment of the son of the wife he loves, Rachel. Though the story does not say how Joseph disposed of his physical property among his sons, McConville (*Deuteronomy*, 330) says Joseph did receive a "double share" when his two sons each received a tribal designation in the Promised Land (Gen. 48:5; Josh. 14:4).

[167] The other times that the Hebrew root translated "rebellious" in 21:20 is used in Deuteronomy, it refers to Israel's rebellion against God (1:26, 43; 9:7, 23–24; 31:27).

[168] When Paul says, "Expel the wicked person from among you" (1 Cor. 5:13), he is alluding to a frequent refrain in Deuteronomy: "you shall purge the evil from your midst" (Deut. 13:5; 17:7, 12; 19:19; 21:21; 22:21, 22, 24; 24:7).

Chapter 13: Choose Life

[169] For another version of the curses and blessing in the Pentateuch, see Leviticus 26.

[170] See Chapter 6 on the ways Israel was to keep the word alive in their community.

[171] On the requirement that they make the altar out of field stones, see Exodus 20:24–26. A structure made of field stones with a ramp leading to the top has been discovered on Mount Ebal. While some scholars associate the structure with the altar built by Joshua in fulfillment of Deuteronomy's requirement (Josh. 8:30–31), others argue that it is a watch tower. For a discussion of the structure, see Adam Zertal, "Has Joshua's Altar Been Found on Mnt Ebal?" *Biblical Archaeology Review*, 11:1 (Jan–Feb 1985): 26–43; *idem.* "How Can Kempinski Be So Wrong?" *Biblical Archaeology Review*, 12:1 (Jan–Feb 1986): 43, 49–53; Aharon Kempinski, "Joshua's Altar: An Iron Age I Watchtower," *Biblical Archaeology Review*, 12:1 (Jan–Feb

1986): 42, 44–49. See also Amihai Mazar, *Archaeology of the Land of the Bible: 10,000–586 B.C.E.*, The Anchor Bible Reference Library (New York: Doubleday, 1990), 348–350.

[172] See McConville, *Deuteronomy*, 389.

[173] Deuteronomy 11 and 27 contain corresponding themes (blessings, curses, call to obedience) that bracket the stipulations of the *Torah* in chapters 12–26.

[174] The twelve tribes listed in 27:12–13 are the actual sons of Jacob, with Levi and Joseph named, rather than the two tribes descended from Joseph—Manasseh and Ephraim.

[175] Note the following links between these cursed behaviors and earlier portions of Deuteronomy: v. 15, making idols (4:15–20; 5:8–9); v. 16, dishonoring parents (5:16; 21:18–21); v. 17, moving boundary markers (19:14); v. 18, leading the blind astray (no references in Deuteronomy, but note the larger concern for the weak; cf. Lev. 19:14); v. 19, depriving the foreigner, orphan, and widow of justice (1:16–17; 16:19–20); vv. 20–23, various sexual offenses (not all of these are listed in Deuteronomy, but see 5:18; 22:30; cf. Lev. 18:7ff.; 20:11ff.); v. 24, striking down a neighbor (5:17; 19:11–13; 21:1–9); v. 25, taking bribes to shed innocent blood (cf., 1:16–17; 16:19–20).

[176] C. A. Keller, "brk," *Theological Lexicon of the Old Testament* 1:268.

[177] C. A. Keller, "'rr," *Theological Lexicon of the Old Testament* 1:180–181.

[178] Laboring for something and then being prevented from enjoying the fruits is sometimes called a "futility curse." Along these lines, see, e.g., Hos. 8:7; Amos 5:11; Mic. 6:14-15; Zeph. 1:13; Hag. 1:6, 9. Note that the things covered in the curses in Deuteronomy 28:30 echo the reasons that excused a man from military service in Deuteronomy 20:5–7. Thus, the special provision to allow them to enjoy the blessings of the land would likewise prove futile. This curse may even suggest that such men would be called up to engage this devastating enemy (since God would no longer be fighting for Israel) and killed.

[179] The mention of cannibalism (vv. 53–57) highlights the severity of the situation leading up to the exile. Lamentations 4:10 indicates that cannibalism was practiced within Jerusalem during the Babylonian siege. A similar event is recounted in 2 Kings 6:28–29.

[180] A similar statement is found in Jeremiah 16:13 in the context of anticipating the Babylonian exile. Note, however, that there is an anticipation of a return from that exile, which will surpass the exodus from Egypt as the saving event of significance (Jer. 16:14–15).

[181] Some Judeans flee to Egypt following the destruction of Jerusalem by Babylon and the assassination of the Babylonian-appointed governor, Gedaliah. Among them is Jeremiah, who is taken there against his will (Jer. 41:16–44:30).

[182] The meaning of "the Lord has not given you a heart to understand or eyes to see or ears to hear" (29:4) in this respect is unclear. Does it mean that they have been hardened like Pharaoh? This is unlikely since it would undermine their intended role as a positive witness and they are repeatedly called upon to obey. It may suggest that the ability to see and respond in faith is a gift of God (cf. 30:6). Along these lines, see Wright, *Deuteronomy*, 286. Or it may mean that "this day" marks a new point. In light of the giving of the *Torah* to the people, they can now understand more fully God's intentions for them.

[183] As a comparison of English versions will show, the translation of 29:19b is notoriously difficult, as is its meaning. For a discussion and possible meanings, see McConville, *Deuteronomy*, 412, 417; Nelson, *Deuteronomy*, 336.

[184] For the association of Admah and Zeboyim with Sodom and Gomorrah, see also Genesis 10:19 and 14:2, 8. Hosea 11:8 refers to the destruction of Admah and Zeboyim without mentioning the other two cities.

[185] Though often obscured in English translations, the Hebrew word for "turn/return" provides a keyword for this text (30: 1, 2, 3, 8, 9, 10) to describe both Israel's action toward God and God's actions toward Israel.

[186] The word Hebrew translated "evil" in the ESV does not have to mean "evil" in the moral sense. It can also mean something along the lines of "harm," which fits the context here better.

[187] On Apostle Paul's use of Deuteronomy 30:11–14 in Romans 10:5–10, see Douglas Moo, *The Epistle to the Romans*, New International Commentary on the New Testament (Grand Rapids: Eerdmans, 1996), 644–660.

[188] The context of national restoration should be kept in mind when interpreting God's claim that "I put to death and bring to life." While it is correct to understand God as the one who has ultimate control over life and death, this verse does not mean that God directly causes every death. In light of the larger context (30:11–20), this

refers to the life and death of the Israelite community as a whole, living under the blessing or curse of God.

[189] Some may wonder here about the "unforgivable sin" (Matt. 12:31; Mark 3:29; Luke 12:10) or the "sin that leads to death" (1 John 5:16–17). The larger contexts of the biblical passages where these concepts occur indicate that this "sin" refers to denying the testimony of the Spirit concerning who Jesus is; that is, a rejection of Jesus as the Christ, the Son of God. Thus, those who commit this sin are those who turn their backs on God by rejecting his salvation in Jesus Christ. In this respect, the "unforgivable sin" is related to the claim that God will not forgive in Deuteronomy 29:20. Both envision one who spits in the face of God by willfully persisting in his or her own way despite the gifts and commands of God.

[190] John Newton, "Amazing Grace" (1779).

[191] Robert Robinson, "Come, Thou Fount of Every Blessing" (1758). Various versions of this verse are found in different hymnals.

Chapter14: The Beginning

[192] Simeon is left out of the blessings for reasons that are not clear. Perhaps it is because that tribe is surrounded by and eventually absorbed into Judah (cf. Josh. 19:8–9). Also, rather than Ephraim and Manasseh receiving blessings as separate tribes, the blessing is directed toward Joseph, the ancestor of these tribes (Gen. 48).

[193] Given the significance the tribe of Judah will have in Israel as the tribe of the Davidic kings, the brevity of this blessing is interesting. Clearly, Judah is not of elevated significance or central concern here (cf. Gen. 49:8–12). Given Deuteronomy's downplaying of the role of a king in Israel (17:14–20), this is not surprising.

[194] In the Old Testament, Yahweh's spirit is often said to come upon those he has called to be empowered so as to fulfill their calling, including some of Israel's judge-deliverers (Judg. 3:10; 6:34; 11:29; 13:25; 14:6, 19; 15:14), certain kings (1 Sam. 10:6; 11:6; 16:13), prophets (2 Kings 2:9–15; Joel 2:28–29), the "servant" in Isaiah (Isa. 42:1; 61:1; cf. Luke 4:18). Though none of these instances refer to the spirit as the "Holy Spirit" (despite the impression left by some translations that capitalize the S in "Spirit"), there are clear parallels and links with the Holy Spirit as described in the New Testament. For a discussion of the Holy Spirit in the Old Testament, see Christopher J. H. Wright, *Knowing the Holy Spirit through the Old Testament* (Oxford: Monarch Books, 2006). On a spirit of wisdom, cf. 1 Kings 3:4–15; Isa. 11:1–2.

[195] This line is taken from the title of J. G. McConville's *Grace in the End: A Study in Deuteronomic Theology* (Grand Rapids: Zondervan, 1993), which traces the theology of Deuteronomy into Joshua, Judges, 1 and 2 Samuel, and 1 and 2 Kings.

[196] The exodus and Promised Land are recurring themes in African-American preaching. However, often against the dominant culture's interpretation of these Old Testament narratives, the U.S. is associated with Egypt and African-Americans with the Israelites escaping bondage and oppression. For a recent work, see Gary S. Selby, *Martin Luther King and the Rhetoric of Freedom: The Exodus Narrative in America's Struggle for Civil Rights* (Waco: Baylor University Press, 2008).

[197] From Martin Luther King Jr.'s sermon delivered on April 3, 1968, sometimes called his "Mountaintop" sermon. The text of this sermon is available in a number of places, for instance: Michael Warner, ed., *American Sermons: The Pilgrims to Martin Luther King Jr.*, The Library of America (New York: Penguin Putnam, 1999), 876–885 (citation above from p. 885). However, the power of the sermon is better experienced through video or audio clips, which can be found online through various Internet search engines or on video sharing Web sites like YouTube.com.

Excursus on Slavery in the Bible

[198] Howard Thurman, *Jesus and the Disinherited* (Boston: Beacon Press, 1976; 1996), 31.

[199] Interestingly, I rarely hear the same arguments made with respect to America's founders for throwing off what they considered unjust bondage to England. Furthermore, I wonder whether those who make such arguments would simply accept slavery were the tables turned. That is, would they accept being slaves and serve to please their masters? Or would they fight enslavement. Since, in their view, the Bible supports (or at least does not condemn) the institution, they would have no moral ground to resist. This is especially true since there is no New Testament justification for taking up arms for the sake of one's own political and personal freedom.

Along these lines, one would also be hard-pressed to find freedoms of the press, assembly, speech, and religion in the Bible. With regard to freedom of religion, a freedom that many Americans believe is worth shedding blood over and fear losing, we would do well to remember that Christians are told to expect persecution for our faith (Phil. 1:29; 2 Tim. 3:12; 1 Pet. 4:16). That we in the American church do not experience serious persecution—at least not in any serious or dangerous form—may suggest how much we have allied ourselves to and identified with the powers of the world.

[200] With respect to the issues of slavery and liberation in the Bible, particularly as presented by modern liberation theologians, see the insightful and challenging essay "Exodus and Liberation" by Jon D. Levenson in his *The Hebrew Bible, the Old Testament, and Historical Criticism: Jews and Christians in Biblical Studies* (Westminster John Knox, 1993), 127–159. This paragraph draws on some of his observations.

[201] For a discussion of slavery in the Old Testament from an ethical standpoint, see Wright, *Old Testament Ethics for the People of God* (Downers Grove, Ill.: InterVarsity, 2004), 333–337. What follows, in part, draws on his discussion.

[202] See Propp, *Exodus 19–40*, 218. Nuzi, a fifteenth century B.C. Mesopotamian city-state, appears to be an exception. A text from there indicates that a slave could take an abusive master to court.

[203] The meaning of the call to punish the killer, literally "to avenge" the slave, in Exodus 21:20 is uncertain. The death penalty is one possibility, which would suggest that the slaves are as important as free Israelites in this regard. For the range of possibilities, see Propp, *Exodus 19–40*, 218–219.

[204] For suggestions on the nature of Ham's offense, see Gordon J. Wenham, *Genesis 1–15*, Word Biblical Commentary, (Waco: Word, 1987), 199–200.

[205] Why the curse is put upon Canaan instead of Ham is unclear. For suggestions, see Wenham, *Genesis 1–15*, 201–202.

[206] Along these lines, see the brief discussion of the damage caused by misunderstanding in Genesis 9:24–29 in W. Sibley Towner, *Genesis*, Westminster Bible Companion, (Louisville: Westminster John Knox, 2001), 99–100.

[207] For a discussion of slavery in the Greco-Roman world of the NT, see Everett Ferguson, *Backgrounds of Early Christianity*, second ed. (Grand Rapids: Eerdmans, 1993), 56–59; James S. Jeffers, *The Greco-Roman World of the New Testament* (Downers Grove, Ill.: InterVarsity, 1999), 220–236. As slavery relates particularly to early Christians in this Greco-Roman setting, see the discussion by Lincoln, *Ephesians*, 415–420, 424–428.

[208] In fact, both take for granted the institution in illustrating their messages (e.g., Matt. 18:23–35; 22:1–14; Luke 17:7–10; Gal. 4.

[209] See Gordon D. Fee, *1 and 2 Timothy, Titus*, New International Biblical Commentary, (Peabody, Mass.: Hendrickson, 1988), 138.

[210] See Lincoln, *Ephesians*, 423.

[211] Either Omesimus was a Christian already or became one after meeting Paul (Philemon 10–11).

[212] All of the interpretative issues in Philemon are beyond the scope of this work. Any good scholarly commentary will discuss them.

[213] This text deals directly with the rich-poor division in the Corinthian church, but the theological principle rules out any divisions on social or economic grounds.

[214] The International Justice Mission is a Christian organization dedicated to using every legal recourse possible to free those who are still enslaved and being enslaved today. More information about this organization and modern-day slavery can be found at their Web site: www.ijm.org.

Excursus on the Ban

[215] In Hebrew, *cherem* or *herem*. There has been a great deal written on this issue, and what follows in this excursus is indebted to the following: Jeph Holloway, "The Ethical Dilemma of Holy War," *Southwest Journal of Theology* 41 (1998): 44–69; David M. Howard Jr., *Joshua*, The New American Commentary, (Nashville: Broadman & Holman, 1998), 180–187; Paul Copan, *Is God A Moral Monster?: Making Sense of the Old Testament God* (Baker, 2011), 158–197; Wright, *Deuteronomy*, 112–115; *idem*, *Old Testament Ethics*, 472–480. A more popular version of this discussion is in Wright's *The God I Don't Understand,* (Grand Rapids: Zondervan, 2008), 73–108. Another helpful resource in struggling with this issue is C.S. Cowles, *et al.*, *Show Them No Mercy: 4 Views on God and Canaanite Genocide* (Grand Rapids: Zondervan, 2003).

[216] The only times that Israel is commanded to destroy everything, people and property, are at Jericho (Josh. 6–7), and, at least by implication, when Saul fights the Amalekites (1 Sam. 15; cf. Exod. 17:8–16; Deut. 25:17–19). Ai and Hazor were the only other cities burned, and, in these conquests, the people were killed but Israel was permitted to keep the plunder (Josh. 8:1–29; 11:1–15).

[217] The dominant view among biblical scholars is that the archaeological evidence does not support the biblical portrayal of the conquests of Jericho and Ai, a conclusion that is strongly rejected by more conservative scholars. For a summary of the perspectives with relevant bibliography, see Tremper Longman III and Raymond Dillard, *An Introduction to the Old Testament*, second ed. (Grand Rapids: Zondervan, 2006), 123–127. For those who deny the historicity of the conquest

accounts, some then explained that ban was never carried out but was invented at a much later time for theological purposes; e.g., to support Josiah's religious reforms or to provide an explanation and give hope to those in exile. See, e.g., Carolyn Pressler, *Joshua, Judges, Ruth*, Westminster Bible Companion (Louisville: Westminster John Knox, 2002), 49–53.

[218] See, e. g., Eugene E. Carpenter, "Deuteronomy" in *Zondervan Illustrated Bible Background Commentary*, vol. 1, ed. John H. Walton (Grand Rapids: Zondervan, 2009), 437.

[219] The translation is according to *Readings from the Ancient Near East: Primary Sources for Old Testament Study*, ed. Bill T. Arnold and Bryan E. Beyer (Grand Rapids: Baker, 2002), 162. Mesha appears in the Bible in 2 Kings 3.

[220] See Copan, *Is God a Moral Monster*, 169–185.

[221] In the case of the Amalekites, the fight against them extends into the period of the monarchy in Israel, where Saul (1 Sam. 15) was to destroy them, and David does destroy all but 400 who escape (1 Sam. 30:17). In the days of Hezekiah, king of Judah, the Simeonites wipe out the remainder of the Amalekites, fulfilling the ban against them (1 Chron. 4:41–43).

[222] Cf. also Deut. 25:17–19; 2 Kings 8:12; Amos 1:13.

Works Cited

Achtemeier, Elizabeth. *The Committed Marriage*. Philadelphia: Westminster, 1977.

Arnold, Bill T. and Bryan E. Beyer, eds. *Readings from the Ancient Near East: Primary Sources for Old Testament Study*. Grand Rapids: Baker, 2002.

Augustine, *Confessions*, Book I, 1. Cited according to the edition *Saint Augustine Confessions*. R. S. Pine-Coffin, trans. New York: Viking Penguin, 1961; reprint 1987.

Bahnsen, Greg L. et al. *Five Views on the Law and Gospel*. Grand Rapids: Zondervan, 1996.

Bell, Daniel M. *Just War as Christian Discipleship: Recentering the Tradition in the Church rather than the State*. Grand Rapids: Brazos, 2009.

Black, Mark C. *Luke*. College Press NIV Commentary. Joplin, Mo.: College Press, 1996.

Blomberg, Craig L. *Neither Poverty nor Riches: A Biblical Theology of Material Possessions*. Grand Rapids: Eerdmans, 1999.

Boring, M. Eugene. *Mark*, New Testament Library. Louisville: Westminster John Knox, 2006.

Brown, William P., ed. *The Ten Commandments: The Reciprocity of Faithfulness*. Louisville: Westminster John Knox, 2004.

Camp, Daniel F. *The Marriage-Friendly Church*. Nashville: 21st Century Christian, 2013.

Camp, Lee C. *Mere Discipleship: Radical Christianity in a Rebellious World*. Grand Rapids: Brazos, 2003.

Camp, Phillip G. "The Lord's Supper as Sabbath Observance," *Restoration Quarterly* 51:2 (2009): 81–92.

Carpenter, Eugene E. "Deuteronomy" in *Zondervan Illustrated Bible Background Commentary*, vol. 1, ed. John H. Walton. Grand Rapids: Zondervan, 2009.

Charles, J. Daryl. *Between Pacifism and Jihad: Just War and the Christian Tradition*. Downers Grove, Ill.: InterVarsity, 2005.

Christensen, Duane L. *Deuteronomy 21:10–34:12*. Word Biblical Commentary. Nashville: Thomas Nelson, 2002.

Claiborne, Shane. *The Irresistible Revolution*. Grand Rapids: Zondervan, 2006.

Cogan, Mordechai. *1 Kings: A New Translation with Introduction and Commentary*. The Anchor Bible. New York: Doubleday, 2000.

Copan, Paul. *Is God a Moral Monster?: Making Sense of the Old Testament God*. Grand Rapids: Baker, 2011.

Cowles, C. S., et al. *Show Them No Mercy: 4 Views on God and Canaanite Genocide*. Grand Rapids: Zondervan, 2003.

Craigie, Peter C. *The Book of Deuteronomy*. New International Commentary on the Old Testament. Grand Rapids: Eerdmans, 1976.

Douglas, Mary. "The Abominations of Leviticus," in *Anthropological Approaches to the Old Testament*, ed. Bernhard Lang. Philadelphia: Fortress, 1985. Pages 100–116.

Durham, John I. *Exodus*, Word Biblical Commentary. Waco: Word, 1987.

Fee, Gordon D. *1 and 2 Timothy, Titus.* New International Biblical Commentary. Peabody, Mass.: Hendrickson, 1988.

_____. *The First Epistle to the Corinthians.* New International Commentary on the New Testament. Grand Rapids: Eerdmans, 1987.

Fee, Gordon D. and Douglas Stuart. *How to Read the Bible for All Its Worth,* 3rd ed. Grand Rapids: Zondervan, 2003.

Ferguson, Everett. *Backgrounds of Early Christianity,* 2nd ed. Grand Rapids: Eerdmans, 1993.

Fikkert, Brian and Steve Corbett, *When Helping Hurts: Alleviating Poverty without Hurting the Poor...and Yourself.* Chicago: Moody, 2009.

Foster, Richard J. *Celebration of Discipline,* rev. ed. San Francisco: Harper San Francisco, 1988.

"Hang Ten? Thou Shalt Avoid Ten Commandments Tokenism" in *Christianity Today* 44:3 (March 6, 2000): 36.

Hayes, Richard B. *The Moral Vision of the New Testament: A Contemporary Introduction to New Testament Ethics.* New York: HarperCollins, 1996.

Hicks, John Mark. *Come to the Table: Revisioning the Lord's Supper.* Orange, Calif.: New Leaf Books, 2002.

Holloway, Jeph. "The Ethical Dilemma of Holy War." *Southwest Journal of Theology* 41 (1998): 44–69.

Howard, David M., Jr. *Joshua,* The New American Commentary. Nashville: Broadman & Holman, 1998.

Jeffers, James S. *The Greco-Roman World of the New Testament.* Downers Grove, Ill.: InterVarsity, 1999.

Jenni, Ernst and Claus Westermann, eds. *Theological Lexicon of the Old Testament*. Translated by Mark E. Biddle. 3 vols. Peabody, Mass.: Hendrickson, 1997.

Johnson, Luke T. *The Acts of the Apostles*. Sacra Pagina. Collegeville, Minn.: The Liturgical Press, 1992.

Kempinski, Aharon. "Joshua's Altar: An Iron Age I Watchtower." *Biblical Archaeology Review*, 12:1 (Jan–Feb 1986): 42, 44–49.

King, Martin L. Jr. "Sermon Delivered April 3, 1968 ('I've Been to the Mountaintop')." In *American Sermons: The Pilgrims to Martin Luther King Jr.*, ed. Michael Warner. The Library of America. New York: Penguin Putnam, 1999.

King, Philip J. and Lawrence E. Stager. *Life in Biblical Israel*. Louisville: Westminster John Knox, 2001.

Levenson, Jon D. *The Hebrew Bible, the Old Testament, and Historical Criticism: Jews and Christians in Biblical Studies*. Westminster John Knox, 1993.

Lincoln, Andrew T. *Ephesians*. Word Biblical Commentary. Dallas: Word Books, 1990.

Longman, Tremper III and Raymond Dillard. *An Introduction to the Old Testament*. 2nd ed. Grand Rapids: Zondervan, 2006.

Mayes, A. D. H. *Deuteronomy*. New Century Bible Commentary. Grand Rapids: Eerdmans, 1979.

Mazar, Amihai. *Archaeology of the Land of the Bible: 10,000–586 B.C.E.* The Anchor Bible Reference Library. New York: Doubleday, 1990.

McBride, S. Dean. "Polity of the Covenant People." *Interpretation* 41 (1987): 229–244.

McConville, J. G. *Deuteronomy*. Apollos Old Testament Commentary. Downers Grove, Ill.: InterVarsity Press, 2002.

_____. *Grace in the End: A Study in Deuteronomic Theology*. Grand Rapids: Zondervan, 1993.

Merrill, Eugene H. *Deuteronomy*. The New American Commentary. Nashville: Broadman and Holman, 1994.

Milgrom, Jacob. *Leviticus 1–16*. The Anchor Bible. New York: Doubleday, 1991.

Miller, Patrick D. *Deuteronomy*. Interpretation, A Bible Commentary for Preaching and Teaching. Louisville: John Knox Press, 1990.

_____. *The Religion of Ancient Israel*. Louisville: Westminster John Knox, 2000.

_____. *The Ten Commandments*. Interpretation Resources for Use in the Church. Louisville: Westminster John Knox, 2009.

Moberly, R. W. L. *Prophecy and Discernment*. Cambridge: Cambridge University Press, 2006.

Nelson, Richard D. *Deuteronomy*. Old Testament Library. Louisville: Westminster John Knox, 2002.

_____. *The Historical Books*. Nashville: Abingdon, 1998.

Olson, Dennis T. *Deuteronomy and the Death of Moses: A Theological Reading*. Eugene, Ore.: Wipf and Stock, 1994.

Pressler, Carolyn. *Joshua, Judges, Ruth*. Westminster Bible Companion. Louisville: Westminster John Knox, 2002.

Propp, William H. *Exodus 19–40: A New Translation with Introduction and Commentary*. The Anchor Bible. New York: Doubleday, 2006.

Roth, Martha T. *Law Collections from Mesopotamia and Asia Minor*. 2nd ed. SBL Writings from the Ancient World Series 6. Atlanta: Scholars Press, 1997.

Sarna, Nahum. *Exploring Exodus: The Origins of Biblical Israel*. New York: Schocken Books, 1986, 1996.

Selby, Gary S. *Martin Luther King and the Rhetoric of Freedom: The Exodus Narrative in America's Struggle for Civil Rights*. Waco: Baylor University Press, 2008.

Shelly, Rubel. *Divorce and Remarriage: A Redemptive Theology*. Abilene, Tex.: Leafwood, 2007.

Sider, Ronald J. *Rich Christians in an Age of Hunger: Moving from Affluence to Generosity*. Dallas: Word, 1997.

Thompson, J. A. *Deuteronomy: An Introduction and Commentary*. Tyndale Old Testament Commentaries. Downers Grove, Ill.:1974.

Thurman, Howard. *Jesus and the Disinherited*. Boston: Beacon Press, 1976; 1996.

Tigay, Jeffrey H. *Deuteronomy: The Traditional Hebrew Text with the New JPS Translation*. Philadelphia: Jewish Publication Society of America, 1996.

Towner, W. Sibley. *Genesis*. Westminster Bible Companion. Louisville: Westminster John Knox, 2001.

Walton, John H. *Ancient Near Eastern Thought and the Old Testament*. Grand Rapids: Baker, 2006.

Walton, John H., Victor H. Matthews, and Mark W. Chavalas, *IVP Bible Background Commentary: Old Testament*. Downers Grove, Ill.: InterVarsity, 2000.

Weinfeld, Moshe. *Deuteronomy 1–11*. Anchor Bible. New York: Doubleday, 1991.

Wenham, Gordon J. *Genesis 1–15*. Word Biblical Commentary. Waco: Word, 1987

Wilkinson, Bruce. *The Prayer of Jabez: Breaking Through to the Blessed Life*. Sisters, Ore.: Multnomah, 2000.

Wright, Christopher J. H. *Deuteronomy*. Understanding the Bible Commentary Series. Grand Rapids: Baker, 1996.

_____. *The God I Don't Understand*. Grand Rapids: Zondervan, 2008.

_____. *Knowing the Holy Spirit through the Old Testament*. Oxford: Monarch Books, 2006.

_____. *The Mission of God: Unlocking the Bible's Grand Narrative*. Downers Grove, Ill.: InterVarsity, 2006.

_____. *Old Testament Ethics for the People of God*. Downers Grove, Ill.: InterVarsity, 2004.

Yoder, John H. *The Politics of Jesus*. 2nd. ed. Eerdmans, 1994.

Zertal, Adam. "Has Joshua's Altar Been Found on Mnt Ebal?" *Biblical Archaeology Review* 11:1 (Jan–Feb 1985): 26–43.

_____. "How Can Kempinski Be So Wrong?" *Biblical Archaeology Review* 12:1 (Jan–Feb 1986): 43, 49–53.

Index to Texts in Deuteronomy

CPSIA information can be obtained
at www.ICGtesting.com
Printed in the USA
LVHW080411290522
719966LV00005B/10